SHARED
PARKING

SECOND EDITION

Mary S. Smith

Urban Land Institute

International Council of Shopping Centers

About ULI–the Urban Land Institute

ULI–the Urban Land Institute is a nonprofit education and research institute that is supported by its members. Its mission is to provide responsible leadership in the use of land in order to enhance the total environment.

ULI sponsors education programs and forums to encourage an open international exchange of ideas and sharing of experiences; initiates research that anticipates emerging land use trends and issues and proposes creative solutions based on that research; provides advisory services; and publishes a wide variety of materials to disseminate information on land use and development. Established in 1936, the Institute today has more than 26,000 members and associates from more than 80 countries representing the entire spectrum of the land use and development disciplines.

Richard Rosan

President

For more information about ULI and the resources that it offers related to parking and a variety of other real estate and urban development issues, visit ULI's Web site at www.uli.org.

About the International Council of Shopping Centers

Founded in 1957, the International Council of Shopping Centers (ICSC) is the global trade association of the shopping center industry. Its more than 54,000 members in the United States, Canada, and more than 96 other countries include shopping center owners, developers, managers, marketing specialists, investors, lenders, retailers, and other professionals as well as academics and public officials. As the global industry trade association, ICSC links with more than 25 national and regional shopping center councils throughout the world.

Michael P. Kercheval

President

For more information about ICSC and the products and services that it offers, including publications and research data, visit ICSC's Web site at www.icsc.org.

Recommended bibliographic listing:
Smith, Mary S. *Shared Parking*, Second Edition. Washington, D.C.: ULI–the Urban Land Institute and the International Council of Shopping Centers, 2005.

ULI Catalog Number: S54
ICSC Catalog Number: 279
International Standard Book Number: 978-0-87420-939-6
Library of Congress Control Number: 2005934519

ULI:
1025 Thomas Jefferson Street, N.W.
Suite 500 West
Washington, D.C. 20007-5201

ICSC:
1221 Avenue of the Americas
New York, NY 10020-1099

Shared Parking Study Team

Team Leader and Principal Author

Mary S. Smith
Senior Vice President
Walker Parking Consultants
Indianapolis, Indiana

Other Contributors

Patrick Gibson
Vice President
Kaku Associates
Santa Monica, California

Ransford S. McCourt
Principal
DKS Associates
Portland, Oregon

Gerald Salzman
Senior Planner
Desman
Chicago, Illinois

Martin J. Wells
President
Wells Associates
McLean, Virginia

Jerry Wentzel
Regional Manager
DKS Associates
Tampa, Florida

Review Committee

Robert T. Dunphy
Senior Resident Fellow, Transportation and Infrastructure
ULI–the Urban Land Institute
Washington, D.C.

William R. Eager
President
TDA Inc.
Seattle, Washington

Kemper Freeman
President
Bellevue Square Managers, Inc.
Bellevue, Washington

Kenneth H. Hughes
President
Hughes Development, L.P.
Dallas, Texas

Jean Lambert
Manager of Global Research
International Council of Shopping Centers
New York, New York

Ronald A. Massott
Senior Parking Specialist
Wilbur Smith Associates
Harrisburg, Pennsylvania

Michael P. McCarty
Senior Vice President
Simon Property Group
Indianapolis, Indiana

Joseph Stallsmith
Director of Civil Engineering
Simon Property Group
Indianapolis, Indiana

William A. Speer
President
Speer Consulting International
Coronado, California

James W. Todd
President
The Peterson Companies
Fairfax, Virginia

ULI Project Staff

Rachelle L. Levitt
Executive Vice President, Policy and Practice
Publisher

Gayle Berens
Vice President, Real Estate Development Practice

Robert T. Dunphy
Senior Resident Fellow for Transportation and Infrastructure
Project Director

Nancy H. Stewart
Director, Book Program

James A. Mulligan
Managing Editor

Duke Johns
Manuscript Editor

Betsy VanBuskirk
Art Director

Byron Holly
Book Designer

Susan S. Teachey/ON-Q Design, Inc.
Book Layout

Craig Chapman
Director, Publishing Operations

Ronnie Van Alstyne
Senior Administrative Assistant

ICSC Project Staff

Jean Lambert
Manager of Global Research

Rudolph E. Millian
Senior Staff Vice President
Director of Professional Development Services

Patricia Montagni
Director of Publications

Michael P. Niemira
Staff Vice President
Chief Economist and Director of Research

Jay Starr
Senior Staff Vice President
Group Publisher, Director of Marketing and Membership

Foreword

Since the first edition of this book was published in 1983, the concept of shared parking has become well established as an important element of mixed-use developments, probably beyond the wildest dreams of its authors. That pioneering study demonstrated that when developments with complementary parking patterns were able to use the same parking, less was required. At the time, there was not even a generally accepted source of documented parking needs for individual land uses, so such data were developed as part of the original study. Over the subsequent two decades, shared parking has become a routine part of the design and approval of mixed-use developments. Parking needs have changed as a result of the evolution in mixed-use developments and changes in transportation, requiring a new look at the shared parking parameters advocated in 1983. With this publication, we are pleased both to validate the original study and to provide current data for a more complex mix of different potential land uses.

It is a tribute to the ground-breaking nature and thoroughness of the original shared parking study that it has taken so long to update it, and ULI could not have done it alone. Growing concerns from within and outside the ULI community made this project a priority for the Policy and Practice Committee. The publication of the third edition of *Parking Generation* by the Institute of Transportation Engineers provided a rich source of current parking data for single land uses that served as a foundation for an updated shared parking study. The International Council of Shopping Centers partnered with us to make the study a reality. A national study team of experts was established and a lead consultant selected to direct and manage the work.

This new publication provides up-to-date parking parameters that will be useful now and well in the future for many users, including local governments, developers, shopping center owners, and lenders. These new guidelines should help those users to integrate parking and development in the most responsible way.

Robert T. Dunphy
Project Director

Acknowledgments

I would like to express my thanks to the many organizations and individuals who helped make this collaboration a success. It would not have been possible without access to the Institute of Transportation Engineers' parking data, generously provided by Tom Brahms, ITE's executive director, and hands-on assistance with the database from Randy McCourt, who chaired the ITE committee. The project was a major cooperative venture between the Urban Land Institute and the International Council of Shopping Centers. Mary Smith, the principal consultant and author, and her colleagues at Walker Parking Consultants were responsible for most of the work, assisted by a study team of five consultants—Pat Gibson, Randy McCourt, Gerry Salzman, Marty Wells, and Jerry Wentzel—who evaluated information on key land uses and provided additional data and case studies from their own files. Ron Massott of Wilbur Smith Associates also worked with the team, and after his retirement he served on the review committee. Pat Gibson and Kaku Associates developed the computer model. I especially appreciate the contribution of the reviewers, who evaluated the findings and patiently plowed through extensive technical data to help validate the final publication.

I would like to thank Rachelle Levitt, who championed this project among many competitive ULI research needs, and acknowledge the tireless advocacy of ULI members Jim Todd and Ken Hughes. I thank ULI's publishing staff for making this a readable and professional publication: Duke Johns, who edited a manuscript with complicated tables and charts; Byron Holly, who designed the book; Susie Teachey, who laid out the book; Jim Mulligan, who skillfully managed this complex work through the editing and production process; and Craig Chapman, who coordinated the book's publication.

To all these and others who had a hand in this work, I extend my sincere appreciation and thanks.

Robert T. Dunphy
Project Director

Contents

Introduction

The Concept of Shared Parking

Shared parking is the use of a parking space to serve two or more individual land uses without conflict or encroachment. The ability to share parking spaces is the result of two conditions:

■ variations in the accumulation of vehicles by hour, by day, or by season at the individual land uses, and

■ relationships among the land uses that result in visiting multiple land uses on the same auto trip.

Although the ULI methodology for shared parking analysis was developed in the early 1980s,[1] the concept of shared parking was already well established: a fundamental principle of downtown planning from the earliest days of the automobile has always been to share parking resources rather than to allocate parking for each use or building. The resurgence of many central cities resulting from the addition of vibrant residential, retail, restaurant, and entertainment developments continues to rely heavily on shared parking for economic viability. In addition, mixed-use projects in many different settings have benefited from shared parking.

Parking is a key element of any site development plan. Parking can consume 50 percent or more of the building and land area of a development. An oversupply of parking can result in excess storm drainage impacts and unnecessarily high expenses (surface stalls can cost $2,000 to $3,000 per space and structured spaces $15,000 to $25,000 or more). Insufficient parking can result in the intrusion of parking into neighborhoods or adjoining properties, excessive vehicle circulation, and unhappy users. Ultimately, great parking alone won't make a mixed-use project successful; however, inadequate or poorly designed parking can limit its potential success.

The key goal of shared parking analysis, then, is to find the balance between providing adequate parking to support a development from a commercial viewpoint and minimizing the negative aspects of excessive land area or resources devoted to parking. Mixed-use developments that share parking result in greater density, better pedestrian connections, and, in turn, reduced reliance on driving, typically because multiple destinations can be accessed by walking. Higher-density development, especially on infill sites, is also more likely to support alternative modes of travel, including transit and carpools.

Concern for the negative impacts of growth has stimulated a search for better ways to develop land. "Smart growth" is a collection of planning principles and strategies designed to facilitate development without sprawl. Smart growth projects typically are designed to create transportation options and reduce driving, especially for short trips. Walkable live/work/play environments, located near established transportation and infrastructure resources, are central to the concept. Some communities are questioning the economic costs of abandoning infrastructure in the city only to rebuild it further out.[2] Ironically, a critical element of such pedestrian-oriented districts is adequate parking.

One of the hottest real estate trends is known as "place making," the development of town centers and urban villages with mixed uses in pedestrian-friendly settings. Another significant trend today is transit-oriented development, which seeks to cluster development near transit stations. With housing located within walking distance of rail transit, some trips and, in turn, some parking spaces can be eliminated.

Shared parking is a critical factor in the success of all these development approaches, and thus the importance of shared parking will continue to grow in future years. This report aims to provide planners, engineers, developers, and agencies with tools to better quantify and understand how shared parking can be successful.

Objective of the Second Edition

The widely accepted methodology for shared parking analysis was established in 1983 with the publication of the first edition of *Shared Parking*. Two decades later, ULI and ICSC convened a working group of parking experts to examine the question of whether shared parking is still appropriate, given changes in society, transportation, and mixed-use development trends. The consensus was that the underlying concept and methodology are still viable, but that an update of the default factors would be appropriate. The following three examples illustrate how changing trends have affected parking needs.

■ When *Shared Parking* was first published, a multiscreen cinema complex had two or three screens. By the late 1990s, new cinema developments had as many as 30 screens. It is far less likely that every seat in a 30-screen cineplex is filled than in a two- or three-screen cinema. The proliferation of these complexes has had a profound impact on the movie industry, and the parking needs of cineplexes will be discussed later in this report.

■ Changing lifestyles have led to a significant increase in the proportion of family meals eaten outside the home, which has caused a marked increase in the proportion of newly developed space that is occupied by restaurants. In 1955, 25 percent of expenditures for food in the United States was spent in restaurants (both limited and full service); in 2003, restaurants' share of the food dollar was 46.4 percent.[3]

■ As more women have joined the workforce, there has been an increase in the proportion of shopping trips that occur in evenings and a significant increase in "trip-chaining," owing to commuters making multiple stops to drop off or pick up children at daycare and to take care of household errands.

A committee of the Institute of Transportation Engineers (ITE) also agreed that the methodology recommended in the first edition of *Shared Parking* is still the correct approach to shared parking analysis, but it called for updating some default values.[4] It found that almost half of all local governments had incorporated shared parking into local codes, either directly or as an option, and many of those codes cited the ULI shared parking methodology.

The development of updated references on the parking needs of individual land uses also made an update of *Shared*

Parking timely. In 1998, ULI and ICSC commissioned an update of *Parking Requirements for Shopping Centers*, the most widely recognized reference regarding that land use. That reference's second edition recommended a 10 percent reduction in the parking ratio for centers over 600,000 square feet and modified its recommendations for centers with more than 10 percent of GLA in restaurant, entertainment, or cineplex uses.[5] In particular, when more than 20 percent of the space in centers is allocated to those uses, shared parking analysis should be employed to determine the appropriate number of parking spaces.

ITE also has updated its *Trip Generation*[6] and *Parking Generation*[7] publications. The third edition of *Parking Generation* includes four times as much data as the second edition, with over 100 land uses now incorporated. This document provides much-needed information on the parking needs of individual land uses, but it simply provides statistical analysis of the data. It makes no recommendations regarding appropriate parking ratios to be used in parking studies, including shared parking analysis. In fact, the limited data in many land use classifications are not statistically reliable, and professional experience and judgment must be employed in their use. One of the purposes of this report is to formulate recommendations regarding the parking ratios to be used in shared parking analysis, using, to the extent appropriate, the data found in *Parking Generation*. Both documents are complementary.

ULI and ICSC concluded that the timely coordination of an updated *Shared Parking* publication with these other documents would result in a vastly improved set of tools for transportation planners to determine the appropriate number of parking spaces for mixed-use developments.

Definition of Terms

A key to understanding the shared parking methodology is the definition of terms and assumptions inherent in the use of those terms.

Parking ratio is the number of parking spaces that should be provided per unit of land use, if parking serves only that land use. The ratios recommended herein are based on the expected peak accumulation of vehicles at the peak hour on a design day (see below), assuming nearly 100 percent modal split to auto use and minimal ridesharing. The recommended ratios also include consideration of effective supply issues.

Parking accumulation is the number of parked vehicles observed at a site.

Parking supply is the total number of spaces available to serve a destination. It may include spaces that are on site, off site, on street, or shared with other uses.

Effective parking supply is the number of occupied spaces at optimum operating efficiency. A parking facility will be perceived as full at somewhat less than its actual capacity, generally in the range of 85–95 percent occupancy. (The range is because regular users learn where spaces are likely to be available at a particular time of day and thus require less of an extra cushion than unfamiliar users.) It is appropriate to have a small cushion of spaces over the expected peak-hour accumulation of vehicles. The cushion reduces the need to search the entire system for the last few parking spaces, thus reducing patron frustration. It further provides for operating fluctuations, misparked vehicles, snow cover, vehicle maneuvers, and vacancies created by reserving spaces for specific users, such as disabled parking. The effective supply cushion in a system also provides for unusual peaks in activities.

A design day or design hour is one that recurs frequently enough to justify providing spaces for that level of parking activity. One does not build for an average day and have insufficient supply for the peak (if not multiple) hours on 50 percent of the days in a year. Conversely, it is not appropriate to design for the peak accumulation of vehicles ever observed at any site with that land use. That peak accumulation might last only for an hour or so, while there are 8,760 hours in a year. A traffic engineer does not design a street system to handle the peak volume that would ever occur; instead, the level of activity that represents the 85th or 90th percentile of observed traffic volumes in peak hours on average days is used for design. This second edition of *Shared Parking* uses the 85th percentile of peak-hour observations for recommended parking ratios, unless otherwise noted. See chapter 3 for further discussion of design hour issues.

Mode adjustment is employed to adjust the base parking ratios for local transportation characteristics. Two factors must be considered in such adjustments: modal split for private auto and auto occupancy, both of which are terms commonly used in transportation planning. The parking ratios herein assume that nearly all users arrive by private auto with typical auto occupancy for the specific use. It should be noted that even in locations without transit, some walking and dropoffs occur, as well as some ridesharing. The base ratios are appropriate for conditions of free parking and negligible use of public transit. The mode adjustment then reflects local transit availability, parking fees, ride sharing programs, and so on. See chapter 3 for further discussion of mode adjustments.

Modal split is the percentage of persons arriving at a destination in different modes of transportation. Among the modes that may be available are commuter rail, light rail, bus, private automobile (including trucks, vans, and SUVs used for personal transportation), carpools and vanpools, walking, and bicycling. The percentage of persons who arrive at the destination by private automobile is generally called "auto mode split" and includes both driver and passengers.

Auto occupancy is the average number of persons per private automobile arriving at the destination. Vehicle occupancy (as employed in transportation planning) refers to the average number of persons per vehicle including all vehicle types, such as public and chartered buses.

Noncaptive ratio is an estimate of the percentage of parkers at a land use in a mixed-use development or district who are not already counted as being parked at another of the land uses. For example, when employees of one land use visit a nearby food court or coffee store, there usually is not any additional parking demand generated. See chapter 3 for further discussion.

Units of Land Uses

Parking ratios are generally stated as a ratio of *x* spaces per *y* units, with the unit being the most statistically valid independent variable for that land use. In the vast majority of uses, the unit is square feet of building area. Other units that may be used are employees, dwelling units, hotel rooms, or seats. This publication uses the most widely accepted independent variable, generally in accordance with *Parking Generation*. The following terms describe specific formulas for parking ratios.

Gross Floor Area (GFA): Total gross floor area, including exterior building walls of all floors of a building or structure. Also referred to as gross square feet or GSF.

Gross Leasable Area (GLA): The portion of GFA that is available for leasing to a tenant. Generally, GLA is equal to GFA less "common" areas that are not leased to tenants, including spaces for circulation to and from tenant spaces (lobbies, elevator cores, stairs, corridors, atriums, and so on), utility/mechanical spaces, and parking areas.

Net Floor Area (NFA): Total floor area, excluding exterior building walls.

Net Rental Area (NRA): The portion of NFA that is rentable to a tenant. Also called net leasable area.

Thus, GFA and GLA are calculated out-to-out of exterior walls, while NFA and NRA are calculated between interior faces of exterior walls. GLA is commonly used for shopping centers, but GFA or NFA is more commonly used for office uses. No matter what calculation method is employed, the vehicular parking and loading areas and the floor area occupied by mechanical, electrical, communications, and security equipment are deducted from the floor area for the purpose of calculating parking needs.

Organization of This Report

Chapter 2 of this report presents key findings, including the recommended default values for shared parking analysis. Chapter 3 discusses the methodology, with an example analysis, and chapter 4 discusses the parking needs of individual land uses and the derivation of the default values. Chapter 5 presents case studies, while chapter 6 discusses the design, operation, and management of shared parking.

Notes

1. ULI–the Urban Land Institute, *Shared Parking* (Washington, D.C.: ULI–the Urban Land Institute, 1983).

2. "About Smart Growth," www.smartgrowth.org/about (October 2003).

3. 2004 Restaurant Industry Forecast, National Restaurant Association.

4. ITE Technical Council Committee 6F-52, *Shared Parking Planning Guidelines* (Washington, D.C.: Institute of Transportation Engineers, 1995).

5. ULI–the Urban Land Institute and the International Council of Shopping Centers, *Parking Requirements for Shopping Centers*, 2nd ed. (Washington, D.C.: ULI–the Urban Land Institute, 1999).

6. ITE Technical Council Committee, *Trip Generation*, 7th ed. (Washington, D.C.: Institute of Transportation Engineers, 2004).

7. ITE Technical Council Committee, *Parking Generation*, 3rd ed. (Washington, D.C.: Institute of Transportation Engineers, 2004).

2 Key Findings

This report presents recommendations for the methodology as well as recommended default values for certain assumptions to be employed in a shared parking analysis.

Methodology

Shared parking methodology provides a systematic way to apply appropriate adjustments to parking ratios for each use in a mixed-use development or district. This methodology is summarized in Figure 2-1. Chapter 3 discusses the importance of each of these steps. Steps 1 and 9, which involve developing an understanding of the project before starting analysis, and developing site design and parking management plans that will facilitate shared parking (after the recommended number of spaces is determined), are often neglected in many shared parking studies. The analysis may reliably project the peak accumulation of vehicles, but if the design and management of the parking system do not facilitate the sharing of spaces, parking may be inadequate. While management practices can often be changed to improve the situation, a poorly designed site for shared parking often cannot be significantly improved, and more spaces may ultimately have to be added. Chapter 6 is devoted to this topic.

One of the key changes in the methodology from the first edition of *Shared Parking* is the separation of parking ratios into visitor/customer, employee/resident, and reserved components. This delineation facilitates application of different noncaptive and mode adjustments, since those characteristics may be distinctly different in certain locations and with certain combinations of land uses.

Most important, if spaces are reserved for specific users, they cannot be shared with other land uses. For example, in some cases where a shared parking analysis was found to be unreliable, it had assumed that residential spaces would be shared, but the residential leasing plan developed later in the process included separated, dedicated stalls for the residents' parking needs. Leasing deals for office and retail tenants may also include reserved parking. Spaces that are reserved for specific users are part of the parking needed for that land use, whether or not a vehicle is present.

The terms "weekday" and "weekend" have also been modified. Weekdays are now defined as extending from 6 a.m. Monday to 5 p.m. Friday. Weekends include Friday evening and all day Saturday. This categorization avoids increasing weekday factors to reflect Friday evening activity at restaurants, cinemas, and other venues where there is considerably more demand on Friday evenings than other weekdays. Parking requirements on Sundays are not considered here, as they are rarely a significant factor in parking planning and there is currently inadequate data on which to base recommended ratios for Sunday conditions at most land uses.

When performed manually, the determination of critical scenarios for peak parking needs is usually an iterative process. Depending on the relative quantities of retail, dining, and entertainment, a shopping center may have peak demand in December or in July. Therefore, with few exceptions, it is important to develop several scenarios for modeling parking needs to assure that the peak hour is identified. ULI and ICSC have made available a shared parking model that greatly eases the number of iterations required to determine the overall peak need for parking. Using the default values recommended in this report, along with user input of quantities of land uses, mode, and noncaptive adjustments, the model calculates the parking needs in each hour of the day from 6 a.m. to midnight, weekdays and weekends, for each month. It then determines the peak hour of the peak month for weekdays and weekends. If necessary, the user can make further manual adjustments to finalize the analysis.

Figure 2-1 Shared Parking Methodology

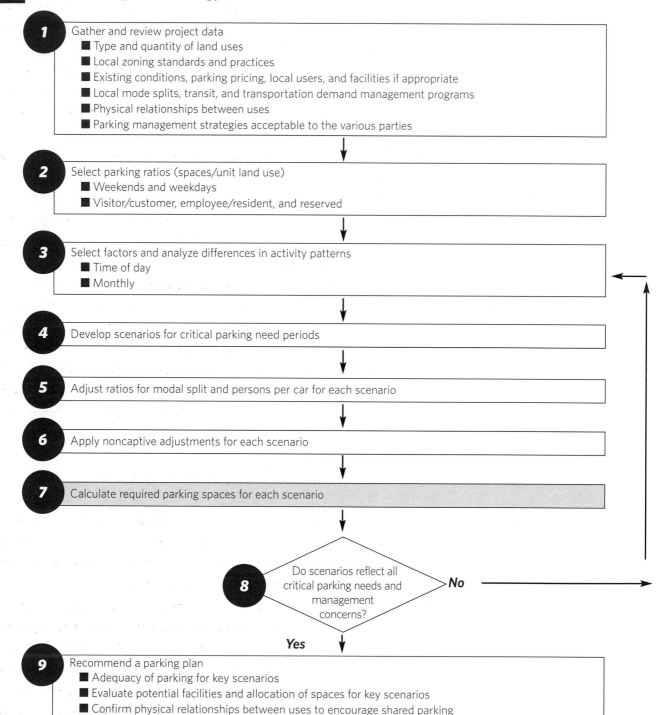

1 Gather and review project data
- Type and quantity of land uses
- Local zoning standards and practices
- Existing conditions, parking pricing, local users, and facilities if appropriate
- Local mode splits, transit, and transportation demand management programs
- Physical relationships between uses
- Parking management strategies acceptable to the various parties

2 Select parking ratios (spaces/unit land use)
- Weekends and weekdays
- Visitor/customer, employee/resident, and reserved

3 Select factors and analyze differences in activity patterns
- Time of day
- Monthly

4 Develop scenarios for critical parking need periods

5 Adjust ratios for modal split and persons per car for each scenario

6 Apply noncaptive adjustments for each scenario

7 Calculate required parking spaces for each scenario

8 Do scenarios reflect all critical parking needs and management concerns? — *No*

Yes

9 Recommend a parking plan
- Adequacy of parking for key scenarios
- Evaluate potential facilities and allocation of spaces for key scenarios
- Confirm physical relationships between uses to encourage shared parking
- Recommend parking management plan to achieve projected shared parking

Note: Step 7 is automatically performed in the ULI/ICSC shared parking model

Another key change in the methodology is that it is strongly recommended that mode and noncaptive adjustments be modified for each scenario. Generally speaking, these factors vary by four combinations of time/day of week:

■ weekday daytime,
■ weekday evening,
■ weekend daytime, and
■ weekend evening.

For example, a significantly higher proportion of the patrons of a restaurant near large concentrations of office workers will be captive on a weekday at noon than would be true that same evening. There may be differences in mode adjustments for employees on weekdays and weekends and by time of day, depending on the service schedules of local transit systems, the perception of security at certain times of the day, and other factors.

Although captive market effects are discussed in this report for a number of land uses, the magnitude will be affected significantly by the combinations of land uses and more specifically the relative quantities. For example, the noncaptive adjustments for a 10,000-square-foot restaurant in a 40,000-square-foot strip shopping center will be distinctly different than the adjustments for a restaurant of that size in a mixed-use project with significant office space or hotel rooms. Even ranges of noncaptive factors for each land use thus would be misleading. Therefore, suggested ranges of noncaptive factors are not tabulated in this report. The sole exception is hotels, where there typically is a rational relationship between the number of guest rooms and the square feet of restaurants and meeting and conference/banquet space. Chapter 3 includes a discussion of how to develop noncaptive adjustments, and examples are provided in the case studies of chapter 5.

Regarding step 5 of the methodology, the wide availability of information regarding modal splits for commuters in a particular community (or even in a census tract) greatly assists in the development of mode adjustments for employees. Information is also available on auto ownership by household that can be identified by community or a more specific area. This information can be obtained through local surveys of comparable conditions. Adjustments for differences in auto occupancy are more likely to affect employee parking than visitor parking. In particular, formal ridesharing programs at employment centers can and will increase the auto occupancy of commuters above that found in low-density suburban developments.

Step 8 is another particularly critical step in the process. Even when one is using the ULI/ICSC model, which will determine the peak demand for the assumptions that have been entered into it, there may be other scenarios that should be factored into parking planning. It may be important to document that one scenario indeed reflects greater demand, in order to encourage a developer's acceptance of the findings or to provide input for parking planning and management. The number of spaces provided in each parking area or facility may be driven by particular needs at specific times of the day that should be documented in order to ensure adequate and convenient parking for tenants.

Parking Ratios and Other Default Factors

This edition of *Shared Parking* significantly increases the number of land uses for which recommended parking ratios are presented, and it subdivides some land uses into more refined categories. These changes are summarized in Table 2-1.

Chapter 4 discusses each land use, the derivation of the parking ratios, and the sources for time of day and monthly factors in detail. The key findings, however, follow. Table 2-2 presents the recommended parking ratios, while Tables 2-3 and 2-4 present recommended monthly factors for customer and employee/resident parking needs, respectively. Tables 2-5 and 2-6 present time-of-day factors for weekdays and weekends, respectively.

Table 2-1 Land Use Changes between First and Second Editions of *Shared Parking*

Land Use[1] in Second Edition	Land Use in First Edition	Comment
Office (701) <25,000 sq. ft.	Single category: Office	Per *Parking Generation*, separation is appropriate.
Office (701) 25,000 to 100,000 sq. ft.		
Office (701) 100,000 to 500,000 sq. ft.		
Office (701) >500,000 sq. ft.		
Data Processing Center		
Medical/Dental Office (720)		
Bank with Drive-in (912)		
Retail	Retail (400,000 sq. ft.)	n/a
Community Center <400,000 sq. ft. (820)	Retail (600,000 sq. ft.)[2]	
Regional Center 400,000 to 600,000 sq. ft. (820)		
Super Regional Center >600,000 sq. ft. (820)		
Fine/Casual Dining (Quality Restaurant, 931; High Turnover with Bar, 932)	Single category: Restaurant	Unpublished study by team member and *Parking Generation* indicated separation is appropriate.
Family Restaurant (High Turnover with No Bar, 932)		
Fast Food (ITE Fast Food, 933)		
Cineplex (444) (>10 screens)	Same	First-edition ratio was applicable for 1-5 screens.
Residential, Rented (221, 222, 224)	Single category: Residential	Per *Parking Generation*, separation is appropriate.
Residential, Owned (230)		Specific time of day and adjustment factors are provided for suburban and transit/CBD oriented locations.
Leisure Hotel (330)—Rooms	Guest Rooms	Per published references, separation is appropriate.
Business Hotel (312)—Rooms	Restaurant/Lounge	
Restaurant/Lounge	Conference Rooms	
Conference Center/Banquet (20 to 50 sq. ft./room)	Convention Area	
Convention (>50 sq. ft./room)		
Convention Center (455)	Not covered	Common in shared parking situations, especially in central business districts.
Health Club (492)	Not covered	Common in shared parking situations.
Performing Arts Center (441)	Not covered	Common in shared parking situations.
Active Entertainment (400 series)	Not covered	Significant trend in retail development; due to wide variation in specific tenants, default values for parking ratios are not provided.
Nightclub	Not covered	Significant trend in retail development.
Arena	Not covered	Common in shared parking situations.
Baseball Stadium	Not covered	Common in shared parking situations.
Football Stadium	Not covered	Common in shared parking situations.

Notes

[1]The ITE *Parking Generation* land use code is provided in parenthesis.
[2]The text of the first edition of *Shared Parking* recommended that, between 400,000 and 600,000 sq. ft., the ratio should be linearly interpolated from 4.0 to 5.0 spaces per thousand sq. ft., which was consistent with the then-current ULI/ICSC publication on *Parking Requirements for Shopping Centers*. The table summarizing the parking ratios, however, identified retail as noted and thus was not completely clear regarding the ratio to be used between 400,000 and 600,000 sq. ft.

Table 2-2 Summary of Recommended Base Parking Ratios (Spaces per Unit Land Use)

Land Use	Weekday Visitor	Weekday Employee	Weekend Visitor	Weekend Employee	Unit	Source
Community Shopping Center (<400,000 sq. ft.)	2.9	0.7	3.2	0.8	/ksf[1] GLA	1
Regional Shopping Center (400,000 to 600,000 sq. ft.)	Sliding scale between 400,000 and 600,000 sq. ft.				/ksf GLA	1
Super Regional Shopping Center (>600,000 sq. ft.)	3.2	0.8	3.6	0.9	/ksf GLA	1
Fine/Casual Dining	15.25	2.75	17.0	3.0	/ksf GLA	2, 3
Family Restaurant	9.0	1.5	12.75	2.25	/ksf GLA	3
Fast-Food Restaurant	12.75	2.25	12.0	2.0	/ksf GLA	2
Nightclub	15.25	1.25	17.5	1.5	/ksf GLA	3
Active Entertainment	Custom to each tenant					
Cineplex	0.19	0.01	0.26	0.01	/seat	3, 2
Performing Arts Theater	0.3	0.07	0.33	0.07	/seat	2
Arena	0.27	0.03	0.3	0.03	/seat	3
Pro Football Stadium	0.3	0.01	0.3	0.01	/seat	3
Pro Baseball Stadium	0.31	0.01	0.34	0.01	/seat	3
Health Club	6.6	0.4	5.5	0.25	/ksf GFA	3, 4
Convention Center	5.5	0.5	5.5	0.5	/ksf GLA	3
Hotel—Business	1.0	0.25	0.9	0.18	/room	2, 3
Hotel—Leisure	0.9	0.25	1.0	0.18	/room	2, 3
Restaurant/Lounge	10.0	—	10.0	—	/ksf GLA	2, 3, 5
Conference Center/Banquet (20 to 50 sq. ft./guest room)	30.0	—	30.0	—	/ksf GLA	2, 3, 5
Convention Space (>50 sq. ft./guest room)	20.0	—	10.0	—	/ksf GLA	2, 3, 5
Residential, Rental	0.15	1.5[2]	0.15	1.5[2]	/unit	2
Residential, Owned	0.15	1.7[2]	0.15	1.7[2]	/unit	2
Office (<25,000 sq. ft.)	0.3	3.5	0.03	0.35	/ksf GFA	2
Office (25,000 to 100,000 sq. ft.) Sliding scale between					/ksf GFA	2
25,000 sq. ft.:	0.3	3.5	0.03	0.35		
100,000 sq. ft.:	0.25	3.15	0.03	0.32		
Office (100,000 to 500,000 sq. ft.) Sliding scale between					/ksf GFA	2
100,000 sq. ft.:	0.25	3.15	0.03	0.32		
500,000 sq. ft.:	0.2	2.6	0.02	0.26		
Office >500,000 sq. ft.	0.2	2.6	0.02	0.26	/ksf GFA	2
Data Processing Office	0.25	5.75	0.03	0.58	/ksf GFA	2, 3
Medical/Dental Office	3.0	1.5	3.0	1.5	/ksf GFA	2, 3
Bank, Branch with Drive-in	3.0	1.6	3.0	1.6	/ksf GFA	2

Notes

Ratios based on peak parking spaces required with virtually 100% auto use and typical ridesharing for suburban conditions.

[1] /ksf = per thousand sq. ft.

[2] 1.0 spaces reserved for residents' sole use, 24 hours a day; remainder shared with visitors and other uses.

Sources:

1. *Parking Requirements for Shopping Centers*, 2nd ed. (Washington, D.C.: ULI–the Urban Land Institute, 1999).
2. *Parking Generation*, 3rd ed. (Washington, D.C.: Institute of Transportation Engineers, 2004).
3. Data collected by team members.
4. John W. Dorsett, "Parking Requirements for Health Clubs," *The Parking Professional*, April 2004.
5. Gerald Salzman, "Hotel Parking: How Much Is Enough?" *Urban Land*, January 1988.

The first edition of *Shared Parking* employed a single ratio of 3.0 spaces/ksf (per thousand square feet) for parking at office uses on weekdays, with 0.5 spaces/ksf on weekends. This edition stratifies office uses into six categories, four for general office with ratios decreasing as size of office space increases (3.8 to 2.8 spaces/ksf on weekdays and 0.38 to 0.28 spaces/ksf on weekends), plus separate new categories for data processing offices and medical and dental offices. In addition, a new category is now provided for bank branches with drive-in facilities.

For retail, the update of *Parking Requirements for Shopping Centers* in 1999 recommended the same parking ratios for less than 400,000 square feet of retail (4.0 spaces/ksf) but lowered the ratio for centers larger than 600,000 square feet from 5.0 spaces/ksf to 4.5 spaces/ksf. This change also results in slightly different ratios when scaled between 400,000 and 600,000 square feet. This edition recommends a similarly scaled ratio of 3.5 to 4.0 spaces/ksf for weekday parking needs, as compared with the flat 3.8 spaces/ksf ratio of *Shared Parking's* first edition. Monthly and time-of-day factors for retail have been modified considerably to represent more recent shopping patterns.

Parking Requirements for Shopping Centers also recommended that where dining and entertainment uses (including cinema) represent more than 20 percent of the total GLA, shared parking methodology should be employed. When dining and entertainment uses constitute 10–20 percent of the GLA, *Parking Requirements for Shopping Centers* recommended that the base ratio for retail be increased by 0.03 for each additional 1 percent of dining/entertainment space over 10 percent. The case studies in chapter 6 indicate that the use of shared parking methodology may be more accurate for shopping centers where dining and entertainment uses exceed 10 percent of the GLA. The case studies also confirm that it is not necessary or appropriate to further stratify retail uses such as discount superstores, big-box retail uses, and supermarkets

and drug stores (using more refined base ratios for each); rather, the base ratios recommended for shopping centers should be employed for all retail tenancies.

Parking ratios for restaurants have also been considerably modified in this edition. The first edition recommended a single ratio of 20.0 spaces/ksf for both weekdays and weekends for restaurant use. This second edition separates restaurants into three categories: fine/casual dining (with bars), family restaurants (no bar), and fast-food restaurants. The Saturday ratio for fine/casual dining remains 20.0 spaces/ksf, but the weekday ratio is now 18.0 spaces/ksf, with ratios of 15.0 on Saturday and 10.5 on weekdays for family restaurants. In addition to the lower ratios, a key reason for this differentiation between restaurants with and without bars is that family restaurants have peak parking needs at noon, while fine/casual establishments peak in the evenings. Differentiation also enables analysts to employ more captive patronage (and thus a lower noncaptive adjustment) for fast-food uses than for restaurants, where the typical patron stays for an hour or more. Ratios of 15 spaces/ksf on weekdays and 14 spaces/ksf on Saturdays are recommended for fast-food restaurants.

The ratios for cineplexes have been lowered from 0.3 on weekends and 0.25 on weekdays to 0.27 and 0.2, respectively, reflecting the significant changes in the movie theater business in the last 20 years.

Separate ratios of 1.65 and 1.85 spaces/unit are now recommended as the starting points for rental and owned residential units (the same ratios are employed weekdays and weekends), rather than the single ratio of "1.0 spaces per auto owned per dwelling unit" recommended in the first edition. The latter was intended to be adjusted according to auto ownership per dwelling unit but was commonly used as simply 1.0 space/unit. For this edition, the study team concluded that it was more appropriate to give ratios reflecting auto ownership for "cornfield" residential projects and to allow adjustment for the specific location of the units. (A cornfield project is a freestanding land use in an area with little or no transit and only weak pedestrian connections with other uses.)

For hotels, while ratios of 1.25 spaces/room (for overnight guests and employees) continue to be used for business hotels on weekdays, a lower ratio of 1.18 spaces/room is now recommended for such hotels on the weekends, and reversed ratios of 1.18 and 1.25 spaces per room are recommended for weekdays and weekends, respectively, at leisure hotels. In addition, while the same ratio of 10 spaces/ksf is still recommended for hotel restaurants/lounges for weekdays and weekends, the recommended ratios for convention areas (now defined as more than 50 ksf/guest room) have been lowered from 30 spaces/ksf both weekdays and weekends to 20 ksf on weekdays and 10 ksf on weekends. The ratios for banquet/meeting space (20 to 50 ksf/guest room) have been converted from 0.5 spaces/seat to 30 spaces/ksf for weekdays and weekends. The sole category with recommended default values for mode and noncaptive adjustments is hotels.

The remaining eight uses presented in this edition were not considered in the first edition. These include nightclubs, active entertainment venues, performing arts theaters, arenas, pro football and baseball stadiums, health clubs, and convention centers.

The time-of-day variations in parking needs continue to be the most significant determinants of the potential for shared parking at project sites. Where uses have been considered in both editions, the time-of-day factors recommended here are significantly different in many cases than those recommended previously.

Seasonal variations also continue to have a large impact on parking, especially for retail demand and cinemas. A significant improvement in the reliability of the methodology has been achieved by considering the period between Christmas and New Year's Day as a "13th month" because cineplex activity patterns are considerably different in the postholiday period than in the holiday shopping season.

Captive markets also have a large influence on parking. Office workers and hotel guests in particular can provide important markets for nearby retail and restaurants without requiring additional parking. Significant levels of carpooling, transit, or pedestrian access can reduce parking demands. Individual estimates must be made for particular local situations.

Conclusion

The shared parking study team evaluated significant amounts of national information that have been found to be appropriate for estimating parking demand. Where good local data exist, however, such as peak parking statistics for single land uses, high transit use, or noncaptive rates, they are preferable to the national data.

■ Shared parking analysis is still a valid method for estimating parking requirements of mixed-use projects. There are now many more components, and this update includes estimates for a much wider range of land uses.

■ Designing for the peak hour of parking demand requires a broad consideration of many potential scenarios, as well as extensive data on the hourly and seasonal variations, much of which is included here.

■ In order for shared parking to be most effective, it is important that all spaces be conveniently located and accessible to all users. Various techniques of managing parking can be used to encourage the sharing of parking.

Table 2-3 Recommended Monthly Adjustment Factors for Customer/Visitor Parking

Land Use	JAN	FEB	MAR	APR	MAY	JUN	JUL	AUG	SEP	OCT	NOV	DEC	Late DEC	Source
Shopping Center	56%	57%	64%	63%	66%	67%	64%	69%	64%	66%	72%	100%	80%	1, 3
Restaurant	85%	86%	95%	92%	96%	95%	98%	99%	91%	96%	93%	100%	95%	1
Fast Food	85%	86%	95%	92%	96%	95%	98%	99%	91%	96%	93%	100%	95%	1
Nightclub	84%	86%	98%	90%	90%	91%	94%	96%	92%	98%	96%	100%	95%	1
Cineplex Weekdays	27%	21%	20%	19%	27%	41%	55%	40%	15%	15%	25%	23%	100%	3
Cineplex Weekends	71%	59%	67%	58%	71%	82%	92%	75%	51%	62%	78%	67%	100%	3
Performing Arts Theater	90%	90%	90%	90%	90%	90%	90%	90%	90%	90%	90%	100%	100%	2
Arena	90%	100%	100%	100%	100%	75%	—	—	60%	65%	90%	95%	95%	2
Pro Football Stadium[1]	—	—	—	—	—	—	—	67%	—	—	—	100%	100%	2
Pro Baseball Stadium	—	—	—	100%	100%	100%	100%	100%	100%	100%	—	—	—	2
Health Club	100%	95%	85%	70%	65%	65%	65%	70%	80%	85%	85%	90%	95%	2, 4
Convention Center[2]	75%	100%	90%	55%	60%	50%	45%	75%	80%	85%	100%	60%	—	2
Hotel—Business	71%	85%	91%	90%	92%	100%	98%	92%	93%	93%	81%	67%	50%	5
Hotel—Leisure	90%	100%	100%	100%	90%	90%	100%	100%	75%	75%	75%	50%	100%	5
Restaurant/Lounge	85%	86%	95%	92%	96%	95%	98%	99%	91%	96%	93%	100%	95%	1
Meeting/Banquet (20 to 50 sq. ft./guest room)	100%	100%	100%	100%	100%	100%	100%	100%	100%	100%	100%	100%	100%	2
Convention (>50 sq. ft./guest room)	75%	100%	90%	55%	60%	50%	45%	75%	80%	85%	100%	60%	—	2
Residential	100%	100%	100%	100%	100%	100%	100%	100%	100%	100%	100%	100%	100%	2
Office, Bank	100%	100%	100%	100%	100%	100%	95%	95%	100%	100%	100%	100%	80%	2, 6

Notes

December = December 1–24; Late December = December 25–31.

[1]Because there is only one weeknight game and no Saturday games per NFL team September through November, and activity patterns are modified at adjacent uses due to the crowds expected, this category is not considered a "design day" for parking planning.

[2]Many convention centers are completely dark between Christmas and New Year's Day.

Sources:

1. U.S. Census Bureau, unadjusted estimates of monthly retail and food service sales, 1999–2002.
2. Data collected by team members.
3. *Parking Generation*, 3rd ed. (Washington, D.C.: Institute of Transportation Engineers, 2004).
4. John W. Dorsett, "Parking Requirements for Health Clubs," *The Parking Professional*, April 2004.
5. Smith Travel Research, www.wwstar.com.
6. Parking study conducted by Patton Harris Rust & Associates for the Peterson Companies, 2001.

Table 2-4 Recommended Monthly Adjustment Factors for Employee Parking

Land Use	JAN	FEB	MAR	APR	MAY	JUN	JUL	AUG	SEP	OCT	NOV	DEC	Late DEC	Source
Shopping Center	80%	80%	80%	80%	80%	80%	80%	80%	80%	80%	90%	100%	90%	1, 2
Restaurant	95%	95%	100%	100%	100%	100%	100%	100%	100%	100%	100%	100%	100%	1, 2
Fast Food	95%	95%	100%	100%	100%	100%	100%	100%	100%	100%	100%	100%	100%	1, 2
Nightclub	90%	90%	100%	100%	100%	100%	100%	100%	100%	100%	100%	100%	100%	1, 2
Cineplex Weekdays	50%	50%	50%	50%	50%	75%	75%	75%	50%	50%	50%	50%	100%	3, 2
Cineplex Weekends	80%	80%	80%	80%	80%	100%	100%	90%	80%	80%	80%	80%	100%	3, 2
Performing Arts Theater	100%	100%	100%	100%	100%	100%	100%	100%	100%	100%	100%	100%	100%	2
Arena	100%	100%	100%	100%	100%	75%	10%	10%	75%	75%	100%	100%	100%	2
Pro Football Stadium[1]	10%	10%	10%	10%	10%	10%	10%	100%	10%	10%	100%	100%	100%	2
Pro Baseball Stadium	10%	10%	10%	10%	100%	100%	100%	100%	100%	100%	10%	10%	10%	2
Health Club	100%	100%	95%	80%	75%	75%	75%	80%	90%	95%	95%	100%	100%	4, 2
Convention Center	85%	100%	100%	65%	70%	60%	55%	85%	90%	95%	100%	70%	10%	5, 2
Hotel	100%	100%	100%	100%	100%	100%	100%	100%	100%	100%	100%	100%	100%	2
Residential	100%	100%	100%	100%	100%	100%	100%	100%	100%	100%	100%	100%	100%	2
Office, Bank	100%	100%	100%	100%	100%	100%	95%	95%	100%	100%	100%	100%	80%	6

Notes

December = December 1–24; Late December = December 25–31.

[1]Because there is only one weeknight game and no Saturday games per NFL team September through November, and activity patterns are modified at adjacent uses due to the crowds expected, this category is not considered a "design day" for parking planning.

Sources:

1. U.S. Census Bureau, unadjusted estimates of monthly retail and food service sales, 1999–2002.
2. Data adjusted by team members.
3. *Parking Generation*, 3rd ed. (Washington, D.C.: Institute of Transportation Engineers, 2004).
4. John W. Dorsett, "Parking Requirements for Health Clubs," *The Parking Professional*, April 2004.
5. Smith Travel Research, www.wwstar.com.
6. Parking study conducted by Patton Harris Rust & Associates for the Peterson Companies, 2001.

Table 2-5

Recommended Time-of-Day Factors for Weekdays

Land Use	User	6 a.m.	7 a.m.	8 a.m.	9 a.m.	10 a.m.	11 a.m.	Noon	1 p.m.	2 p.m.
Shopping Center—Typical	Customer	1%	5%	15%	35%	65%	85%	95%	100%	95%
Peak December	Customer	1%	5%	15%	30%	55%	75%	90%	100%	100%
Late December	Customer	1%	5%	10%	20%	40%	65%	90%	100%	100%
	Employee	10%	15%	40%	75%	85%	95%	100%	100%	100%
Fine/Casual Dining	Customer	—	—	—	—	15%	40%	75%	75%	65%
	Employee	—	20%	50%	75%	90%	90%	90%	90%	90%
Family Restaurant	Customer	25%	50%	60%	75%	85%	90%	100%	90%	50%
	Employee	50%	75%	90%	90%	100%	100%	100%	100%	100%
Fast Food	Customer	5%	10%	20%	30%	55%	85%	100%	100%	90%
	Employee	15%	20%	30%	40%	75%	100%	100%	100%	95%
Nightclub	Customer	—	—	—	—	—	—	—	—	—
	Employee	—	—	—	5%	5%	5%	5%	10%	10%
Cineplex—Typical	Customer	—	—	—	—	—	—	20%	45%	55%
Late December	Customer	—	—	—	—	—	—	35%	60%	75%
	Employee	—	—	—	—	—	—	50%	60%	60%
Performing Arts Theater	Customer	—	—	—	1%	1%	1%	1%	1%	1%
No matinee	Employee	—	10%	10%	20%	20%	20%	30%	30%	30%
Arena	Customer	—	—	—	1%	1%	1%	1%	1%	1%
No matinee	Employee	—	10%	10%	20%	20%	20%	30%	30%	30%
Stadium	Customer	—	—	—	1%	1%	1%	5%	5%	5%
8 p.m. start	Employee	—	10%	10%	20%	20%	20%	30%	30%	30%
Health Club	Customer	70%	40%	40%	70%	70%	80%	60%	70%	70%
	Employee	75%	75%	75%	75%	75%	75%	75%	75%	75%
Convention Center	Visitor	—	—	50%	100%	100%	100%	100%	100%	100%
	Employee	5%	30%	33%	33%	100%	100%	100%	100%	100%
Hotel—Business	Guest	95%	90%	80%	70%	60%	60%	55%	55%	60%
Hotel—Leisure	Guest	95%	95%	90%	80%	70%	70%	65%	65%	70%
Restaurant/Lounge	Customer	—	10%	30%	10%	10%	5%	100%	100%	33%
Conference/Banquet	Customer	—	—	30%	60%	60%	60%	65%	65%	65%
Convention	Customer	—	—	50%	100%	100%	100%	100%	100%	100%
	Employee	5%	30%	90%	90%	100%	100%	100%	100%	100%
Residential	Guest	—	10%	20%	20%	20%	20%	20%	20%	20%
Residential	Reserved	100%	100%	100%	100%	100%	100%	100%	100%	100%
Residential	Resident	100%	90%	85%	80%	75%	70%	65%	70%	70%
Office	Visitor	—	1%	20%	60%	100%	45%	15%	45%	100%
Office	Employee	3%	30%	75%	95%	100%	100%	90%	90%	100%
Medical/Dental Office	Visitor	—	—	90%	90%	100%	100%	30%	90%	100%
	Employee	—	—	60%	100%	100%	100%	100%	100%	100%
Bank	Customer	—	—	50%	90%	100%	50%	50%	50%	70%
	Employee	—	—	60%	100%	100%	100%	100%	100%	100%

3 p.m.	4 p.m.	5 p.m.	6 p.m.	7 p.m.	8 p.m.	9 p.m.	10 p.m.	11 p.m.	Midnight	Source
90%	90%	95%	95%	95%	80%	50%	30%	10%	—	1
100%	95%	85%	80%	75%	65%	50%	30%	10%	—	1
100%	95%	85%	70%	55%	40%	25%	15%	5%	—	1
100%	100%	95%	95%	95%	90%	75%	40%	15%	—	2
40%	50%	75%	95%	100%	100%	100%	95%	75%	25%	2
75%	75%	100%	100%	100%	100%	100%	100%	85%	35%	2
45%	45%	75%	80%	80%	80%	60%	55%	50%	25%	2
75%	75%	95%	95%	95%	95%	80%	65%	65%	35%	2
60%	55%	60%	85%	80%	50%	30%	20%	10%	5%	3
70%	60%	70%	90%	90%	60%	40%	30%	20%	20%	2
—	—	—	25%	50%	75%	100%	100%	100%	100%	2
10%	20%	45%	70%	100%	100%	100%	100%	100%	100%	2
55%	55%	60%	60%	80%	100%	100%	80%	65%	40%	2, 6
80%	80%	80%	70%	80%	100%	100%	85%	70%	55%	2, 6
75%	75%	100%	100%	100%	100%	100%	100%	70%	50%	2
1%	1%	1%	1%	25%	100%	100%	—	—	—	2
30%	30%	30%	100%	100%	100%	100%	30%	10%	5%	2
1%	1%	1%	10%	25%	100%	100%	85%	—	—	2
30%	30%	30%	100%	100%	100%	100%	30%	10%	5%	2
5%	5%	5%	10%	50%	100%	100%	85%	25%	—	2
30%	30%	30%	100%	100%	100%	100%	100%	25%	10%	2
70%	80%	90%	100%	90%	80%	70%	35%	10%	—	2, 4
75%	75%	100%	100%	75%	50%	20%	20%	20%	—	2, 4
100%	100%	100%	50%	30%	30%	10%	—	—	—	2
100%	90%	70%	40%	25%	20%	20%	5%	—	—	2
60%	65%	70%	75%	75%	80%	85%	95%	100%	100%	5
70%	75%	80%	85%	85%	90%	95%	95%	100%	100%	2
10%	10%	30%	55%	60%	70%	67%	60%	40%	30%	5, 3
65%	65%	100%	100%	100%	100%	100%	50%	—	—	2
100%	100%	100%	50%	30%	30%	10%	—	—	—	2
100%	90%	70%	40%	20%	20%	20%	20%	10%	5%	2
20%	20%	40%	60%	100%	100%	100%	100%	80%	50%	2
100%	100%	100%	100%	100%	100%	100%	100%	100%	100%	2
70%	75%	85%	90%	97%	98%	99%	100%	100%	100%	2
45%	15%	10%	5%	2%	1%	—	—	—	—	2
100%	90%	50%	25%	10%	7%	3%	1%	—	—	3
100%	90%	80%	67%	30%	15%	—	—	—	—	2
100%	100%	100%	67%	30%	15%	—	—	—	—	2
50%	80%	100%	—	—	—	—	—	—	—	3
100%	100%	100%	—	—	—	—	—	—	—	2

Sources:
1. Confidential data provided by shopping center managers.
2. Developed by team members.
3. *Parking Generation*, 3rd ed. (Washington, D.C.: Institute of Transportation Engineers, 2004).
4. John W. Dorsett, "Parking Requirements for Health Clubs," *The Parking Professional*, April 2004.
5. Gerald Salzman, "Hotel Parking: How Much Is Enough?" *Urban Land*, January 1988.
6. Parking study conducted by Patton Harris Rust & Associates for the Peterson Companies, 2001.

Table 2-6

Recommended Time-of-Day Factors for Weekends

Land Use	User	6 a.m.	7 a.m.	8 a.m.	9 a.m.	10 a.m.	11 a.m.	Noon	1 p.m.	2 p.m.
Shopping Center—Typical	Customer	1%	5%	10%	30%	50%	65%	80%	90%	100%
Peak December	Customer	1%	5%	10%	35%	60%	70%	85%	95%	100%
Late December	Customer	1%	5%	10%	20%	40%	60%	80%	95%	100%
	Employee	10%	15%	40%	75%	85%	95%	100%	100%	100%
Fine/Casual Dining	Customer	—	—	—	—	—	15%	50%	55%	45%
	Employee	—	20%	30%	60%	75%	75%	75%	75%	75%
Family Restaurant	Customer	10%	25%	45%	70%	90%	90%	100%	85%	65%
	Employee	50%	75%	90%	90%	100%	100%	100%	100%	100%
Fast Food	Customer	5%	10%	20%	30%	55%	85%	100%	100%	90%
	Employee	15%	20%	30%	40%	75%	100%	100%	100%	95%
Nightclub	Customer	—	—	—	—	—	—	—	—	—
	Employee	—	—	—	5%	5%	5%	5%	10%	10%
Cineplex—Typical	Customer	—	—	—	—	—	—	20%	45%	55%
Late December	Customer	—	—	—	—	—	—	35%	60%	75%
	Employee	—	—	—	—	—	—	50%	60%	60%
Performing Arts Theater	Customer	—	—	—	1%	1%	1%	1%	17%	67%
With matinee	Employee	—	10%	10%	20%	20%	20%	30%	100%	100%
Arena (two shows)	Customer	—	—	—	1%	1%	1%	1%	25%	95%
	Employee	—	10%	10%	20%	20%	20%	30%	100%	100%
Stadium (1 p.m. start; see	Customer	—	—	1%	1%	5%	5%	50%	100%	100%
weekday for evening game)	Employee	—	5%	10%	20%	30%	30%	100%	100%	100%
Health Club	Customer	80%	45%	35%	50%	35%	50%	50%	30%	25%
	Employee	50%	50%	50%	50%	50%	50%	50%	50%	50%
Convention Center	Visitor	—	—	50%	100%	100%	100%	100%	100%	100%
	Employee	5%	30%	33%	33%	100%	100%	100%	100%	100%
Hotel—Business	Guest	95%	90%	80%	70%	60%	60%	55%	55%	60%
Hotel—Leisure	Guest	95%	95%	90%	80%	70%	70%	65%	65%	70%
Restaurant/Lounge	Customer	—	10%	30%	10%	10%	5%	100%	100%	33%
Conference/Banquet	Customer	—	—	30%	60%	60%	60%	65%	65%	65%
Convention	Customer	—	—	50%	100%	100%	100%	100%	100%	100%
	Employee	5%	30%	90%	90%	100%	100%	100%	100%	100%
Residential	Guest	—	20%	20%	20%	20%	20%	20%	20%	20%
Residential	Reserved	100%	100%	100%	100%	100%	100%	100%	100%	100%
Residential	Resident	100%	90%	85%	80%	75%	70%	65%	70%	70%
Office	Visitor	—	20%	60%	80%	90%	100%	90%	80%	60%
Office	Employee	—	20%	60%	80%	90%	100%	90%	80%	60%
Medical/Dental Office	Visitor	—	—	90%	90%	100%	100%	30%	—	—
	Employee	—	—	60%	100%	100%	100%	100%	—	—
Bank	Customer	—	—	25%	40%	75%	100%	90%	—	—
	Employee	—	—	90%	100%	100%	100%	100%	—	—

3 p.m.	4 p.m.	5 p.m.	6 p.m.	7 p.m.	8 p.m.	9 p.m.	10 p.m.	11 p.m.	Midnight	Source
100%	95%	90%	80%	75%	65%	50%	35%	15%	—	1
100%	95%	90%	80%	75%	65%	50%	35%	15%	—	1
100%	95%	85%	70%	60%	50%	30%	20%	10%	—	1
100%	100%	95%	85%	80%	75%	65%	45%	15%	—	2
45%	45%	60%	90%	95%	100%	90%	90%	90%	50%	2
75%	75%	100%	100%	100%	100%	100%	100%	85%	50%	2
40%	45%	60%	70%	70%	65%	30%	25%	15%	10%	2
75%	75%	95%	95%	95%	95%	80%	65%	65%	35%	2
60%	55%	60%	85%	80%	50%	30%	20%	10%	5%	3
70%	60%	70%	90%	90%	60%	40%	30%	20%	20%	2
—	—	—	25%	50%	75%	100%	100%	100%	100%	2
10%	20%	45%	70%	100%	100%	100%	100%	100%	100%	2
55%	55%	60%	60%	80%	100%	100%	100%	80%	50%	2, 6
80%	80%	80%	70%	80%	100%	100%	100%	85%	70%	2, 6
75%	75%	100%	100%	100%	100%	100%	100%	70%	50%	2
67%	1%	1%	1%	25%	100%	100%	—	—	—	2
100%	30%	30%	100%	100%	100%	100%	30%	10%	5%	2
95%	81%	1%	1%	25%	100%	100%	—	—	—	2
100%	100%	30%	100%	100%	100%	100%	30%	10%	5%	2
85%	25%	—	—	—	—	—	—	—	—	2
100%	25%	10%	5%	5%	—	—	—	—	—	2
30%	55%	100%	95%	60%	30%	10%	1%	1%	—	2, 4
50%	75%	100%	100%	75%	50%	20%	20%	20%	—	2, 4
100%	100%	100%	50%	30%	30%	10%	—	—	—	2
100%	90%	70%	40%	25%	20%	20%	5%	—	—	2
60%	65%	70%	75%	75%	80%	85%	95%	100%	100%	5
70%	75%	80%	85%	85%	90%	95%	95%	100%	100%	2
10%	10%	30%	55%	60%	70%	67%	60%	40%	30%	5
65%	65%	100%	100%	100%	100%	100%	50%	—	—	5
100%	100%	100%	50%	30%	30%	10%	—	—	—	2
100%	90%	75%	60%	55%	55%	55%	45%	45%	30%	5
20%	20%	40%	60%	100%	100%	100%	100%	80%	50%	2
100%	100%	100%	100%	100%	100%	100%	100%	100%	100%	2
70%	75%	85%	90%	97%	98%	99%	100%	100%	100%	2
40%	20%	10%	5%	—	—	—	—	—	—	2
40%	20%	10%	5%	—	—	—	—	—	—	3
—	—	—	—	—	—	—	—	—	—	2
—	—	—	—	—	—	—	—	—	—	2
—	—	—	—	—	—	—	—	—	—	3
—	—	—	—	—	—	—	—	—	—	2

Sources:
1. Confidential data provided by shopping center managers.
2. Developed by team members.
3. *Parking Generation*, 3rd ed. (Washington, D.C.: Institute of Transportation Engineers, 2004).
4. John W. Dorsett, "Parking Requirements for Health Clubs," *The Parking Professional*, April 2004.
5. Gerald Salzman, "Hotel Parking: How Much Is Enough?" *Urban Land*, January 1988.
6. Parking study conducted by Patton Harris Rust & Associates for the Peterson Companies, 2001.

Shared Parking Principles

A key step in gaining acceptance for shared parking is understanding the factors that result in the reduced need for parking spaces for a particular combination of land uses. Shared parking analysis (see Figure 2-1) provides a systematic way to apply appropriate adjustments. This chapter reviews the factors and adjustments in the same sequence presented in Figure 2-1. The methodology has been modified slightly from that recommended in the first edition of this publication, based on a number of considerations explained below.

Local circumstances, both routine and nonroutine, cause parking generation to vary significantly from any one day to any other day. These circumstances, including competition, strength of tenants, changes in the local economy, and demographics, change over time. The goal of any shared parking analysis is to arrive at a projection of parking needs that is reasonably reliable and consistent with accepted transportation planning principles and practices. The use of 85th percentile conditions rather than average ones has been incorporated into this book's recommendations, in order to provide an acceptable level of confidence in the output. A 5 percent or even 10 percent change in any one factor for any one land use is unlikely to have a significant impact on the bottom line.

Conversely, misunderstanding the principles of shared parking or rote application of the default values and factors recommended here, absent professional judgment and knowledge regarding the specific local conditions, can result in unrealistic projections. This report's recommendations should be considered simply a starting point for the analysis of shared parking by experienced and knowledgeable professionals.

Step 1: Gather and Review Project Data

Shared parking analysis entails projecting parking needs for a specific combination of land uses, whether for an individual development project or a parking district or area that shares parking resources. Understanding the precise nature of the land uses, transit availability, parking pricing and transportation demand management considerations, and the interaction of the land uses is necessary to yield reasonably reliable results.

Thus, in order to enhance the analysis, it is important to:

■ determine the type and quantity of each land use;

■ review local zoning practices to determine accepted practices;

■ survey existing conditions, local users, and facilities as appropriate;

■ research the modal split, ridesharing programs, transit availability, and transportation demand management practices in the project's environs;

■ understand the physical relationships of the land uses; and

■ discuss parking management strategies with all the stakeholders, to ensure that shared parking can occur as assumed in the study phase.

In determining the types and quantities of each land use, it is critical to probe for complete and accurate information. For example, a project with 1 million square feet of "retail" space may in fact have only 800,000 square feet of shops, along with 50,000 square feet of active entertainment space, another 75,000 square feet of restaurants of various types (including a food court), and a 75,000-square-foot cineplex with 3,300 seats; thus, approximately 20 percent of the space would not be "retail." Another example of a complex land use often oversimplified and considered as a single generator is a hotel. Although zoning ordinances typically require parking spaces on the basis of the number of guest rooms, hotels may or may not have restaurants and meeting and convention facilities that significantly affect parking needs. Moreover, the activity patterns at hotels oriented to leisure travelers are somewhat different from those oriented to business travelers.

Local zoning policies regarding shared parking vary significantly. Some ordinances are simply silent on the topic, which means that a variance from local requirements is necessary to achieve a reduction in the number of required parking spaces. Local officials may need to be briefed on the concept. Some ordinances accept shared parking analysis performed in accordance with a standard methodology such as this publication's; others allow shared parking only according to specific formulas and stated reductions. Even in the latter case, it is beneficial to perform an independent analysis and then discuss any differences with officials to determine whether a variance to the local standard may be appropriate.

If local zoning requirements for parking appear to be unrealistic, it may be necessary to collect data locally to support the assumptions in the analysis. This may include surveys of parking accumulation at sites with similar characteristics to those proposed for a project.

When new uses are being added to an existing site or district, a model can be developed with assumptions for various factors. Then the model's results can be compared against observed parking accumulations for the existing combination of uses for a given day and season. When the new development is layered on top, reasonably reliable projections of future parking needs will result. When the project is a completely new, freestanding development, the projection of parking needs must rely heavily on the knowledge, experience, and professional judgment of the individual performing the analysis.

The availability and quality of local public transportation and transportation demand programs, as well as parking pricing, will affect the peak accumulation of parked vehicles. Often one step in an already iterative process can be avoided in the early data collection phase by evaluating the local modal split and making appropriate adjustments in persons per car expected in the project area.

The physical relationships among land uses will also have a significant impact on the success of shared parking provisions. These concerns are both physical (vertical versus horizontal connections, distances between land uses and planned parking, proximity to transportation, and so on) and functional design (user friendliness). Even though multiple uses may be located at a single development site, if there is a sea of asphalt for surface parking surrounding each use, it may be difficult to get those bound for a retail/dining/entertainment complex to park at a nearby office building and walk to the destination. It may be necessary to use management strategies such as valet parking or to run a shuttle to more distant parking areas when it is required to meet demand. Chapter 6 includes further exploration of these issues.

Step 2: Select Parking Ratios

The methodology requires the selection for each significant land use of a parking ratio, which is the number of spaces that would be needed if the land use were located by itself in an area with little or no transit and weak pedestrian connections with other uses (the so-called cornfield development). This book recommends parking ratios for a variety of land uses often found in shared parking situations. Where uses not discussed here are included in a shared parking situation, appropriate parking ratios must be developed.

Note that this second edition includes more land uses than the first edition and features more stratification of land uses within broad categories. Individual changes will be further discussed in the section on the development of factors for each land use; the changes and additions are also summarized in Table 2-1.

This book's recommended parking ratios aim to represent the peak accumulation of vehicles at the peak hour on a design day for that land use, as those terms have been defined in chapter 1. Unless otherwise noted in the discussion of a particular land use, the 85th percentile of observed peak-hour accumulations (ignoring seasonality) was employed in determining the parking ratios. The first edition of *Shared Parking* employed the 90th percentile of the peak-hour occupancies observed. In a 1990 article, an Institute of Transportation Engineers (ITE) committee recommended use of the 85th percentile as an appropriate design standard.[1] Weant and Levinson[2] and Smith[3] generally recommended the 85th percentile, as did the Parking Consultants Council.[4] The third edition of *Parking Generation* presents 33rd and 85th percentile values as well as the average values for each land use, to frame the variation in parking ratios and for determining appropriate parking ratios from the data set.

The issue of the appropriate design day/hour for parking has become more of a controversy in recent years as smart growth principles have become more widely accepted. Some planners argue that parking supplies should be based on the average of the peak-hour occupancies observed in order to avoid underused spaces. Others believe that "more is better" and that communities should be protected from the negative impacts of parking shortages with an effective supply factor over and above expected accumulations on most if not all days.

As noted previously, designing a parking system so that every space is occupied at a regularly occurring peak hour will result in a conclusion by owners and users, if not the community at large, that the parking is inadequate. Some have argued that recommended parking ratios should be based on the 85th percentile observation plus an additional effective supply factor of 5–10 percent. Those disagreeing point out that in many cases a system may then have enough spaces to accommodate the 100th percentile accumulation, albeit inefficiently due to increased search time for available spaces.

After considerable debate, the study team for this second edition of *Shared Parking* adopted the 85th percentile of peak-hour observations in developing recommended parking ratios. However, it should be noted that relatively few land uses in *Parking Generation* have a large enough sample size that the 85th percentile value as published was deemed reliable enough to be used directly, without further consideration. In the majority of land uses, the judgment of the *Shared*

Parking team was required to finalize the ratios. Individual considerations for each land use are discussed in chapter 4.

The *Shared Parking* team believes that using the 85th percentile will provide an adequate supply cushion in most locations. But a parking supply based on this ratio will be inadequate for a certain number of locations that perform above the average. For example, some new commercial developments have a "honeymoon" period of high activity after opening, only to settle into a more typical pattern after locals have had a chance to patronize the site. Conversely, there may be a period of time as long as three years during which patronage gradually climbs to a stabilized level. Competitive factors in a local marketplace may also affect whether or not a particular destination will perform above the 85th percentile of all the comparable destinations nationwide. The first entry into a marketplace that satisfies unmet consumer demand will often perform better than average. If exceptional performance by one venue is sustained, competitors will usually enter the marketplace and performance may subsequently become more typical or average.

When a proposed new concept does not quite fit established land use categories and perhaps is being beta tested at a particular development, adjustment from parking ratios for the most closely related land use may be required. While the owners of such venues may be loathe to reveal their business plan, a special parking ratio can be developed by combining likely peak-hour density of patrons and employees with assumptions for modal split and persons per car.

Customizing parking ratios for a particular tenant, however, particularly when it lowers the ratio, is usually not advisable from a longer-term perspective. One of the truisms of almost any business catering to consumer demand is that what is fashionable today can be forgotten tomorrow.

Separate parking ratios should be employed for weekends and weekdays, and thus they are provided here for the land uses included in this report. Weekdays are typically defined as the period of Monday through Friday, and weekends are typically defined as Saturday and Sunday. However, many entertainment venues are as busy on Friday nights as on Saturday nights, while few land uses generate parking needs on Sundays similar to that on Saturdays. Among the land uses that consistently do have peak activity on Sundays are places of worship and professional football stadiums. The parking for either of those uses usually overwhelms the demand from any other use at the peak hours, and thus shared parking is not generally a critical issue for Sunday conditions and there is little published data on Sunday parking needs. Therefore no recommendations are made for Sunday parking demand in this book. For the purposes of this report, "weekday" is defined to be the period from midnight Monday morning to 5 p.m. Friday afternoon. "Weekend" includes Friday evening and all day Saturday.

The adjustment of parking needs for combinations of uses is easier to understand and more reliably predicted if the parking ratios are broken into the components of visitor/customer and employee/resident demand. Other analysts have termed this long-term and short-term demand. Technically speaking, however, some customers (such as hotel guests) park as long or longer than employees, and part-time employees often qualify as short-term parkers (by most definitions, those who stay less than three or four hours). Therefore, this report's recommended parking ratios are broken into visitor/customer and employee/resident components.

The modal splits to private auto for customers and employees are likely to be somewhat different in areas where there is good public transportation. Employees of tenants in an office complex are more likely to use public transportation or to carpool than visitors to those same tenants. There are also some differences in the time-of-day adjustments, depending on whether the user is an employee/tenant. The employees, performers, and staff at a performing arts center will arrive several hours before a scheduled performance, and a small number of staff will be present during normal business hours to handle the daily activities of managing the facility.

Perhaps the most important reason to separate the employee and visitor parking ratios is to facilitate parking management for a mixed-use complex or activity district. For example, when Downtown Silver Spring, an urban retail/entertainment project, was developed in Silver Spring, Maryland, it was determined that the parking added for the project should accommodate only customer parking needs. The downtown area has multiple parking options for employees at various price points; adding significant spaces for employees in this core location was not deemed necessary or appropriate. This sharing of existing parking resources enabled the project to be more financially viable while maintaining the existing environment that priced employee parking according to market forces, and thus encouraged alternate modes and reduced traffic in the core areas.

The *Shared Parking* study team further decided to add another category: reserved parking. A space reserved for a specific individual or group of users cannot be used by other parkers and thus cannot be shared. In the vast majority of new urban residential developments, there is perceived to be a need to provide dedicated, reserved spaces for residents of the development in order to sell or lease the residential units. Because reserving spaces for residents is so common, a separate category is provided here to highlight the likelihood that shared parking is not being assumed. If reserved spaces are to be provided for other tenants such as office building tenants, time-of-day factors can be adjusted to reflect the fact that the space is required whether occupied or not. The breakdown of the ratios for reserved and shared parking is further discussed in the sections on residential and office parking needs.

Step 3: Select Factors and Analyze Differences in Activity Patterns

The parking needs of individual land uses vary by time of year, day of week, and hour of the day. The fact that parking needs may peak at different times generally means that fewer parking spaces are required to serve a mixed-use project than if each land use has its own dedicated parking. An obvious example is that restaurant parking needs will peak at night, while office parking needs will peak in the daytime.

It is widely accepted that the parking needs of individual land uses do not all peak at the same time, and there are numerous studies and references for the peak parking needs of any one land use. The difficulty for the development community has been in determining the factors for accumulation of vehicles at one land use when another is likely to peak. While the third edition of *Parking Generation* provides information on data points by time of day, the amount of data for many land uses remains statistically weak, and information on seasonality of data is often not available in the ITE database. Furthermore, the separation of data into more specific but smaller groupings (for example, separating big-box retail uses into as many as ten separate land use codes) makes it more difficult to determine the design day and hour because the data become less statistically reliable as they are subdivided.

For most land uses, the time-of-day and seasonality adjustments will have a greater impact on the accumulation of vehicles than mode and noncaptive adjustments. Therefore, it makes sense to evaluate the time-of-day and seasonality variables first, narrowing down the number of scenarios to be run before applying noncaptive and mode adjustments. Rationality and common sense can then be employed to decide whether additional hours, days, or seasons should be studied.

The process of determining which hour on which day results in the overall peak accumulation of parked vehicles is often iterative, but it is important to select a number of hours, days, and months for initial analysis, apply factors appropriate to each scenario, and then determine the overall peak accumulation. Presuming a peak accumulation day/time/season and then applying factors for only that one condition may not yield the true peak hour for the combination. For example, many shopping centers built today often have significant dining and entertainment space. In fact, the anchor tenant of a shopping center may be a cineplex rather than a department store. In such cases, the peak accumulation of vehicles at the shopping center may occur on a Saturday night in July or between Christmas and New Year's Day, when schools are closed.

The ULI methodology provides recommended default monthly and time-of-day adjustment factors for the accumulation of vehicles, in addition to the separated parking ratios for weekend and weekday conditions.

Monthly Activity Patterns

While peak parking needs for retail uses occur during the holiday shopping season, demand for other uses may be considerably lower during that season. For example, conventions and seminars are less likely to be scheduled for the period between Thanksgiving and New Year's Day, and business travel is significantly reduced in the last half of the month of December. The holiday shopping season further comprises part but not all of two months: November and December. Cineplex demand during the holiday shopping season is typically quite a bit lower, but will rise again during the period between Christmas and New Year's Day. This has traditionally made the development and acceptance of default values for the month of December difficult. For these reasons, this book has posited a "13th month," hereafter denoted as "Late December," for the period between Christmas and New Year's Day, reflecting high attendance at active entertainment venues, lower demand at office and other employment-centered destinations, and moderate demand for retail.

In addition to the traffic and parking data available from ITE, there are more sources available than in the past on the seasonality of various commercial activities. For example, several firms now track and report the revenue from movie ticket sales on a monthly basis. To the extent possible, these data have been employed to adjust and update the factors for seasonality.

It is important to recognize that some localities have different seasonal activity patterns. In communities in Florida and Arizona, where there are heavy concentrations of "snowbirds," the peak parking needs for most uses, including retail, may occur in February and March. Conversely, major conventions may not be scheduled during high season in such locales because the hotels are likely to be filled with leisure travelers.

Time-of-Day Patterns

Time-of-day activity generally does not exhibit as much variation due to location as do monthly factors. However, adjustment for time-of-day factors may still be appropriate for an unusual destination or situation. A cineplex in an area heavily populated by senior citizens may have higher demand for afternoon matinees, for example.

There are relatively few statistically valid sources for time-of-day adjustment factors in the public domain. Typically, the peak-hour parking accumulation or a recommended parking ratio is published. Although the third edition of *Parking Generation* includes significantly more data than in the past, it often has only a handful of data points for nonpeak hours. The collective resources of the consulting team for this publication were employed to test and adjust default factors published in a variety of places, as well as to develop the factors for newly added land uses.

Step 4: Develop Scenarios for Critical Parking Need Periods

With few exceptions, several scenarios should be developed for modeling parking needs to assure that the peak hour is identified. For a shopping center with retail, dining, a cineplex, and a relatively small amount of office uses, the following scenarios might be developed:

- weekend evening in July
- weekend afternoon and evening in December before Christmas
- weekend afternoon and evening in Late December

One should not presume that the peak hour for this shopping center is going to be Saturday afternoon in December and run only that single scenario. Conversely, if office parking needs clearly will exceed the combined demand from other uses, it would be appropriate to review weekdays in July and October as well.

The first checkpoint in this process is to consider the demand that each land use would generate in a stand-alone mode. This is not simply the square footage, but the quantity of land use times the parking ratio before application of any factors. Then, knowing what the peak times of day and season are for each use, scenarios can be generated that could reasonably result in peak accumulations of vehicles. Certainly any land use that generates less than 10 percent of the total demand when one sums the peak demand of each use is unlikely to drive the overall peak accumulation of vehicles.

It may then be necessary to test several hours for each scenario to determine the peak hours of each of those days. Often this can be achieved by checking a key hour for the land uses that appear to drive demand, eliminating some scenarios and focusing on those that seem likely to result in peak demand by checking multiple hours on those days.

It may be advisable to consider other days for parking management planning, even if they do not generate the overall peak demand for the project or area. While shared parking analysis is typically performed to determine the overall peak number of spaces required, it is often important to examine multiple periods to formulate the overall parking plan. For example, one might design sufficient parking for a project's office buildings for their design day and then allow that parking to be shared by the other uses on evenings and weekends. Exploring additional scenarios thus may assist in devising successful parking management plans.

The previously mentioned project, Downtown Silver Spring, offers a good example. Even though the number of new spaces built with the project was based on the peak customer demand, the parking study did investigate whether there were sufficient spaces in the vicinity for employees on both weekdays and weekends. There also needed to be some means of discouraging employee parking in the spaces intended for customers, particularly since the project is located only a few blocks from a Metro station for the Washington, D.C., rail transit system. Such issues are discussed in more detail later in this book; however, they do affect decisions regarding the number of spaces to be constructed and which spaces can be shared at what times.

In sum, the more scenarios that are developed, the better the understanding of the parking conditions and the greater the likely success of a shared parking analysis and parking management plan.

Step 5: Adjust Ratios for Modal Split and Persons per Car

All the parking ratios recommended in this book are intended to reflect conditions in suburban settings with little or no transit and with minimal employee ridesharing. Adjustments for reduced use of automobiles owing to alternative modes of transportation, formal ridesharing programs, or an atypical ratio of persons per car resulting from carpooling can be made by a mode adjustment. As previously defined, the mode adjustment reflects both modal split to automobiles and persons per car.

Table 3-1	Examples of Journey-to-Work Data			
Transportation Mode	**Chicago, Illinois**	**Rosemont, Illinois**	**Schaumburg, Illinois**	**Elgin, Illinois**
Population (per Census)	2,900,000	4,224	75,386	94,487
Workers (Employed in the City) over 16 Years Old	1,300,000	18,345	77,260	46,625
Commuted by Private Vehicle (Car, Truck, or Van)	60.3%	87.1%	95.2%	93.7%
Drove Alone	49.0%	79.0%	85.3%	83.2%
Carpooled	11.3%	10.5%	9.9%	10.5%
In Two-Person Carpool	8.6%	8.1%	7.4%	7.9%
In Three-Person Carpool	1.6%	1.0%	1.5%	1.3%
In Four-Person Carpool	0.6%	0.5%	0.6%	0.6%
In Five- or Six-Person Carpool	0.3%	0.1%	0.3%	0.5%
In Seven-or-More-Person Carpool	0.2%	0.1%	0.1%	0.2%
Workers per Private Vehicle	1.12	1.06	1.06	1.07
Public Transportation	31.5%	8.7%	1.3%	1.4%
Bus or Trolley Bus	11.5%	4.1%	0.7%	0.8%
Streetcar or Trolley Car	0.2%	—	0.1%	0.1%
Subway or Elevated	9.5%	3.5%	0.2%	0.1%
Railroad	9.6%	0.8%	0.1%	0.2%
Ferryboat	—	—	—	—
Taxicab	0.7%	0.3%	0.2%	0.2%
Motorcycle	—	0.1%	—	—
Bicycle	0.4%	0.1%	0.2%	0.2%
Walked	4.8%	1.3%	1.2%	2.0%
Other Means	0.9%	0.6%	0.6%	0.6%
Worked at Home	2.1%	1.5%	1.5%	2.0%
Mean Travel Time to Work (minutes)	38.9	38.7	31.5	24.7

Source: 2000 U.S. Census Bureau data.

Nearly all the recommended ratios are based on observed accumulations of parked vehicles, and thus the modal split and persons per car at that ratio are implicit in the number but not known. *Parking Generation* is careful to note that even in suburban settings, the sites studied may be served by transit to some degree. Moreover, there will often be a small number of dropoffs and walk-ins and some ridesharing, even where public transit is not available. Minuscule adjustments should be avoided; if there are data suggesting that the actual employee split is precisely 98.5 percent private auto,

they should be disregarded because some ridesharing, dropoffs, and walking are inherent in the base ratios for employee parking. The mode adjustments are intended for significant changes in modal split or persons per car.

Because of wider availability of census and transportation information, it is easier now to adjust for local modal splits for employees than in the past. Table 3-1 presents sample journey-to-work data from the 2000 census. Similar information is available by metropolitan area, county, or even census track (usually zip codes) within a county.

The four cities shown in Table 3-1 were selected to show the range of modal split to private auto and carpooling over a spectrum from a major urban area to a distant suburb. All three suburbs are located along the Northwest Tollway extending from Chicago.

Rosemont is the first suburb beyond the city limits, about 19 miles from Chicago's downtown (known regionally as the Loop). Rosemont is geographically small, with a fairly densely developed area of mid-rise office buildings and hotels adjacent to O'Hare International Airport. Rosemont has a stop on the subway line from the Loop to O'Hare and also has relatively strong local and regional bus service. It was chosen to represent a transit-oriented employment center, but one on a spoke rather than at the hub of the transit system.

Schaumburg (32 miles from the Loop) is an edge city with a significant employment base in mid-rise office towers along two intersecting interstates, drawing suburb-to-suburb commuters from a large area. There is also rail transit service through Schaumburg, and transit links from the trains to employment centers are provided.

Elgin was originally a separate city, but it has been swallowed by suburban growth in the last 15 to 20 years. It is the last stop on one of the commuter rail lines to the Loop, 41 miles away. Its commercial developments are low-rise, and its local employment base is oriented far more toward industrial, warehouse, and distribution businesses than Schaumburg's. It employs proportionately more people who live in smaller, more rural communities yet farther west.

The use of public transit declines by roughly half with each additional ten-mile distance from the Loop. Note also the higher level of carpooling in Elgin, which is more ethnically and commercially diverse; a higher proportion of its residents are locally employed and can reasonably carpool as compared with those of Schaumburg.

Even with this type of data in hand, adjusting for mode still requires careful thought and professional judgment. For example, the above census data on modal splits are by place of work, but data are also available by place of residence. Place-of-residence data include all employed residents living in an area, even if they commute an hour or more to a larger city. Place-of-residence data are thus more appropriate for analyzing residential land uses, while the place-of-work data are somewhat more reliable for assessing employment at destinations. In either case, one probably still has to adjust for the specific location of the project within a community. When a certain percentage of employees working in a community commute by private vehicle, a somewhat lower percentage will commute to an activity center well served by transit, even within the same zip code, while a higher proportion will commute to a suburban office building that is not as well served by transit. The data for Chicago above are for the entire city; modal split to private auto for destinations within the Loop is considerably lower, while other activity centers probably have modal splits more similar to those in Rosemont.

Two different considerations are required to make an appropriate mode adjustment: one for modal split and the other for persons per car. How one makes those adjustments depends on what data are available. For example, let us assume that we have conducted surveys of another office building in the same activity center, and that we know that a 90 percent modal split to private auto is expected with 1.5 persons per car. Note that if one has data on a specific ratio of persons per car, the adjustment for persons per car is an inverse relationship. If the base parking ratios have a nearly 100 percent modal split to private auto, and nearly 100 percent of the commuters drive alone, the adjustment to the base parking ratio would be (90%/100%) x (1.0/1.5) = 0.60. One might then round the ratio back up to 0.65 to reflect the fact that a small amount of ridesharing, walking, and drop-offs is inherent in the base parking ratio, particularly for employees.

If one does not have reliable data for a similarly sited project, one must make some assumptions. Let us consider a hypothetical large office building in Schaumburg, Illinois, which has reasonably good bus transit service. Many commuters, however, will have to transfer between buses in downtown Schaumburg to reach this location. While the census data indicate that 95.2 percent of employees working in this community commute by private auto, that percentage reflects those who take bus and commuter rail service to employment downtown. The local government is requiring the developer to institute transportation demand management measures in this particular activity center, but no data on modal split or ridesharing are yet available. Thus, the modal split to private auto at the project site will be lower than for commuters to areas without such programs, but higher than for commuters to the regional central business district served by transit. It would then be reasonable to assume that this location will be in the middle of the range of percentage using transit. A projection of 95 percent of the employees at the office building commuting by private auto would appear to be a reasonable starting point, equivalent to the percentage currently commuting to downtown Schaumburg by private auto. It is somewhat more difficult to adjust the workers-per-car ratio, but if 10 percent of the 95 percent commuting by private auto will arrive as passengers due to the ridesharing programs, that leaves 85 percent among all employees as drivers. Because the parking ratios assume a nearly 100 percent modal split to private auto and very little ridesharing, or nearly 100 percent drivership, the overall reduction in parking needs due to modal split and persons per car would then be achieved by multiplying the employee parking ratio by 0.85. The equivalent persons per auto of this assumption is 95%/85% or 1.12, somewhat higher than the locality's average ratio of 1.06 persons per auto for all commuters, which seems reasonable for a project that will have a coordinated ridesharing program. For the

visitor component, a much lower adjustment for transit usage would be expected: perhaps 0.95 (a 5 percent reduction of parking needs as compared with a more typical "cornfield" site).

Understanding the types of employees generally associated with a land use is also important in adjusting such ratios. For example, hotel and retail employees are more likely to use transit, to carpool, or to be picked up and dropped off than office employees at the same location. However, the parking ratios already reflect the typical modal splits for a particular type of use, even though the setting is assumed to be a suburban location with little or no transit. Adjustments should be made only when the auto occupancy for that use would be unusually affected.

Step 6: Apply Noncaptive Adjustments

Both formal studies and general experience have proven that some reduction of customer parking needs occurs in a mixed-use project due to patronage of multiple land uses. The term "captive market" has been borrowed from market researchers to describe people who are already present in the immediate vicinity and are likely patrons of a second use. For example, a parking demand analysis may consider that employees in a complex or district may already have parked at another land use and thus will not generate any parking demand when they patronize a coffee store or shop for a few minutes while on a break. If an office is located on a "cornfield" site, most employees will not leave the property during breaks, and therefore the office parking ratio at lunchtime and other breaks already reflects the use of that parking space by that employee.

Determining appropriate noncaptive factors is the step that requires the greatest professional judgment and experience. It is important to understand the difference between sequential and simultaneous trips when estimating the effects of captive market influences on the parking supply.

The development community uses the term "captive" for patrons who are already nearby and may be more easily attracted to a land use. The traffic engineer similarly uses "captive" for patrons who are already present for another purpose and thus do not generate another vehicle trip to the site. The parking planner must therefore determine for each time period whether the captive patrons are already counted as parked for another land use and thus do not generate the need for additional parking spaces at that particular hour. The following examples further explain these issues.

■ When a traffic engineer estimates that 20 percent of a cinema's patrons are also going to eat at the restaurants in a retail/entertainment center, it is clearly legitimate to reduce the number of inbound and outbound trips to the project to reflect the fact that new trips to the restaurants will not be made via automobile (but rather are already accounted for in the trip generation estimates for the cinema). However, if a family goes to a movie and then goes to dinner (i.e., a sequential trip), the overall parking demand for the project is not reduced either during the movie or while they dine. The car is parked in the project's parking supply for 90–120 minutes for the movie and for 60 minutes or more for dinner.

■ With this same trip combination, if the parents have a leisurely dinner while the children go to a movie, this simultaneous trip to two destinations within the center would indeed result in reductions in both trip generation and parking demand. In this case, the car would be counted as parked at the restaurant, and a reduction in the parking demand would be applied to the cinema.

■ The employee who stays to dine and attend a movie after work would not be captive from a parking perspective. That employee may be more likely to patronize the on-site restaurant and cinema than to stop at a restaurant or cinema somewhere else on the way home (thus reducing automobile trips to and from the project); however, the time-of-day factors in this book assume that an employee leaves after the end of normal working hours. Thus, a parking space is needed to serve an employee's visit to the restaurant and the cineplex in the evening. During the daytime, an employee patronizing a restaurant may be considered captive, as 90 percent of employees are assumed to stay on site during the lunch hour in the time-of-day factors for employee parking at office buildings.

The key then is to evaluate what percentage of the users at one land use are already counted as being parked for another land use at that particular hour.

Market studies documenting visits to multiple destinations within an existing project can be helpful in determining the noncaptive adjustments for parking needs at a project. Normally, such market studies are not designed to distinguish between sequential and simultaneous visits. The responder is usually asked simply to name all the venues visited on a particular trip to the center. To quantify sequential trips, the questioner must ask where each person arriving in a vehicle is or was at specific times, which is significantly more time-consuming for both questioner and respondent.

When the study team calibrated the shared parking model to actual conditions at one successful retail/entertainment complex, detailed market studies and customer interviews were available identifying the percentage of patrons that visited multiple venues in the complex. When these percentages were entered directly into the shared parking model as estimates of the captive market, the model seriously underestimated the parking demand revealed by actual occupancy counts. The interview percentages thus had to be reduced by 50 percent when used as noncaptive estimates, to get the model to correctly predict parking demand at the center. This complication illustrated the effects of sequential versus simultaneous trips and the need for caution in estimating high levels of captive market even when survey data are available.

Because captive market effects typically reduce the parking needs, the factor employed to adjust the parking ratio is actually the percentage of customers who are not considered captive, or the noncaptive ratio. For example, if 10 percent of the patrons for a food court are expected to be employees of other land uses, the noncaptive ratio is 90 percent.

In addition to evaluation of simultaneous versus sequential visits to destinations, the magnitude of noncaptive adjustments is affected significantly by the combinations of land uses and more specifically the relative quantities. For example, the noncaptive adjustments for a 10,000-square-foot restaurant in a 40,000-square-foot strip shopping center will be distinctly different from the adjustments for the same size restaurant in a mixed-use project with significant office space or hotel rooms. Even then, one must carefully evaluate the potential for patronage of one use by another. With a 10,000-square-foot restaurant in a complex with 100,000 square feet of office space and 30,000 square feet of retail, one would expect there to be no more than 350 employees at the office (estimated from 3.15 employee parking spaces per 1,000 square feet with 1.08 persons per car) and 25 employees at the retail stores (estimated from the weekday parking ratio of 0.70 employee spaces per 1,000 square feet of retail). Any visitor to either land use who eats lunch will be present in a sit-down restaurant for nearly an hour and therefore should be considered to be parked at the restaurant at the noon hour. The restaurant would have about 250 seats (at an estimated 25 seats per thousand square feet). If a noncaptive adjustment of 30 percent is assumed, it is effectively stating that 75 of the 375 employees, or about 20 percent, from the complex eat at the restaurant every day of the week. A 90 percent noncaptive ratio at the restaurant (25 or 10 percent of the 250 seats filled by employees from the complex at lunchtime) would be much more reasonable for this combination. If, instead, the restaurant is a 1,000-square-foot deli with seating for less than 50 people and provides carryout service as well, 75 percent or more of the patrons could be employees of the complex. If the deli is located in a 100,000-square-foot suburban office building without any retail, virtually 100 percent of the patrons may be captive office employees.

Thus, using ranges of noncaptive factors for each land use would be misleading; in fact, they would be meaningless, since the ranges could be extremely broad: zero to 100 percent of the patrons of a restaurant may be noncaptive on daytime weekdays, as demonstrated above. Therefore, suggested ranges of noncaptive factors are not tabulated in this book. Instead, the analyst must evaluate the reasonableness of the captive market estimates for each development by comparing potential patronage from other uses with the expected patronage at peak hours.

There is sometimes confusion regarding whether a patron is captive or simply uses the mode of walking. These distinctions are far easier to understand in self-contained developments, as those who walk from other uses within the project would be considered captive, while those who walked from uses outside the project would be considered to affect the mode adjustment. The issue is considerably more murky in a downtown area; some visitors to a land use may walk from offices, residences, and other land uses and thus could be considered either as captive patrons or as customers who walked to the complex. The important thing is not to double count such patrons both as captive and as noncaptive customers who do not drive and park.

The need to carefully apply such factors to the specific peak hours being modeled necessarily makes shared parking analysis a complex undertaking, often requiring that multiple hours be individually evaluated to determine the overall peak accumulation of demand. It is for this reason that the methodology for shared parking analysis recommended in this edition has been slightly modified to clearly indicate that noncaptive adjustments should be made after time-of-day and seasonal variations have been evaluated and scenarios for demand have been developed.

It has been argued that a combination of land uses can result in higher parking needs than would result if the uses were spatially separated and have dedicated parking. This phenomenon is associated with the synergy of the development. Stays may be longer, which adds to the parking need without adding vehicle trips or stops in a chain of trips. However, considering whether visits are sequential rather than simultaneous and adjusting accordingly for noncaptive effects will account for this type of synergy. Moreover, while it is true that individual tenants may do more business in a multitenant or mixed-use setting than they would elsewhere (for example, a restaurant that does a brisk lunchtime business thanks to a nearby office building), it remains statistically unlikely that a parking ratio based on the 85th percentile of peak-hour accumulations observed at individual land use sites will be significantly exceeded for all the tenants or land uses present.

A current trend in shopping center design is to group several restaurants together rather than distributing them throughout the center.[5] Distributing them throughout was thought to encourage longer stays by shoppers and thus to support the retail tenancies. Grouping the restaurants together, however, not only extends the shopping trip but is now believed to be more effective at increasing overall mall traffic at hours when parking demand for retail normally drops off. Apparently, patrons are more likely to come to a shopping center with a primary purpose of dining if they know that several restaurants are close together and that therefore they will have easy alternatives if the first choice is too busy. Excess demand for a more popular restaurant will thus divert to another restaurant, or people will shop until their table is available, but this scenario does not necessarily increase the overall parking ratio for the group of restaurants to exceed the 85th percentile value. In fact, such synergy is at the heart of the original concept of the shopping center, whereby all tenants benefit from the competition.

Step 7: Calculate Required Parking Spaces for Each Scenario

This step simply involves totaling the parking needs for each land use to estimate the overall shared parking need for each scenario.

Step 8: Determine Whether Scenarios Reflect All Critical Parking Needs

This step is often overlooked but is key to the reliability of the projections. If calculations are being performed manually, it is often advisable to check other hours on the day that appears to be the design day (the day with the peak overall accumulation). If several scenarios are relatively close, more hours on several days may need to be tested.

Step 9: Recommend a Parking Plan

The final step that is unfortunately often omitted is to develop a comprehensive parking plan that assures the success of shared parking principles. Chapter 6 of this book is devoted to this topic.

Example

A hypothetical example project has been constructed from a number of different land uses that might be included in a new mixed-use development.

Step 1: Gather and Review Project Data

The uses proposed for this example include:

- Office: 100,000 square feet of Class A office space in a single building
- Retail: 7,500 square feet
- Family restaurant (no bar): 5,000 square feet
- Fast food (ice cream, coffee, and so on): 1,000 square feet

- Medical office: 13,500 square feet (in second floor over one retail/restaurant building)
- Casual dining: 10,000 square feet (including 1,000 square feet of patio)
- Bank: 4,000 square feet with drive-through on outlot
- Fine dining: 10,000 square feet (including 1,000 square feet of patio)
- Hotel: 200 rooms, no restaurant (owing to alternative dining venues on site) but 4,000 square feet of meeting rooms

The setting is assumed to be suburban, with no transit and no walk-in customers or employees. Further, it is assumed that outdoor patio dining is available all year, increasing the seating capacity of the various restaurants. The local zoning ordinances are presumed to allow shared parking analysis according to the ULI methodology. All parking will be free and uncontrolled. Walking distances will be less than 1,000 feet from most parking spaces to any destination.

Table 3-2 Parking Ratios and Unadjusted Demand for Each Land Use

Land Use	Quantity of Land Use	WEEKDAYS Base Ratio	Units	Unadjusted Parking Spaces	WEEKENDS Base Ratio	Units	Unadjusted Parking Spaces
Community Shopping Center (<400,000 sq. ft.)	7,500	2.90	/ksf[1] GLA	22	3.20	/ksf GLA	24
Employee		0.70		5	0.80		6
Fine/Casual Dining	20,000	15.25	/ksf GLA	305	17.00	/ksf GLA	340
Employee		2.75		55	3.00		60
Family Restaurant	5,000	9.00	/ksf GLA	45	12.75	/ksf GLA	64
Employee		1.50		8	2.25		11
Fast Food	1,000	12.75	/ksf GLA	13	12.00	/ksf GLA	12
Employee		2.25		2	2.00		2
Hotel—Business	200	1.00	/room	200	0.90	/room	180
Meeting/Banquet (20 to 50 sq. ft./guest room)	4,000	30.00	/ksf GLA	120	30.00	/ksf GLA	120
Employee	200	0.25	/room	50	0.18	/room	36
Office (100,000 sq. ft.)	100,000	0.25	/ksf GFA	25	0.03	/ksf GFA	3
Employee		3.15		315	0.32		32
Medical/Dental Office	13,500	3.00	/ksf GFA	41	3.00	/ksf GFA	41
Employee		1.50		20	1.50		20
Bank (Drive-in Branch)	4,000	3.00	/ksf GFA	12	3.00	/ksf GFA	12
Employee		1.60		6	1.60		6

Note
[1] /ksf = per thousand sq. ft.

Steps 2 and 3: Select Parking Ratios and Separate into Customer and Employee Components

Table 3-2 summarizes the parking ratios and the unadjusted number of spaces required for each individual land use. The breakdown of square footage among the restaurant types is based on a preliminary leasing plan. It is assumed that tenants and business plans for the bank and hotel are known; the hotel will be a business-oriented hotel.

Steps 4 and 5: Select Factors and Analyze Differences in Activity Patterns, Then Develop Scenarios

The sum of the unadjusted demands for each land use indicates that, even after adjustment, weekday demand will be greater than weekend demand. Therefore, the scenarios will first consider weekday demand. The key drivers of demand

according to Table 3-2 will be office (including bank and medical office, about 419 spaces), hotel (370 spaces), and restaurant uses (about 432 spaces). The hotel will have a greater mode adjustment because of its shuttle service to the airport, and the restaurant and retail uses will have demand reduced by noncaptive adjustments in the daytime. At first blush, then, office will be the key driver of this project in the daytime, while the hotel and restaurants will drive evening demand. Table 3-3 summarizes the monthly factors for the uses.

First, all months with significantly lower hotel factors (January, February, November, and both Decembers) were eliminated from consideration as peak months. June clearly will produce higher demand than March, April, or May, eliminating those months. Due to lower office demand, July and August should be a little lower than June. October should

| Table 3-3 | Monthly Variation in Parking Demand (in Percentages) |

Land Use	JAN	FEB	MAR	APR	MAY	JUN	JUL	AUG	SEP	OCT	NOV	DEC	Late DEC
Community Shopping Center	56	57	64	63	66	67	64	69	64	66	72	100	80
Employee	80	80	80	80	80	80	80	80	80	80	90	100	90
Fine/Casual Dining	85	86	95	92	96	95	98	99	91	96	93	100	95
Employee	95	95	100	100	100	100	100	100	100	100	100	100	100
Family Restaurant	85	86	95	92	96	95	98	99	91	96	93	100	95
Employee	95	95	100	100	100	100	100	100	100	100	100	100	100
Fast Food	84	84	94	93	98	97	100	99	92	98	94	100	95
Employee	95	95	100	100	100	100	100	100	100	100	100	100	100
Hotel—Business	71	85	91	90	92	100	98	92	93	93	81	67	50
Meeting/Banquet	100	100	100	100	100	100	100	100	100	100	100	100	100
Employee	100	100	100	100	100	100	100	100	100	100	100	100	100
Office	100	100	100	100	100	100	95	95	100	100	100	100	80
Employee	100	100	100	100	100	100	95	95	100	100	100	100	80
Medical/Dental Office	100	100	100	100	100	100	95	95	100	100	100	100	80
Employee	100	100	100	100	100	100	95	95	100	100	100	100	80
Bank	100	100	100	100	100	100	95	95	100	100	100	100	80
Employee	100	100	100	100	100	100	95	95	100	100	100	100	80

Figure 3-1 Variation in Parking Requirements by Time of Day (Weekday in June)

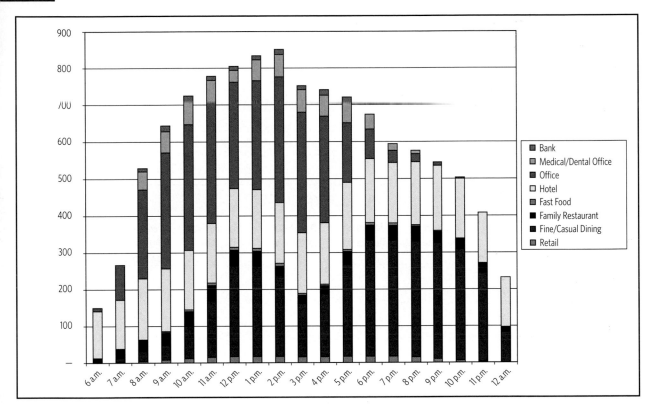

exceed September. Between October and June, restaurant demand will be 1 percent or five parking spaces higher, while hotel guest-room demand will be 7 percent or 21 spaces lower. Considering that the restaurant demand will be lowered by noncaptive ratios in the daytime, and office and hotel demand will not be so adjusted, it appears that June should be considered the peak month. Therefore the selected month for further analysis was June.

The next step is to review time-of-day factors. These were applied against the maximum demand for each land use, adjusted for June conditions, as a test to identify key hours. The resulting table would be too complex to present in this publication, and so the results are presented graphically in Figure 3-1. From the graph it appears that the peak parking need occurs at 2 p.m. However, noncaptive and mode adjustments could change that.

Steps 6 and 7: Adjust Ratios for Modal Split and Persons per Car, and Noncaptive Market Adjustments

Some of the restaurant and retail patronage will come from office and hotel users. On weekdays in the daytime, the retail, fine/casual dining, and bank customer needs are reduced to 90 percent, while family restaurant parking needs are reduced to 85 percent. Fast-food parking need is reduced to 50 percent. Per Salzman, the meeting room activity is reduced to 60 percent for noncaptive market effects and 25 percent as a mode adjustment for a weekday daytime.[6] The mode adjustment for the hotel rooms is a reduction of 33 percent for a hotel in an office park.

Steps 8 and 9: Calculate Demand and Recheck for Critical Periods

With the noncaptive market and mode adjustments, 2 p.m. was found to be the peak hour, as shown in Table 3-4. As a check, 2 p.m. in June and October were also rechecked with the various adjustments, as shown in Table 3-5.

| Table 3-4 | Estimated Weekday Peak-Hour Parking Requirements |

Land Use	Unadjusted Demand	Month Adjustment June	Peak Hour Adjustment 2 p.m.	Noncaptive Daytime	Mode Adjustment Daytime	June 2 p.m.
Community Shopping Center	22	67%	95%	90%	100%	13
Employee	5	80%	100%	100%	100%	4
Fine/Casual Dining	305	95%	65%	90%	100%	170
Employee	55	100%	90%	100%	100%	50
Family Restaurant	45	95%	50%	85%	100%	18
Employee	8	100%	100%	100%	100%	8
Fast Food	13	97%	90%	50%	100%	6
Employee	2	100%	95%	100%	100%	2
Hotel—Business	200	100%	60%	100%	66%	79
Meeting/Banquet	120	100%	65%	60%	75%	35
Employee	50	100%	100%	100%	100%	50
Office	25	100%	100%	100%	100%	25
Employee	315	100%	100%	100%	100%	315
Medical/Dental Office	41	100%	100%	100%	100%	41
Employee	20	100%	100%	100%	100%	20
Bank	12	100%	70%	90%	100%	8
Employee	6	100%	100%	100%	100%	6
Subtotal: Customer/Guest Spaces	783					395
Subtotal: Employee/Resident Spaces	461					455
Total Parking Spaces	1,244					850
Shared Parking Reduction	31%					

Table 3-5
Estimated Weekday Parking Requirements at 2 and 6 p.m. in June and October

Land Use	June 2 p.m.	June 6 p.m.	October 2 p.m.	October 6 p.m.
Community Shopping Center	13	13	12	13
Employee	4	4	4	4
Fine/Casual Dining	170	262	171	264
Employee	50	55	50	55
Family Restaurant	18	32	18	32
Employee	8	8	8	8
Fast Food	6	5	6	5
Employee	2	2	2	2
Hotel—Business	79	99	74	92
Meeting/Banquet	35	54	35	54
Employee	50	20	50	20
Office	25	1	25	1
Employee	315	79	315	79
Medical/Dental Office	41	27	41	27
Employee	20	13	20	13
Bank (Drive-in Branch)	8	—	8	—
Employee	6	—	6	—
Subtotal: Customer/Guest Spaces	395	493	390	488
Subtotal: Employee/Resident Spaces	455	181	455	181
Total Parking Spaces	850	674	845	669

While the October projections were not substantially different from June, the latter was confirmed to be the peak month.

For parking management reasons, reduced noncaptive market factors for evening hours at the restaurants were also checked. As previously noted, an employee in an office building who stays for dinner is no longer considered captive, because he or she would otherwise have left the site and dined elsewhere. However, because the hotel in our example has no restaurant, there will be some captive restaurant patrons in the evening. Therefore the noncaptive adjustments were halved for weekday evenings. The retail parking was also considered to be 95 percent noncaptive in the evening to the hotel and restaurant patrons, and the fast-food parking was estimated to be 50 percent noncaptive. A check of the parking demand in the evenings found that 6 p.m. was the peak hour in the evening, due to some late-working office employees, but that noon was a higher peak. Another check was made of Saturday afternoon and evening demand, to be sure that we had the peak. The model indicates that July has higher demand than June on weekends, and that the peak weekend hour for the project is at 8 p.m., due to the hotel and restaurant activities (see Table 3-6).

Table 3-6 Estimated Parking Requirements on Weekdays and Weekends

Land Use	WEEKDAYS June 2 p.m.	WEEKDAYS June 6 p.m.	WEEKENDS July Noon	WEEKENDS July 8 p.m.
Community Shopping Center	13	13	12	10
Employee	4	4	5	4
Fine/Casual Dining	170	262	167	317
Employee	50	55	45	60
Family Restaurant	18	32	63	38
Employee	8	8	11	10
Fast Food	6	5	6	3
Employee	2	2	2	1
Hotel—Business	79	99	75	109
Meeting/Banquet	35	54	41	63
Employee	50	20	36	20
Office	25	1	3	—
Employee	315	79	27	—
Medical/Dental Office	41	27	12	—
Employee	20	13	19	—
Bank	8	—	10	—
Employee	6	—	6	—
Subtotal: Customer/Guest Spaces	395	493	389	540
Subtotal: Employee/Resident Spaces	455	181	151	95
Total Parking Spaces	850	674	540	635

Therefore, while the overall parking need will peak in the daytime on weekdays, a significantly higher parking need will occur in the evening (rather than daytime) on weekends. The peak hour in the daytime on weekends is noon. Both patterns reflect the predominance of restaurants in the leasing plan.

The extra iterations noted above in checking for additional peak months and hours are commonly needed in situations where the key drivers of parking do not vary much by month and there are several times of day with similar factors. When retail or another single use with wider variations in monthly and time-of-day adjustments drive demand, it is somewhat easier to identify the scenarios for peak-hour parking requirements.

Our example analysis projects that the peak parking needs will occur on a weekday in June at 2 p.m. at 850 spaces. Compared with the sum of the unadjusted spaces for the individual land uses, or 1,244 spaces, shared parking analysis has reduced the estimated peak-hour spaces required for this hypothetical project by about 32 percent.

Step 10: Recommended Parking Plan

On the example's site plan (see Figure 3-2), the buildings are placed around a central water feature (ponds) that double as the retention facility for stormwater runoff. Walkways around and bridges across the ponds and stream will provide pleasant walking paths between uses. Outdoor patio dining areas face the water features, further enhancing the pedestrian environment.

Owing to the convenience orientation of the retail/restaurant/medical office building and the nearby bank, surface parking is to be provided adjacent to both. Surface parking is also provided near the restaurants on the other side of the pond, with a parking structure for shared parking between the hotel and office building, as well as some additional restaurant parking.

It is recommended that all employees at the complex be required to park in the surface lots west of the office building and in the parking structure. This will require some monitoring and enforcement, as discussed in chapter 6. To determine the visitor parking at the retail/medical office building as well as the nearby bank building, the maximum parking needed on weekdays and weekends should be gauged by reviewing both daytime and evening time frames (see Table 3-7). Note that the family restaurant and 5,000 square feet of fine/casual dining GLA are tenants in the retail/medical office building.

Figure 3-2 Site Plan for Example Project

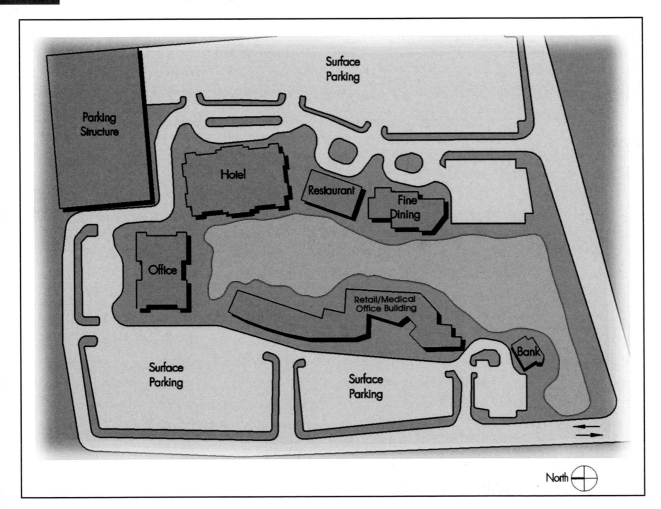

Table 3-7 Estimated Parking Requirements for the Retail/Restaurant/Medical Office Building

Land Use	WEEKDAYS		WEEKENDS	
	December 1 p.m.	December 6 p.m.	December Noon	December 8 p.m.
Community Shopping Center	20	13	20	15
Employee	5	4	6	5
Fine/Casual Dining	51	65	43	81
Employee	13	14	11	15
Family Restaurant	34	32	64	38
Employee	8	8	11	10
Fast Food	6	5	6	3
Employee	2	2	2	1
Medical/Dental Office	37	27	12	—
Employee	20	13	20	—
Bank	5	—	11	—
Employee	6	—	6	—
Subtotal: Customer/Guest Spaces	153	142	156	137
Subtotal: Employee/Resident Spaces	54	41	56	31
Total Parking Spaces	207	183	212	168

Note that the peak demand for the retail/medical office building and bank area is in December.

It is recommended that at least 150 spaces be provided for customers/visitors in the surface lot in front of the retail/medical office and bank buildings. The recommended number of parking spaces in the surface lots to the west and north of the office building, east of the hotel, and in the parking structure is 455 spaces for all employees in the daytime plus the office visitor parking in the daytime, or another 25 spaces, for a total of about 475 spaces. The remaining 225 or so spaces would be in surface parking in front of the restaurants on the east side of the pond. The demand for visitor parking on a weekend evening in July on the east side of the pond is about 384 spaces, but hotel parkers can conveniently use the parking structure. Some of the restaurants' demand

in the evening could also be met by using the parking structure in a self-park mode; valet parking in the evening with storage in the parking structure would be appropriate for the fine-dining restaurant, which is most distant from the parking structure.

Comparison with the First Edition of *Shared Parking*

If this project had been evaluated by using the first edition's recommended default values, with the same mode and non-captive adjustments, the base ratios and unadjusted peak parking needs would have been as shown in Table 3-8. Because the first edition did not have ratios for medical offices or banks, those land uses have been combined with office.

The parking ratios for all uses except office in this example have decreased somewhat, resulting in slight decreases

Table 3-8   Parking Ratios and Maximum Demand for Each Land Use (First Edition)

| Land Use | Quantity | WEEKDAYS | | | WEEKENDS | | |
		Base Ratio	Unit	Maximum Parking Spaces	Base Ratio	Unit	Maximum Parking Spaces
Community Shopping Center	7,500	3.80	/ksf[1] GLA	29	4.00	/ksf GLA	30
Restaurant	26,000	20.00	/ksf GLA	520	20.00	/ksf GLA	520
Hotel—Business	200	1.25	/room	250	1.25	/room	250
Meeting/Banquet	4,000	30.00	/ksf GLA	120	30.00	/ksf GLA	120
Office	117,500	3.00	/ksf GLA	353	0.50	/ksf GLA	59
Total Parking Spaces, first edition				1,272			979
Total Parking Spaces, second edition				1,244			969

Note

[1] /ksf = per thousand sq. ft.

in the unadjusted parking need for both weekdays and weekends. The next step is to project peak accumulation with shared parking (see Table 3-9).

After all adjustments, however, the difference between the first and second edition's projections for weekday daytime conditions is significantly different (a 79-space increase) than the 28-space decrease in the sum of the unadjusted demands. This result reflects significant changes in time-of-day and seasonality factors from the first edition. The evening demand on weekdays also has declined 67 spaces from that projected by the first edition, because the stratification of restaurant ratios results in overall lower ratios for the mix of restaurant types in this example.

Table 3-9   Estimated Weekday Peak-Hour Parking Requirements (First Edition)

Land Use	Maximum Demand	Month Adjustment June	Peak-Hour Adjustment 1 p.m.	Noncaptive Daytime	Mode Adjustment Daytime	June 1 p.m.	June 8 p.m.
Community Shopping Center	29	75%	100%	90%	100%	20	18
Restaurant	520	100%	70%	90%	100%	328	494
Hotel—Business	250	100%	30%	100%	66%	50	149
Meeting/Banquet	120	100%	100%	60%	75%	54	54
Office	353	100%	90%	100%	100%	318	25
Total Parking Spaces, first edition	1,272					771	741
Total Parking Spaces, second edition	1,244					850	674

Table 3-10 Estimated Weekend Peak-Hour Parking Requirements (First Edition)

Land Use	Maximum Demand	Month Adjustment June	Peak-Hour Adjustment 8 p.m.	Noncaptive Evening	Mode Adjustment Evening	June 8 p.m.	June Noon
Community Shopping Center	30	75%	55%	95%	100%	12	21
Restaurant	520	100%	100%	95%	100%	494	222
Hotel—Business	250	90%	90%	100%	77%	156	61
Meeting/Banquet	120	100%	100%	70%	75%	63	63
Office	59	100%	20%	100%	100%	12	35
Total Parking Spaces, first edition	979					737	402
Total Parking Spaces, second edition	969					635	540

While the sum of the unadjusted demands has declined ten spaces for weekends and the projected afternoon demand on weekends has decreased by 102 spaces, the evening demand has increased by 138 spaces. (June values for the first edition are shown in Table 3-10, even though the second edition model projects higher demand in July on weekends.)

In sum, the first edition's default values would have identified 8 p.m. on a weekday in June as the peak demand, with nearly identical demand in the daytime and evening on weekdays (771 and 741 spaces, respectively) and only a little less demand (737) in the evening on weekends. The overall peak would be considered as weekday evening parking demand. The second edition's updated model projects more demand in the daytime (851 spaces) but less in the evening (674). The differences in these projections are more clearly outlined in Table 3-11. Overall, an analysis using the first edition would have recommended that 771 parking spaces be provided, as compared with 857 spaces per the second edition. In sum, the two models' default values clearly result in significant differences in individual projections.

Table 3-11 Estimated Parking Requirements in June (First Edition versus Second Edition)

Land Use	WEEKDAYS				SATURDAYS			
	First Edition 1 p.m.	Second Edition 8 p.m.	First Edition 2 p.m.	Second Edition 8 p.m.	First Edition 6 p.m.	Second Edition 2 p.m.	First Edition Noon	Second Edition 8 p.m.
Retail	20	17	18	17	21	18	12	14
Restaurant	328	254	494	364	222	287	494	419
Hotel Rooms	50	129	149	119	61	111	156	131
Meeting/Banquet	54	35	54	54	63	41	63	63
Office	318	415	25	120	35	81	12	—
Total Parking Spaces	771	850	741	674	402	538	737	627

It should be noted that this example was intentionally constructed to highlight the factors that have changed significantly between the first and second editions of *Shared Parking*. The second edition aims to address issues more common in small and more complex projects than those addressed in the first edition. The first edition had a single lower ratio for office uses and did not address the differences in parking demand at medical offices and banks. Second, the first edition treated overnight guest and employee demand at a hotel in a single ratio with one set of time-of-day factors. This approach results in much lower daytime parking demand associated with hotel rooms than occurs with the second edition model. The first edition also recommended the same demand ratios for restaurant and meeting/banquet space on both weekdays and weekends, and recommended a 100 percent time-of-day factor for the hotel meeting/banquet space from 9 a.m. to 9 p.m. on both weekdays and weekends. The detailed study by Salzman, however, indicates that significantly lower demand in meeting space at hotels is appropriate for daytime parking demands. The stratification of the restaurant ratios into three separate categories, with lower ratios for family restaurants and fast-food uses as well as lower demand on weekdays, also results in significantly different restaurant demand at various hours.

Notes

1. "Using the ITE Parking Generation Report," *ITE Journal*, July 1990, pp. 25–31.

2. Robert Weant and Herbert S. Levinson, *Parking* (Westport, Conn.: Eno Foundation for Transportation, 1990).

3. Mary S. Smith, "Zoning Requirements," in *The Dimensions of Parking*, 3rd ed. (Washington, D.C.: ULI–the Urban Land Institute, 1993), pp. 47–53.

4. Parking Consultants Council, *Recommended Zoning Ordinance Provisions for Parking and Off-Street Loading Spaces* (Washington, D.C.: National Parking Association, 1992).

5. Sheila Muto, "Restaurant Malls," www.realestatejournal.com (October 15, 2003).

6. Gerald Salzman, "Hotel Parking: How Much Is Enough?" *Urban Land*, January 1988, pp. 14–17.

Analysis of Single Land Uses

The overall parking ratios developed for this publication are based on a variety of sources, as noted in the summary tables at the end of chapter 2. The breakdown between visitor and employee demand components is based on information in *Parking Generation, Parking Requirements for Shopping Centers*, and other published references where possible.[1] For some uses, *Parking Generation* has data on employees per square foot or other unit of land use. Adjustments must be made, however, for peak-hour presence, since the data generally reflect total employment. There is only one land use—hotel—with extensive data on employee parking needs, both peak hour and accumulation throughout the day, reported in an intensive study that was published in 1988.[2]

Monthly factors for visitor demand were developed primarily from *Parking Generation*, and were based either on parking accumulation studies (where there was adequate sample size) or on Internet sources, such as the U.S. Census Bureau's unadjusted estimates of retail sales (for retail and restaurant uses), national movie theater ticket sales, and national hotel occupancy data. The available published references were deemed inadequate for several land uses. Additional study and research were therefore required for these land uses, resulting in significantly more text being devoted to the derivation of the recommended ratios and factors. One example is cineplexes; both the film industry and the design of cineplexes have changed significantly in the last decade or so. Similarly, visitor parking ratios and factors, both monthly and time-of-day, for places of assembly (performing arts theaters, convention centers, arenas, and stadiums) were developed by the *Shared Parking* study team based on evaluation of attendance and parking records at representative facilities.

Because almost no statistically reliable data are available on parking needs by time of day, factors were developed by the study team. One exception is office uses, whose parking demand is predominantly employee-driven; thus, the time-of-day factors found in *Parking Generation* were used for office employee demand, while the visitor factors were developed by the team. Where the available data appeared to be weak, a more conservative assumption was made to generate factors.

Retail

Without doubt, the parking needs of retail uses are the most extensively researched and well-documented of any land use. *Parking Requirements for Shopping Centers* includes data from more than 490 centers, with peak accumulation counts taken at 169 centers during the 1998 holiday shopping season. *Parking Generation* includes data from more than 125 sites with independent, freestanding retail uses. Note that ULI defines a shopping center as any combination of three or more tenants providing goods and services to the public under the same leasing and with common area management. In most cases, there is also single ownership of the property, although anchors may own their buildings.

The second edition of *Parking Requirements for Shopping Centers* is thus the basis for this book's recommended parking ratios for most retail situations in shared parking analysis. The first edition of that publication adopted the 20th highest hour in a year as the design hour for parking needs. There are more than 3,000 operating hours per year at most shopping centers; with the 20th highest hour as the design hour, over half of the available spaces would be vacant during 40 percent of the year's operating hours. During 19 hours of the year, distributed over ten days, some patrons would be unable to find parking spaces upon arriving at the center. After analysis of the data collected for the second edition, the study team decided to continue with that standard. The 20th highest hour is considerably higher than the standard of the 85th percentile of peak-hour observations across all days of the year that is used here for most other land uses. However, the average of the observed accumulations at 169 centers in the design hour (rather than the 85th percentile) was employed for the recommended ratios.

Parking, vehicular, and pedestrian-count data for the holiday shopping season of 1997 were evaluated for 32 centers across the country to determine the 20th highest hour. It was determined that the second or third busiest hour on the second Saturday before Christmas (that is, seven to 14 days before Christmas) best represented the 20th highest hour.

After identification of the peak hour, surveys of parked vehicle accumulations were conducted at 169 centers across the United States from 1 p.m. to 3 p.m. on the second Saturday before Christmas (which was December 13, 1998). The average accumulation of vehicles was then employed to derive the recommended ratios. The resulting recommended parking ratios for centers without significant dining and entertainment uses were as shown in Table 4-1, with the recommendation from the first edition of *Shared Parking* also shown for reference. (The recommended parking ratios from the first edition of *Parking Requirements for Shopping Centers* were employed for the first edition of *Shared Parking*.)

Table 4-1 Recommended Parking Ratios for Shopping Centers (without Significant Dining and Entertainment)

Center Size, sq. ft. GLA	Parking Spaces per 1,000 sq. ft. of Occupied GLA	
	1980 study	1998 study
Less than 400,000	4.0	4.0
400,000 to 599,999	4.0–5.0 sliding scale	4.0–4.5 sliding scale
Over 600,000	5.0	4.5

Source: ULI/ICSC, *Parking Requirements for Shopping Centers*, 2nd ed., 1999.

Where more than 10 percent but less than 20 percent of the GLA is occupied by dining and entertainment uses, the second edition of *Parking Requirements for Shopping Centers* recommended that the parking ratio be increased linearly by 0.3 spaces/ksf (per thousand square feet) for each percent above 10 percent. When there is more than 20 percent dining and entertainment in a shopping center, shared parking analysis is recommended.

The average ratio in the 20th highest hour for centers of less than 100,000 square feet was actually 3.7 spaces/ksf. However, there is a wide diversity of tenancies and types of centers with less than 400,000 square feet, including neighborhood and community centers, power centers anchored by big-box retail operations, upscale fashion/specialty centers, theme/entertainment centers, and factory outlet centers. *Parking Requirements for Shopping Centers* therefore did not subdivide the category of centers less than 400,000 square feet.

Parking Requirements for Shopping Centers recommended that 20 percent of the parking demand be considered to be generated by employees of a shopping center; that assumption was employed by the study team to split the parking ratios for retail into this book's customer and employee ratios, although some figures are rounded.

Some analysts have argued that retail tenancies should be tabulated in more specific categories with differing parking ratios. In shopping centers, there may be any combination of the following:
■ fashion retailers;
■ service-oriented uses such as dry cleaners, banks, optometrists, tax preparation firms, and the like;
■ convenience uses such as grocery stores, pharmacies, and video stores;
■ discount superstores and big-box retailers offering furniture, books, electronics, and building materials/garden supplies;
■ fast-food stores and food courts that serve snacks ranging from coffee to ice cream and hamburgers to tacos;
■ restaurants, with any combination of fine dining, casual (with bar), and family (without bar); and
■ cineplex.

One of the problems with too much refinement of land use types within shopping centers is that the majority of tenants (and thus land uses) usually are not known during early planning phases, when parking supply requirements are established. Tenants also change as leases expire. It is unrealistic to expect center owners to modify parking supply every time a new tenant moves in, and local zoning officials are equally adverse to such a process.

Nearly all anchors, whether fashion, grocery, or big-box stores, have different parking ratios than the smaller specialty stores filling out the remainder of a center. The Institute of Transportation Engineers (ITE) *Parking Generation* publication provides at least some information on parking generation at nearly all these individual land uses, but the data are tabulated in over 20 different land use codes, resulting in relatively small samples for each code.

It is clear that the variation in ratios is relatively small, and the higher ratios of some tenants are generally balanced by the lower ratios of others. Using the average ratio on a December Saturday (similar to the design day for shopping centers), the observed peak accumulation of discount stores (ITE land use code 815) is 4.47 spaces/ksf GFA. The recommended ratio would therefore only be 10–12 percent higher than the ratio for the smaller shopping centers where they frequently are located, and the same as the ratio for large centers (over 600,000 square feet). The other land uses lack adequate samples for separating December data points; therefore, the 85th percentile has been used for the recommended ratios. For supermarkets (land use code 850), the recommended ratio is 6.72 spaces/ksf GFA. For home improvement centers (land use code 862), the recommended ratio is 4.4 spaces/ksf GFA. Most other uses, including big-box specialty stores and convenience uses commonly found in centers with grocery and discount super-centers, have parking generation ratios lower than 4.0 spaces/ksf, which would balance out the higher uses. More important, the focused data collection for *Parking Requirements for Shopping Centers* found an average ratio of 3.7 spaces/ksf at centers of under 100,000 square feet GLA, as previously noted. Two case studies in chapter 5 further explore this issue.

Although fast-food uses, including food courts, have parking ratios that are two to three times the individual retail ratios, noncaptive factors typically reduce the parking demand of fast-food uses sufficiently that the overall shopping center ratio is a reasonable proxy.

Restaurants and entertainment uses, however, have sufficiently greater ratios than retail that do affect parking demand when they represent a significant portion of a shop-

ping center's tenants. The parking ratios of cineplexes (when converted to a GLA basis) are about three times that of shopping centers overall; the parking ratios of restaurants are four to five times that of shopping centers. As previously noted, *Parking Requirements for Shopping Centers* recommends using the parking ratios noted in Table 4-1 for all retail uses, as well as for restaurants, fast food, and entertainment incorporated into the shopping center, as long as the dining and entertainment uses do not exceed 10 percent of the GLA. The case studies presented in chapter 5 essentially demonstrate that when more than 10 percent of the GLA is occupied by dining and entertainment uses, the captive patronage for the latter uses during peak shopping hours does not reduce the parking ratios enough for the overall ratio of the center to approach the shopping center ratios recommended in this book.

Figure 4-1 Retail Sales by Month

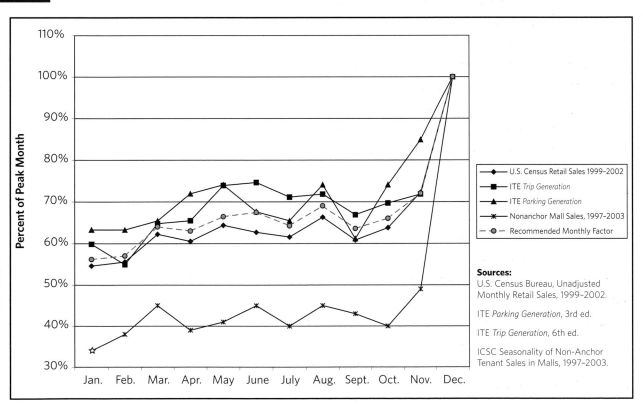

Sources:
U.S. Census Bureau, Unadjusted Monthly Retail Sales, 1999–2002.

ITE *Parking Generation*, 3rd ed.

ITE *Trip Generation*, 6th ed.

ICSC Seasonality of Non-Anchor Tenant Sales in Malls, 1997–2003.

Therefore, it is recommended that stratification of retail into subcategories of retail tenancies and separation of dining and entertainment uses not be employed for shared parking analysis unless more than 20 percent of the center is occupied by dining and entertainment uses. The exception to this guideline would be when there is spatial separation of the tenants, whether they are big-box retailers, restaurants, or fast-food stores, on a separated pad or "outlot." The key factor is that walking between uses is not likely. In those cases, spatially separated stores should be evaluated using appropriate ratios for the planned tenant.

For seasonal adjustments, data from the U.S. Census Bureau for calendar years 1999, 2000, 2001, and 2002 were reviewed. Figure 4-1 presents the unadjusted retail sales[3] after elimination of the following subcategories:

■ food services (restaurants, fast food, and drinking establishments);
■ motor vehicle sales, service, and parts;
■ gas stations;
■ food and beverage sales (grocery and liquor stores);
■ building materials and garden supplies; and
■ nonstore sales (catalog, Internet, and fuel dealers).

Unadjusted sales were used for this analysis, because the adjusted figures are modified for seasonal variations, which would defeat the purpose of using the data to identify seasonal variations. The sales data are also not adjusted for inflation, but because they have been converted to the percentage of sales in the peak month of each year, inflation has been factored out of the analysis. Also illustrated in Figure 4-1 is the seasonality found in ITE's *Parking Generation* and *Trip Generation* data. As noted previously, some of the ITE data are relatively old and may not fully reflect today's shopping patterns, particularly for November and December. Finally, another line represented in the graph shows the nonanchor mall sales for the period 1997 to 2003. These data were collected annually by the International Council of Shopping Centers (ICSC) from the same 489 malls, providing a year-on-year trend analysis. The nonanchor tenant sales in the remainder of the year are a significantly smaller percentage of December as compared with the U.S. Census sales and ITE data, but they follow a similar pattern.

Note also that years 1999 and 2000 were prior to the recession that is generally acknowledged to have begun early in 2001. For the first nine months of 2001, sales tracked similarly to 2000, and then there was a slight dip in the 2001 sales in September and October that could be related to the terrorist attacks of September 11, 2001. By November of that year, sales were again tracking similar to those in 2000.

Sales data and trip generation data will not necessarily correspond precisely to parking accumulation. For example, the average amount spent per customer and the length of stay per shopping trip are both undoubtedly greater during the holiday shopping season than at other times of the year. The ratio of parking spaces required per sales dollar will be lower in December than in the rest of the year. The adjustment factor of parking spaces needed in other months as compared with the design-day parking ratio is thus going to be higher than the percent of sales by month. Conversely, longer trips in December mean that parking needs will be higher per trip than in the remainder of the year, and therefore the monthly factors should be lower than indicated by trip generation statistics. A line between the sales and trip data has been charted, in rounded figures, for the recommended default factors for seasonal variations (see Table 2-3 in chapter 2). The factor for Late December is based on information from the ICSC weekly sales data from 1997 to 2002.

Similar graphs for food and liquor store sales in 1999 to 2002 show a significantly less pronounced peak in December, resulting in higher factors in other months as a percentage of December sales than for shopping centers as a whole. In Figure 4-2, the average percentage of the peak-

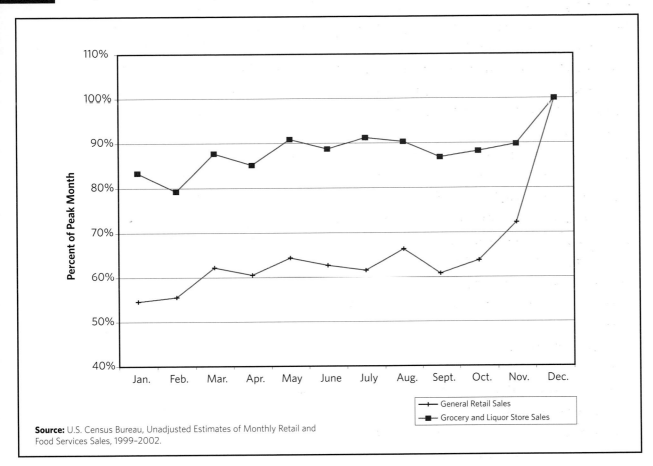

Source: U.S. Census Bureau, Unadjusted Estimates of Monthly Retail and Food Services Sales, 1999-2002.

month sales for the four years of general retail and grocery/liquor sales are compared. The percentages shown in the figure can be used when such uses dominate a center.

Time-of-day factors also appear to be different for convenience retail and shopping centers in the ITE database, but some of the samples are rather small, and most of the non-December data are relatively old. The *Shared Parking* study team also felt some concern regarding the patterns for shopping centers on both weekday and Saturday evenings in December as summarized in *Parking Generation*: there were significantly fewer data points after 7 p.m., and both curves

spiked significantly at 8 p.m. It seemed possible that the centers where data were available for 8 p.m. had a significant portion of space leased to cineplexes and/or restaurants; the portion of GLA in those land uses was not delineated.

Figure 4-3 presents data from pedestrian counts taken at entries to nine shopping centers every day in December in one year. The firm contributing these data requested confidentiality. The evening pattern on weekdays in early December is significantly different than later in the month; this is believed to represent a somewhat more normal pattern for shopping in the remainder of the year.

Figure 4-3

Pedestrian Counts at Shopping Center Entries

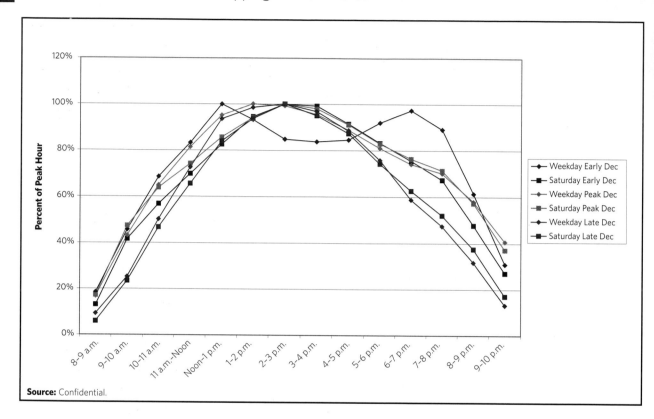

Source: Confidential.

The recommended hourly factors are based on a review of both the *Parking Generation* data, which are older and may not reflect today's shopping patterns, and an estimate of parking needs at the shopping centers in the pedestrian counts, assuming an average two-hour length of stay. Shopping hours do vary regionally, and manual adjustments may be appropriate. For example, in California, Arizona, and Nevada, most stores in shopping centers close at 6 p.m. on Saturday evenings.

Restaurants and Nightclubs

The first edition of *Shared Parking* included a single category for dining uses. The third edition of *Parking Generation* has three categories (Quality Restaurants, High-Turnover Restaurants, and Fast-Food Restaurants, with a further sub-

division of High-Turnover into two subcategories: those with bars and those without). Further evaluation of the data, however, has indicated that the parking needs of Quality Restaurants and High-Turnover Restaurants with Bars are not statistically different. The three categories of restaurants considered in this report have therefore been renamed to facilitate a fuller understanding of the categories and are defined as follows.

Fine/Casual Dining

Fine or gourmet restaurants are called "upscale" by the National Restaurant Association and "Quality Restaurants (931)" by ITE. They are distinguished by several characteristics, including more leisurely dining, and thus lower turnover; higher price points; and reservations by the vast majority of diners. They are less likely to be chain restaurants, although there are exceptions such as the Ruth's Chris and Benihana steakhouses. Few serve breakfast (except possibly Sunday brunch), and some do not serve lunch. While some may have lounge or bar areas, they are secondary to the restaurant use. Casual dining facilities are popular, moderately priced restaurants that are often chains, generally do not accept reservations (although some have call-ahead programs), and have active bar lounge areas where people gather to socialize or wait for tables. ITE calls them High-Turnover Restaurants with Bar (code 932). The typical length of stay by dining patrons is about an hour. These restaurants commonly serve lunch and dinner, and some may serve brunch but few serve breakfast. The past few years have seen a trend to promote carryout service at many of these restaurants, and therefore the absence of carryout is no longer a distinguishing characteristic.

Family Restaurants

These restaurants are typically lower priced, do not accept reservations, and lack bars or lounges, although some may serve bottled beer or wine with meals. ITE calls them High-Turnover Restaurants without Bar. Many serve breakfast as well as lunch and dinner; others do not serve dinner. The price point of the menu is typically lower than those at casual dining establishments as defined above. Many offer both carryout and dine-in options. Examples include pancake houses, cafeteria-style restaurants, and diners and coffee shops (not today's coffee stores), as well as many moderately priced ethnic restaurants.

Fast Food

At these restaurants, food is ordered at a counter and then either carried out of the store or to a table. They typically do not serve alcoholic beverages. In addition to carryout and fast-food restaurants, this category would include sandwich shops, coffee stores (such as Starbucks), ice cream shops, and so on. Both the National Restaurant Association and the U.S. Census Bureau call these "limited-service restaurants."

The *Shared Parking* study team added a further category for nightclubs/bars and other drinking places, since these land uses are increasingly found in mixed-use projects. Nightclubs typically have a performance or active entertainment component such as a dance floor. Bars and other drink-

Table 4-2 Observed Parking Accumulations for Quality/Casual Restaurants (Spaces/ksf[1] GFA)

	Fine/Casual Dining		Family Restaurants	
	Weekdays	Saturdays	Weekdays	Weekends
Study Days	49	80	51	32
Range	4.8–29.3	5.5–29.7	1.0–21.8	4.5–19.3
85th Percentile	18.0	20.0	10.5	14.8
Average	12.5	14.8	6.7	10.6
Recommended Ratio	18.0	20.0	10.5	15.0

Note
[1] /ksf = thousand sq. ft.

Source: Custom sort of ITE *Parking Generation* database.

ing places may serve sandwiches and bar food but do not have full-service menus, and children may not be permitted to enter these establishments in some states.

One concern of the study team regarding the ITE data is that Friday evenings are considered weekdays. The peak parking accumulations in the ITE data for "sit-down restaurants" were therefore retabulated to combine Friday and Saturday data, and the results are presented in Table 4-2. These data also indicate that family restaurant needs peak in the daytime rather than the evening, and thus they should be treated separately in shared parking analysis.

ITE's *Parking Generation* has separated various kinds of fast-food restaurants into several subcategories, as illustrated in Table 4-3. Although there is some range to the data, a parking ratio of 15 spaces/ksf is recommended for weekdays and 14 spaces/ksf for weekends, whether or not a fast-food restaurant has a drive-in window.

No published sources were found for parking needs at nightclubs and drinking places. It is reasonable to assume that their densities of patron activity would be similar to those of a casual dining establishment, and therefore those

ratios have been employed. Employee parking needs have been reduced by 50 percent to reflect minimal food service. The time-of-day factors, however, have been adjusted to reflect an evening opening on weekdays and an 11 a.m. opening on weekends.

A consultant study (not published as of this writing)[4] that focused on hourly parking accumulations at 13 family restaurants and several casual dining establishments was employed for the hourly adjustment factors. ITE only has significant data from hamburger eateries for fast-food uses; those patterns are similar to those for family restaurants.

The consultant study found that employee demand represents about 15 percent of the overall demand at casual restaurants; the ITE data tabulate total employees but do not appear to reflect employees present at any one time. The employee parking factors by time of day are based on typical weekday and Saturday staffing plans that were provided to the consultant team on a confidential basis by one of the well-established casual dining chains.

Seasonal adjustments are based on U.S. Census Bureau sales data for 1999–2002 (see Figure 4-4). It is believed that

Table 4-3 Observed Parking Accumulations for Fast-Food Restaurants (Spaces/ksf[1] GFA)

| | Hamburger | O T H E R | | All |
	Weekdays	Weekdays	Weekdays	Saturdays
Drive-through	No	No	Yes	Yes
Observations	8	14	46	24
Peak Hour	Noon	Varies	Noon	Noon–3 p.m.
Range	7.1–14.6	1.4–29.2	1.5–23.3	3.0–18.0
85th Percentile	14.5	12.3	14.8	13.6
Average	12.4	8.2	9.9	9.5

Note
[1] ksf = thousand sq. ft.

Source: ITE, *Parking Generation*, 3rd ed., Land Use Codes 933 and 934.

Figure 4-4 Monthly Restaurant Sales Patterns, 1999–2003

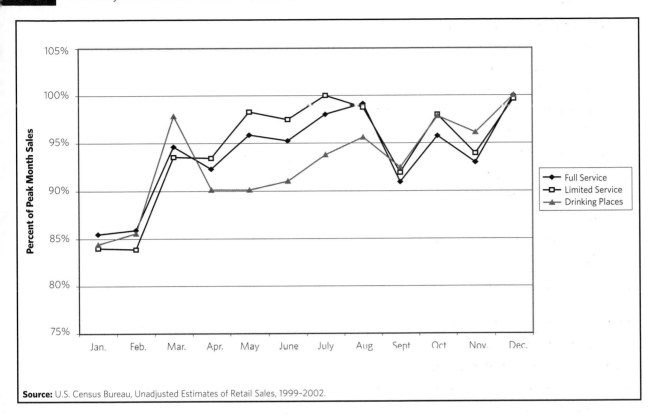

Source: U.S. Census Bureau, Unadjusted Estimates of Retail Sales, 1999–2002.

parking at restaurants is more directly proportional to sales than for retail establishments, and therefore these factors have been used without further adjustment. The Census Bureau tracks food service sales in three categories: full-service restaurants, limited-service restaurants, and drinking places. The full-service restaurant pattern was used for both categories of sit-down restaurants, the limited service pattern was used for fast-food restaurants, and the drinking places pattern was used for nightclubs/drinking places. A notable sharp peak in drinking-place sales occurs in March, which may be attributable to St. Patrick's Day, Mardi Gras, and spring-break travel and revelry.

Active Entertainment

This category encompasses a wide variety of active or interactive entertainment uses, from bowling alleys and go-cart tracks to amusement arcades and virtual reality venues. These uses are increasingly being added to shopping centers, converting them to retail/dining/entertainment venues. For example, the Xanadu project being developed at the Meadowlands in the metropolitan New York/New Jersey area will have about 2.2 million square feet of leasable space, of which only about 15 percent will be traditional retail fashion tenants. Among the planned uses is a "snow dome," an indoor ski hill that will be used year-round for skiing, tubing, and snowboarding. Children's entertainment uses include Wannado (which provides an active environment for role-playing in a variety of settings, including a retired commercial airplane),[5] a roller rink, sports simulations, and miniature golf. Other planned attractions include an indoor mini–Formula One racing venue, a Ferris wheel similar to London's Eye, a skydiving simulator with a vertical wind tunnel, bowling, and billiards.[6] The project also includes a hotel, 1.75 million square feet of office space, and a minor-league baseball park. The parking spaces built with the project will not only serve these uses but also events at Continental Arena and Giants Stadium.

The difficulty of developing a single parking ratio for such diverse active entertainment uses is that each use has differing densities of customers and employers per square foot. ITE's *Parking Generation* offers a few data points for several uses (bowling alleys, miniature golf) but they are not sufficient to determine an overall ratio for the combination of such uses that may be present in a project such as the Meadowlands' Xanadu.

In general, active entertainment uses will not be as densely occupied as restaurants, cinemas, and performing arts facilities, and they may not even be as densely occupied as retail. Some, however, have restaurant and banquet/conference facilities overlooking the activity areas. It is recommended that if less than 10 percent of the GLA of a shopping center is occupied by active entertainment uses, or if less than 20 percent is occupied by restaurants and entertainment uses, then those uses need not be tabulated separately. In other cases, custom ratios for the specific tenants should be developed. The ratios typically would be developed by projecting the persons per car and the maximum presence of customers and employees at peak hours per square foot of each use. Time-of-day factors may need to be adjusted; some venues that attract children and families in the daytime will attract adults in the evening, while others will have little activity after 8 or 9 p.m., particularly on weekdays during the school year. Noncaptive factors may also vary substantially; parents may allow older children to visit some destinations on their own while the parents shop or dine. In other cases,

children will be dropped off, and thus there should be a mode adjustment. Wannado, for example, is a kids-only venue where children are checked into the facility and parents are given wristbands with pagers to notify them when the children are finished playing. On weekdays, a high proportion of visitors will arrive by school bus. The appropriate adjustment for Wannado thus would be zero percent noncaptive, making mode adjustments moot.

Cineplexes

Because cineplexes are frequently major components of mixed-use projects today, special attention has been paid to this land use for the second edition of *Shared Parking*. The term cineplex has been employed to make it clear that the use portrayed is a large facility with multiple screens, rather than the single-screen movie theater of the past. In the 1980s, multiscreen cineplexes began opening across the nation. Initially, two or three screens were considered "multiscreen"; by the mid-1990s, some new cineplexes had as many as 30 screens. Between 1990 and 1999, the number of screens (not counting drive-ins) in the United States increased by 59 percent, from 22,904 to 36,448.[7] In the same period, however, the number of admissions (tickets sold) increased by only 24 percent, from 1.19 billion to 1.47 billion. The overbuilding of the 1990s forced several chains into bankruptcy and also affected older theaters with fewer screens. There was a contraction to 34,490 screens by 2001, and in that year analysts projected that between 10 and 15 percent of movie theaters would have to close.[8] However, the number of screens increased to 35,170 in 2002, to 35,361 in 2003, and to 36,012 in 2004. A new box-office record was achieved in 2002 with 1.63 billion tickets sold; 2003 was similar, with 1.57 billion tickets sold.[9] In 2004, 1.53 billion tickets were sold.

One reason that a greater contraction in the number of screens has not occurred as of this writing is that new cineplexes with stadium seats and other amenities can still be successfully developed in many markets. Older theaters are renovating to add stadium seating, food services, and the like to remain competitive, and thus the fight for market share continues to spur both new construction and renovation. However, the number of screens per new project has settled into the eight-to-20 range; the return on investment for cineplexes with more than 20 screens is not deemed attractive in most markets. Some older cineplexes that cannot be expanded or renovated are being forced to close or to change their focus, resulting in increases in the average number of screens per site from 3.78 in 1995 to 5.18 in 1999, 6.15 in 2002, 6.2 in 2003, and 6.4 in 2004.

New movies are shown on multiple screens at each cineplex on their opening days, purportedly to try to use widely reported box-office sales from the first weekend as free publicity for subsequent weeks. Movies that are less successful

disappear from screens quickly, and relatively few have enough appeal to draw customers for more than a few weeks. At the same time, films are being released more uniformly throughout the year rather than just in the summer and holiday periods.[10]

Parking Generation's data in land use code 444 (movie theaters) comes from only seven sites, all but one of which were observed prior to 1985 and all at locations with ten or fewer screens. The 85th percentile ratio of parked vehicles was 0.36 spaces per seat for six sites on Fridays, 0.23 spaces per seat for seven sites on Saturdays, and 0.15 spaces per seat for four sites with Sunday data. The high Friday data point appears to be out of line with other data, including North American ticket sales as charted in Figure 4-5. (By definition in this publication, Friday evening is considered to be part of the weekend, but Friday daytime is included with weekdays.)

Figure 4-5 North American Movie Ticket Sales, 1997–2002

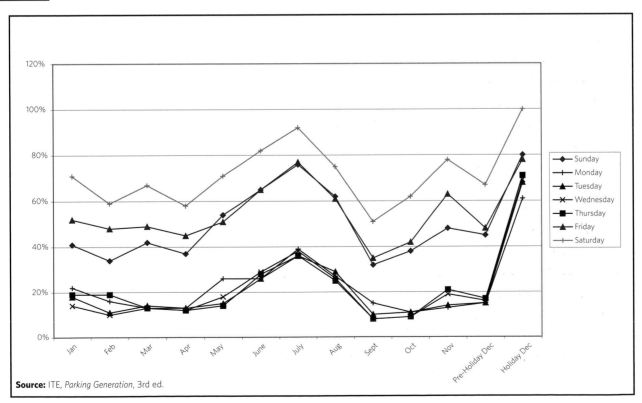

Source: ITE, *Parking Generation*, 3rd ed.

When the default factors in *Shared Parking*'s first edition database were compared with several different, more recent sources, the study team concluded that the seasonality and time-of-day factors were no longer reliable for today's conditions. The ticket sales data published in the third edition of *Parking Generation* indicate that Saturdays in general have about a 25 percent higher demand than Fridays, and Sundays in most months have ticket sales equal to or slightly higher than Fridays. Ticket sales through the remainder of the week are generally 25 percent of those on Saturdays and half of those on Fridays and Sundays. The exception is Late December, when ticket sales on Mondays through Thursdays run about 70 percent of those on Saturdays, while Friday and Sunday ticket sales run about 80 percent of those on Saturday.

Data collected by Patton Rust Harris & Associates for the Peterson Companies at stand-alone cineplexes in Late December 2000 and two weeks later in January 2001 indicate that one of the reasons for higher ticket sales between Christmas and New Year's Day is significantly higher demand for the afternoon hours, as compared with the January data (see Figure 4-6).[11] The Late December weekday daytime figures may be higher because a large proportion of adults are on vacation during this period and thus are more likely to visit a cineplex in the daytime as a family.

The three blue lines in Figure 4-6 represent observed parking patterns at four multiscreen cineplexes in Late December 2000, while the black lines show counts in January 2001. Three sites were in different cities in Virginia, and the fourth was in Florida. The three Virginia cineplexes had 2,500 to

Figure 4-6 Parking Patterns in January and Late December

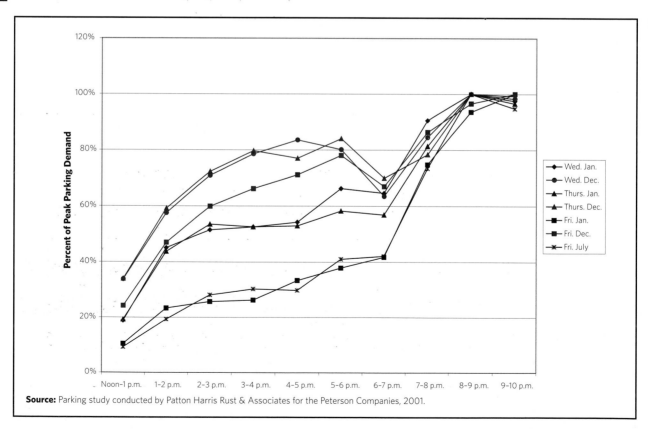

Source: Parking study conducted by Patton Harris Rust & Associates for the Peterson Companies, 2001.

4,200 seats with 12 to 14 screens; the Florida cineplex had 20 screens and 4,000 seats. The peaking of activity on Wednesdays and Thursdays was not as pronounced as on Fridays; in other words, proportionately more of the total attendance on Fridays was in the evenings. The parking generation on Friday afternoons was comparable to that on Thursday afternoons. It was therefore deemed appropriate to consider Friday and Saturday evenings to have similar parking demand, but to use the Thursday data for weekday time-of-day factors.

Also shown are data on ticket sales by hour in July, provided by one of the major cineplex chains for the same study. The Friday July pattern is similar to the Friday January pattern, when children are still in school, rather than the Friday Late December pattern. It is for this reason that the same time-of-day factors are recommended in this book for July as for other months, with special factors only for Late December.

The analysis of North American movie ticket sales indicated that the top sales days of the year are, in order, the day after Thanksgiving, the Saturday during Late December, the day after Christmas, and Saturdays in July. The 20th highest hour (the design hour employed for shopping center parking needs) appears to occur on Saturdays in July. Ticket sales on the second Saturday before Christmas (the design day for shopping centers) are less than half of those on Saturdays in July.

Table 4-4 presents a summary of the peak accumulation of vehicles observed in the Patton Harris Rust & Associates study, as well as those found in the *Parking Generation* (third edition) database and a few additional studies contributed by study team members. Note that the definition of the design day is the 85th percentile of all observations. One of the studies found an average of 2.0 persons per car on Fridays, 2.14 persons per car on Saturdays, and 1.84 persons per car on Wednesdays.[12]

| Table 4-4 | Observed Peak Parking Accumulations in Cineplexes (Spaces per Seat) |

	Parking Generation		WSA Study		WPC Study		PHR&A Study			
	FRI	SAT	WED JUN	FRI/SAT JUN	WED AUG	SAT AUG	WED/ THURS JAN	WED/ THURS DEC	FRI JAN	FRI DEC
Sites	6	7	1	2	1	4	4	4	4	4
Range	0.11-0.46	0.11-0.23	0.04	0.18-0.23	0.04	0.8-0.16	0.03-0.14	0.13-0.30	0.2-0.34	0.16-0.36
85th Percentile	0.36	0.23	—	0.23	—	0.16		0.18		0.26
Average Ratio	0.26	0.19	0.04	0.21	0.04	0.11	0.07	0.18	0.25	0.24

Sources: ITE, *Parking Generation*, 3rd ed.; Wilbur Smith Associates, unpublished study of movie theater parking patterns, Pigeon Forge, Tennessee, June 2001; Walker Parking Consultants, unpublished study of movie theater parking patterns, 2003; Patton Harris Rust & Associates, *Fairfax Corner Shared Parking Study*, including Addendum 2, February 2001.

Parking ratios of 0.27 spaces per seat for Friday and Saturday evenings and 0.2 spaces per seat for weekdays are recommended. These compare with the ratios of 0.3 spaces per seat on Saturdays and 0.25 spaces per seat on weekdays recommended in the first edition of *Shared Parking*. When one considers that the average vehicle occupancy for cineplex patrons is about 2.0 persons per car on weekend evenings, the first edition's parking ratios would indicate that only two-thirds of the seats would be occupied in the design hour on a Saturday night in July. Cineplexes have very low ratios of employees per seat, typically less than 0.01 employees per seat.

The recommended time-of-day factors are based on the same references as the recommended parking ratios, while seasonal factors are based on the analysis of North American ticket sales for 1997–2002. Both sets of factors have changed significantly from those in the first edition, as illustrated in Figures 4-7 and 4-8. Because of the significant differences in monthly variations that have been documented via ticket sales, it is recommended that different monthly factors be employed for weekday and weekend activity at cineplexes. For this edition of *Shared Parking*, the Saturday sales pattern was employed for weekend factors, while the Monday-through-Thursday average was used for weekdays.

Figure 4-7 Cineplex Time-of-Day Factors

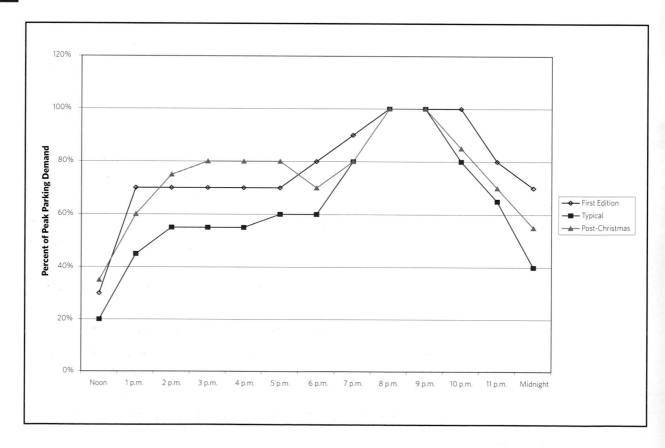

Figure 4-8 Cineplex Seasonal Adjustments

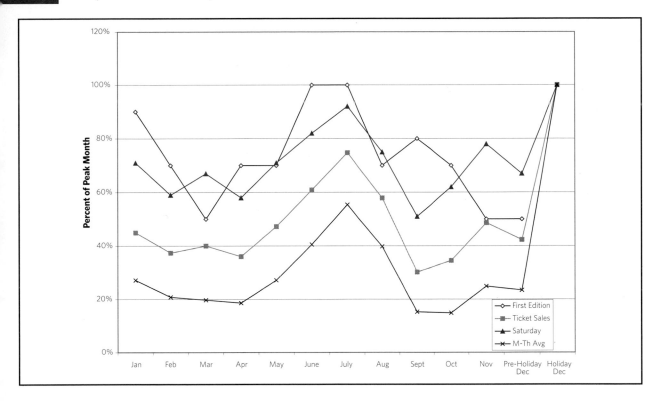

Performing Arts Theaters

This category includes venues for live plays, musical performances, and individual concerts and comedy shows. Some venues are single-purpose, hosting one symphony, ballet, or repertory company. Others are multiuse and may house touring plays, concerts, and local events such as high school graduations, lectures, and motivational speakers. The most common location in which shared parking occurs for these venues is downtown. Increasingly, however, these venues may be located in urban or suburban entertainment complexes that combine retail, dining, and entertainment components.

Live performances occur at everything from outdoor amphitheaters to large indoor auditoriums to smaller night-club settings. The *Parking Generation* database for live theaters (land use code 441) includes surveys for one day at four different theaters in a rural Tennessee resort area in 1997. Three of the theaters had attendance at roughly 50 percent of capacity, while the fourth had nearly 100 percent of capacity. The latter theater programmed three shows, with some overlap of arriving and departing attendees between the first two; the peak parking accumulation was 0.51 spaces during that overlap. All four had similar peak accumulations during the prime evening performance, averaging 0.38 spaces per occupied seat for the evening show (see Figure 4-9). The theater with an afternoon show but no overlap had a ratio of 0.25 spaces per occupied seat for the matinee. No tour bus activity was observed at any of the theaters.

Owing to the lack of data on a range of theater types to include in this category, the recommended parking ratio is based on a sold-out show in the evening, with no overlap of attendees between shows, no tour buses or significant

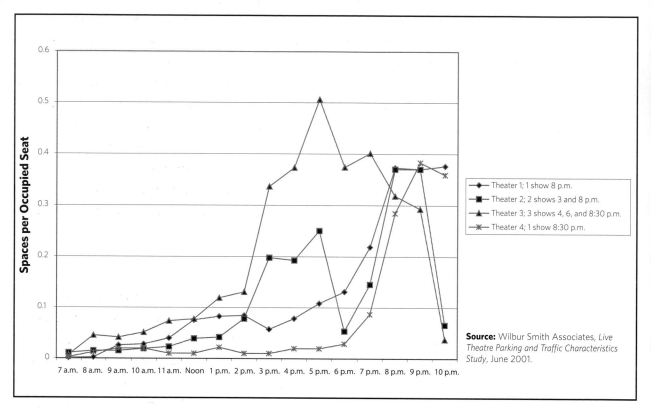

Legend:
- Theater 1; 1 show 8 p.m.
- Theater 2; 2 shows 3 and 8 p.m.
- Theater 3; 3 shows 4, 6, and 8:30 p.m.
- Theater 4; 1 show 8:30 p.m.

Source: Wilbur Smith Associates, *Live Theatre Parking and Traffic Characteristics Study*, June 2001.

use of local transit, and a ratio of 0.08 employees and performers per seat. The vehicle occupancy for ticketed attendees is assumed to be three persons per car, with 1.2 persons per car for employees. The customer-parking ratio is thus 0.33 spaces per seat, and the employee-parking ratio is 0.07 employees per seat, for an overall ratio of 0.4 spaces per seat.

To determine time-of-day and monthly adjustment factors, the study team reviewed performance calendars posted on the Internet by performing arts theaters in multiple cities. Broadway shows and some other venues do have matinees almost every Wednesday, but most theaters that host touring productions or mount their own shows do not regularly schedule weekday matinees. Some theaters have children's productions on weekdays that are oriented to school groups,

which means that most children will arrive by bus. On rare occasions (no more than one afternoon a month), some theaters host a lecture or motivational group. Given the rarity, no afternoon show is assumed for weekdays. If a venue is likely to have weekday matinees, the weekend adjustments could be used for weekdays; the matinee factors when applied against the lower weekday factors would result in yet lower afternoon parking demand on weekdays.

The design day for Saturdays is assumed to include an evening show and a matinee, with the matinee having two-thirds of the peak-hour demand as the evening. The design day for weekdays is assumed to be a single show with 90 percent of the demand of a Saturday evening, or 0.3 spaces per seat for patrons.

Individual performing arts facilities may have a specific focus, and all factors should be carefully reviewed to determine whether each factor is appropriate for the particular circumstances. In some cases, there should be an adjustment for a different ratio of persons per cars. Conversely, the focus of a theater can change over time, and tying parking needs to a specific production company or focus may not be appropriate.

On weekdays, there will be administrative employees during normal business hours, as well as rehearsals and other activities on days when there are not matinees. The Tennessee study cited above formed the basis of this edition's time-of-day factors. Internet searches revealed that theaters that feature touring productions will frequently host them for a month or more and then have a "dark" period before another event opens. Repertory theaters, ballet companies, and other groups that mount significant productions locally may have as much as a month between productions. Of course, a show that runs on Broadway for a year or more will have a long continuous run between dark periods.

A review of weekly ticket sales for Broadway theaters as reported by the League of American Theatres and Producers indicates that the busiest week of the year on Broadway is the week between Christmas and New Year's Day, a period that has about 10 percent higher attendance than the second busiest week, which occurs over the Thanksgiving holiday weekend.[13] Theater attendance on Broadway is clearly lowest in September; attendance in September 2003 averaged less than 60 percent of the peak week the prior year. During the summer tourist season, Broadway ticket sales average about 70 percent of the peak week.

The study team's review of the calendars of theaters of other types (symphony, university-based, touring shows, repertory theaters, and so on) indicated that December, both pre- and post-Christmas, is clearly the busiest time (none scheduled significant dark time for this period). It appears that relatively few events occur in the summer; for example, some symphonies switch to outdoor venues in the summer months, and many repertory and university theaters are largely dark in the summer. However, other theaters (including dinner theaters) typically operate year-round, with only brief dark periods between shows.

To reflect the likelihood of sellouts with holiday shows in December, and the lower likelihood of sellout events the remainder of the year, the monthly factor is set at 90 percent for all months except December, pre- and post-holiday. If a well-established performing arts theater or company is in place or relocating to a development site, it should be fairly easy to obtain a typical schedule in order to customize the monthly factors.

Arenas

With the exception of arenas on college campuses, new arenas today are often located in or near downtowns for several reasons. Generally, there is already a well-developed transportation and parking infrastructure, and arenas serve to increase the nightlife in downtown environments. Increasingly, mixed-use, dining, and entertainment-oriented areas are built with or around arena sites. Conseco Fieldhouse in Indianapolis was developed adjacent to the city's already vibrant retail, dining, and entertainment district. Staples Center in Los Angeles was developed adjacent to the existing convention center, and an urban retail, dining, and entertainment district is being developed across the street. Although Continental Arena at the Meadowlands in New Jersey is more than 20 years old, the previously mentioned Xanadu project is being developed on its adjacent parking lots, which will be replaced with shared structured parking.

Arenas typically are used for more than sporting events; a common figure is 150 to 200 event days a year, and there may be more than one event per day. The types of events vary substantially, with a resulting wide variation in parking needs. Generally, arenas host three main event types:

Table 4-5 Attendance at Continental Arena Events, Meadowlands, N.J., 2000-2002

	2000	2001	2002
Number of Events	217	201	243
Maximum Attendance per Seat	1.04	1.00	1.00
85th Percentile Attendance per Seat	0.85	0.90	0.90
Average Attendance per Seat	0.65	0.61	0.55

Source: New Jersey Sports and Exposition Authority.

■ Sporting events have a mix of singles and families.

■ Family shows have the highest ratio of persons per car.

■ Concerts typically have the lowest ratio of about 2.0 persons per car.

There also will be a handful of what are known as "flat shows," using the arena floor for consumer shows, graduations, and large meetings and convocations.

To assist in the development of parking ratios and seasonality factors, the New Jersey Sports and Exposition Authority, owner of Continental Arena, provided attendance for all events for calendar years 2000, 2001, and 2002. The arena, with 20,049 seats, is home to the New Jersey Nets (NBA), New Jersey Devils (NHL), and Seton Hall (college) basketball teams. It also has hosted arena football teams (Red Dogs in 2000, Gladiators in 2001–2002) playing from April to July and an indoor lacrosse team (Storm) playing from November through March since fall 2001. The total number of events is summarized in Table 4-5.

Playoffs will lengthen the sports seasons; in 2000 and 2001, the Devils advanced to the Stanley Cup finals; in 2002, they advanced to the first round of the playoffs. The Nets advanced to the NBA finals in 2002. One reason for the lower number of event days in 2001 was that the nine-day run of a family show scheduled to occur shortly after September 11, 2001, was canceled.

About 15 percent of the events occurred on the same day as another event; only 3 percent were third shows. Nearly all the days with three events were family shows (circus, ice show, and the like) The vast majority of multishow days occurred on Saturdays or Sundays. More than 77 percent of the events occurred in the evening; nearly all morning and most afternoon shows on weekdays were family shows or motivational speakers and graduations.

Over 25 percent of the events were pro basketball games, and about 20 percent were hockey. Sporting events comprised about 60 percent of the annual events. Another 25 percent were family shows, and 15 percent were concerts. The remaining events included private events, several college graduations, religious assemblies, and motivational speakers.

This arena is located near and shares parking resources with Giants Stadium. Despite its location in the metropolitan New York/New Jersey area, it is not currently served by regular public transit. Parking data from arena events in 2002 have been evaluated, as summarized in Table 4-6. Although the Authority does not track the attendance that arrives via bus, the number of charter buses parked at each event was recorded. New Jersey Transit also provided information on ridership of the service it provides from the Port Authority Terminal in Manhattan.

Table 4-6 Parking and Charter Bus Data for Continental Arena Events, Meadowlands, N.J., 2002

	Nets	Devils	College Basketball	High School	Storm/ Gladiators	Family Shows	Concerts	Other
Events	62	45	15	3	13	56	28	8
Average Attendance	15,087	15,095	7,706	6,215	5,671	8,190	13,603	10,533
Parked Cars/Attendee	0.30	0.30	0.24	0.26	0.11	0.23	0.30	0.27
Buses/Event	18.9	3.7	3.3	—	2.8	36.9	2.7	8.4
Buses/1,000 Attendees	1.3	0.2	0.4	—	0.5	4.5	0.2	0.8

Source: New Jersey Sports and Exposition Authority.

The events that generated the highest attendance (Nets, Devils, and concerts) all had average parking ratios of 0.30 spaces per occupied seat, but the Nets had significantly more buses per 1,000 occupied seats than either of the other two uses. This would indicate that the Nets games have a lower number of persons per car among those who drive and park. Assuming 50 seats per bus, there can be no more than about 5 percent of Nets fans who travel via charter bus, while no more than 1 percent of Devils and concert fans arrive via bus. It appears that those three uses averaged over 3.0 persons per car. College basketball and high school sporting events generated about 0.25 spaces per occupied seat, with family shows slightly lower, about 0.23 spaces per occupied seat. There were not a significant number of buses transporting students and fans for college and high school sporting events.

Family shows generated significantly more buses than any other use, and 15 percent or more of the family show patrons may be arriving via bus. However, more detailed analysis indicates that one or two shows in each run of family shows attracted the majority of buses. For example, an ice show in January 2002 drew a total of 606 buses over 11 shows, posting a total attendance of 88,977. An accumulation of 434 buses (over 70 percent) came to a single show

at 10:30 a.m. on a Thursday morning. Three of the shows drew only three to five buses. In sum, a high rate of bus arrivals is an exception, not a regular condition meriting consideration on a design day.

The two newer sporting teams, the Storm and the Gladiators, generated significantly fewer parked vehicles per ticket sold; persons and corporations may be purchasing seats to support the teams, but the tickets are not always used. The higher ratio of bus usage for "other" events was directly related to a religious assembly that generated half of the attendance and virtually all the bus arrivals in this category.

The recommended parking ratio for arenas assumes a pro basketball game with 90 percent of seats occupied on a weekend evening, no overlap of attendees between events, no tour buses or significant use of public transit by attendees, and a ratio of 0.03 employees per seat. There typically are far fewer employees/performers per seat found at arenas than at performing arts theaters, and most arenas reserve only very limited parking for players and key employees. Event employees (ushers, parking, vendors) typically must choose either to pay event-parking rates (and thus are considered part of the customer parking ratio) or to take transit.

The vehicle occupancy for arena public parking is assumed to be 3.0 persons per car, with 1.1 persons per car for employees. Because most arenas are located in urban areas, with significantly less parking than at the Meadowlands, a mode adjustment for both spectators and employees may be appropriate. The patron parking ratio is therefore 0.3 spaces per seat, and the employee parking ratio is 0.03 employees per seat, for an overall ratio of 0.33 spaces per seat. With about 15 percent of events occurring on weekend afternoons, a show or game in the afternoon on a weekend is included in the time-of-day adjustments; the data indicate that the 85th percentile weekend afternoon event is a pro basketball game with about 95 percent attendance compared with the design-day evening event, or 0.29 spaces per seat. Analysis of weekend and weekday patterns indicates that the weekday parking ratio should be 90 percent of the weekend ratio, or 0.27 spaces per seat.

The vast majority of spectators arrive in the hour before the start of an event; in fact, it has been found that season ticket holders with parking passes often arrive in the last 30 minutes before the event. Unless the game is close, 15 percent of patrons typically leave before the end of the game. Most arenas are designed to allow all users to depart within 45 minutes after the event, although many facilities are adding bars and clubs within the building to capture food and beverage sales from those willing to arrive early or stay later.

Arenas tend to be busiest during the school year, which encompasses the pro basketball and hockey seasons; if a pro basketball team goes to the finals, there could be high-attendance games in June. Figure 4-10 presents the events at Continental Arena over the three-year period as an indication of seasonality.

Figure 4-10 Seasonality of Continental Arena Events, Meadowlands, N.J., 2000–2002

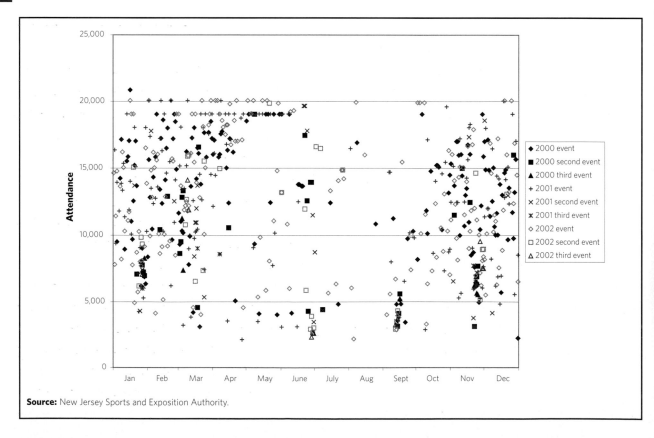

Source: New Jersey Sports and Exposition Authority.

Table 4-7 Seasonality Factors for Continental Arena

Month	Attendance Average	Event Days Average	Events Average	ATTENDANCE PER EVENT		Percent Peak Month 85th Percentile	Recommended Factor
				Average	85th Percentile		
January	306,256	22	27	11,205	15,850	88%	90%
February	290,537	19	21	14,058	18,000	100%	100%
March	396,786	23	47	12,939	18,000	100%	100%
April	240,655	14	11	15,695	18,000	100%	100%
May	167,109	13	11	14,745	18,000	100%	100%
June	136,643	8	13	10,788	13,179	73%	75%
July	55,321	4	5	11,064	11,082	62%	—
August	29,445	2	2	12,619	10,862	60%	—
September	72,145	8	11	6,559	10,319	57%	60%
October	155,101	13	13	12,245	15,220	85%	85%
November	339,550	24	32	10,723	15,884	88%	90%
December	228,581	17	19	12,245	16,452	91%	95%
Late December	63,002	4	5	12,068	16,864	94%	95%

Source: New Jersey Sports and Exposition Authority.

Seasonality factors were based on a more specific evaluation of the number of events and the likelihood of sellout at Continental Arena, as shown in Table 4-7. The slowest months are July, August, and September, similar to the patterns observed for performing arts theaters.

Recommended seasonal factors generally reflect the 85th percentile attendance in each month, except for July and August. In those two months there were very few events (an average of five and two, respectively), which is not frequent enough to be considered a typical day. Therefore, no events are assumed for those months.

The most significant issue with shared parking for arenas is often parking management. See chapter 6 for a discussion of these issues, with a specific discussion of parking management tactics for shared parking with arenas.

Stadiums

The trend today for professional baseball and football stadiums is to locate them in mixed-use areas or in downtown locations for the same reasons that arenas are located in such areas. Two recent examples of mixed-use developments in concert with new stadiums are in Pittsburgh and Cincinnati. Both have downtowns located near a major river; and in both cases separate new football and baseball stadiums have recently been developed several blocks apart on the riverfront, with space between for the development of retail, dining, office, residential, outdoor plazas with an amphitheater, and of course shared parking for all the uses. Both areas also provide a significant amount of lower-cost parking for commuters bound for downtown buildings.

Football stadiums are generally much larger and have more limited use than other stadiums, especially if they are not domed. Football stadiums serving a professional team are often used primarily on Sundays, with perhaps one Monday or Thursday evening game a season. Preseason games may occur on Thursdays, Fridays, or Saturdays; post-season games and one game in December may also occur on Saturdays. Weeknight games and playoff and championship games are generally considered special cases and are not considered in parking planning. Even a regular-season Sunday football game may not be considered the design event for sharing with retail/entertainment uses, since the public generally avoids patronizing any other uses during football games because of the traffic congestion that inevitably occurs when tens of thousands of fans flood the area. Stadiums that host college football games or other sports such as baseball or pro soccer may be of more concern when parking is to be shared with nearby retail/dining/

entertainment venues, since Saturday patronage is important to the economic viability of these uses. The appropriate design day for estimating parking needs for an overall development may thus be a Saturday baseball or college football game.

Other issues with planning parking for football stadiums are tailgating and the accommodation of motor homes, which is relatively difficult in the structured parking that is more likely with mixed-use development near stadiums.

Giants Stadium at the Meadowlands is in the unusual position of hosting two pro football teams (the Giants and the Jets) and the MetroStars (Major League Soccer), as well as several college and high school football games each year. In 2001, it was also home to the New Jersey Hitmen, an extreme football team. The Meadowlands has control of

Figure 4-11   Seasonality of Events at Giants Stadium, Meadowlands, N.J., 2000–2002

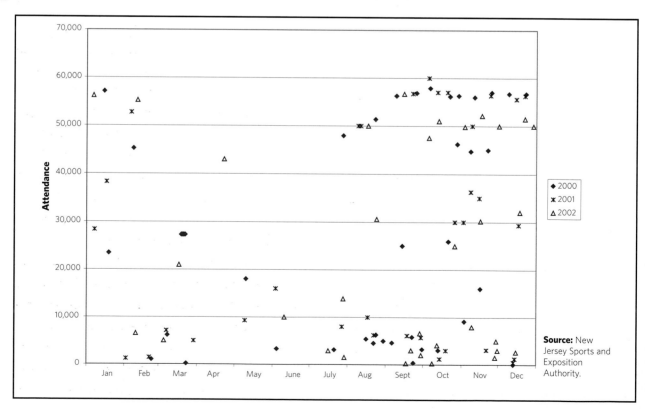

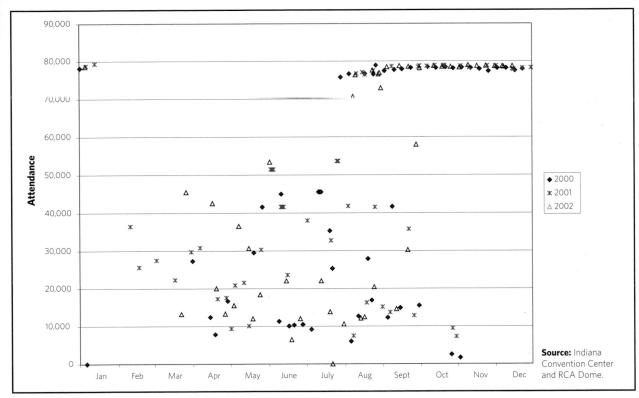

Source: Indiana Convention Center and RCA Dome.

enough parking to serve almost every event (approximately 27,700 parking spaces, a ratio of 0.35 spaces per stadium seat), and it maintains parking records by event. It thus provided a rich data source for this publication. Although *Shared Parking* did not originally intend to evaluate data on soccer stadiums, information was received on both U.S. pro league and "international friendly" games that is occasionally discussed here. Soccer is not shown as a land use type in the summary tables, however.

In addition to sporting events, Giants Stadium averages five concerts and several marching band competitions each year. Even with an unusually high number of teams, it hosts an average of only 50 events a year, as summarized in Figure 4-11.

The stadium has about 80,000 seats (79,646 seats in 2000 and 2001, expanded to 80,242 seats in 2002). Typically, over 97 percent of the seats are sold for pro foot-

ball games. Preseason games in August usually have a reported attendance of about 95 percent of capacity.

The configuration of Giants Stadium for Major League Soccer (MLS) reduces the capacity to about 25,000, while the configuration for concerts typically has about 50,000 seats. Soccer games and concerts are more likely to occur on weekdays than football and also typically occur in the evenings. Concerts occur in the summer months. The pro soccer league season runs April through September. In addition to major-league soccer, Giants Stadium hosts a number of international soccer games each year, some of which were scheduled as double headers with major-league games, while others occurred outside the pro soccer league's season.

Giants Stadium is not domed, and thus has almost no activity other than football in the winter months. Similar data on events attendance, however, were received for the

RCA Dome, home to the Indianapolis Colts. The RCA Dome has 57,837 seats for football games and can accommodate as many as 32,000 for basketball games. It hosts one major college football game a year, the Circle City Classic, featuring two historically black colleges. A number of high school football games are scheduled each fall, including multiclass state high school football championships. The RCA Dome also hosted the National Collegiate Athletic Association (NCAA) basketball championships in 2000 and the World Basketball championships in 2002, as well as a number of championships in gymnastics, volleyball, tae kwon do, and other Olympic sports. A gathering of 25,000 attended a Jubilee Mass in September 2000. The dome is also the annual home of one of the nation's largest high school marching band competitions.

The RCA Dome does not attract as many concerts as Giants Stadium, averaging only one per year. Conversely, it hosts several large indoor motor vehicle competitions, such as monster truck, tractor pull, and motor cross events, typically in the early spring when open stadiums in northern climates would be dark.

In total, the dome hosted 41 events in 2000 and 34 each in 2001 and 2002. Some events extended for multiple days.

Figure 4-12 charts the seasonality of RCA Dome events over the same three-year period presented for Giants Stadium.

Table 4-8 summarizes the distribution of pro football games at the two stadiums by day of week (remember that Giants Stadium houses two pro teams). The Thursday, Friday, and Saturday games at both stadiums all occurred in the preseason of late July, August, or early September.

Giants Stadium has adequate parking for its needs, and it keeps records of parking of both autos and buses for each event (see Table 4-9). Typically, less than 2 percent of ticket holders arrive by bus, but this stadium has the highest parking supply ratio among pro football venues, and it was not well-served by public transit at the time the data were collected. A default value of 85 percent modal split to auto is recommended as a typical starting point for football stadiums in a downtown setting with transit available on Sundays or where there is limited parking.

With minimal arrivals by bus, football games at Giants Stadium generated 0.29 parked vehicles per attendee, as compared with soccer games, which generated an average of 0.16 parked cars per seat. Major League Soccer is being heavily marketed to families with young soccer players; this would contribute to a high ratio of persons per car. The ratio

| Table 4-8 | Distribution of Pro Football Games by Day of Week |

	Giants Stadium			RCA Dome		
	2000	**2001**	**2002**	**2000**	**2001**	**2002**
Thursday	—	1	2	1	—	—
Friday	1	1	1	—	—	—
Saturday	3	4	3	1	1	2
Sunday	15	13	15	8	7	9
Monday	2	2	—	1	—	—
Total	21	21	21	11	8	11
Percent on Sunday	71%	62%	71%	73%	88%	82%

Sources: New Jersey Sports and Exposition Authority; Indiana Convention Center and RCA Dome.

Table 4-9 Giants Stadium Parking Data, 2002

	Football	Pro Soccer	International Soccer	College	Concerts
Events	21	17	3	3	1
Average Attendance	78,224	17,846	49,922	60,602	58,000
Parked Cars/Attendee	0.29	0.16	0.22	0.23	0.31
Buses/Event	27.0	4.1	13.7	177.7	28.0
Buses/1,000 Attendees	0.35	0.22	0.27	2.93	0.48
Estimated Maximum Percent by Bus	2%	1%	1%	15%	2%

Source: New Jersey Sports and Exposition Authority.

for soccer on weekends was a little lower at 0.16 spaces per occupied seat, while the ratio on weeknights was 0.17 spaces per seat. However, it is also likely that part of the low ratio of spaces per seat resulted from season-ticket holders not attending every game. Three international "friendlies" during the off-season, all featuring teams from other countries, attracted significantly more attendance (an average of almost 50,000 per event) and averaged 0.22 spaces per seat. All the friendlies occurred on weeknights. Similarly, the three college games at Giants Stadium in 2002 were all special events with out-of-town teams: Notre Dame vs. Maryland, Army vs. Navy, and Hampton vs. Alcorn State. Students and fans were bused from distant campuses and hotels.

Football stadium arrivals typically occur over two hours, fairly evenly distributed over that period, although season ticket holders tend to arrive later if they have a pass for parking in a reserved area. The number of persons per car for pro football games ranges from 2.7 to 4.0. The recommended parking ratio for pro football stadiums is based on an average vehicle occupancy of 3.3 persons per car, or 0.3 spaces per seat. Very limited parking is provided for employees and players at most stadiums. In such cases, concession workers and other part-time staff must choose to pay for public parking or to take public transportation and thus should not be included in employee parking projections. The nominal employee parking ratio is estimated to be 0.01 spaces per seat for a total ratio of 0.31 spaces per seat. To factor in time-of-day variables, 85 percent of the departures can be assumed to occur within one hour after a game; this estimate presumes adequate roadway capacity to absorb the vehicles. It typically takes one and a half to two hours to clear all the vehicles from Giants Stadium parking lots.

The Jets played a postseason game at the stadium in January 2000; the Giants played two postseason games at the stadium in January 2001 and then played a game rescheduled for January 2002 because of the World Trade Center tragedy. The preseason football games at Giants Stadium in August had slightly lower paid attendance (98 percent) than season games; they also had significantly lower parking generation at 0.19 spaces per reported attendance. This pattern was probably due to season ticket holders not attending the preseason games. The games on Labor Day weekend had particularly low parking ratios. Preseason games occurred on Thursdays, Fridays, or Saturdays, which also may have contributed to lower attendance. Based on the Giants stadium experience, the monthly factor for August would be 61 percent of the games within the season. For August weekday evenings, a monthly factor of 67 percent is recommended for pro football.

Table 4-10 Distribution of Non-NFL Events at the RCA Dome by Month

Month	2000	2001	2002	Average Attendance
January	1	2	0	30,026
February	2	3	2	23,338
March	6	2	2	15,362
April	0	0	1	43,000
May	1	1	0	13,650
June	1	1	1	9,767
July	1	1	3	5,880
August	5	2	4	12,480
September	5	2	4	5,694
October	4	4	4	25,332
November	4	4	5	20,531
December	1	3	2	10,978

Source: Indiana Convention Center and RCA Dome.

Table 4-10 summarizes the non–National Football League (NFL) events at the RCA dome by month over the three-year period. The NCAA basketball tournament in March 2000 would not be considered a normal event for parking planning purposes. Three or fewer events in a month also do not represent sufficient activity to be modeled in a shared parking analysis. Most of the events from August through November occurred on Saturdays and can be considered significant enough to be included in a shared parking model for Saturdays. Clearly, these types of activities are far less likely to sell out a stadium than pro or college football, and therefore the recommended monthly adjustment factor for pro football stadiums for Saturday activity in September through November is 50 percent.

Monthly factors for football stadiums must be adjusted according to whether or not a particular stadium is likely to be used for more than a dozen football games and a handful of other events each year. College football generally begins in early September and winds down by the end of November. The pro football season begins in August, and playoffs extend the season through most of January.

Whether serving major- or minor-league teams, baseball stadiums typically have 80 home games a year, not counting the postseason. The typical design day for shared parking purposes is a nearly sold-out Saturday night game. The assumed average vehicle occupancy is 2.9 persons per seat, yielding a ratio of 0.34 spaces per seat. The parking ratio for weekdays is assumed to be 90 percent of the ratio for weekends or 0.31 spaces per seat and is assumed to occur in the evening, given that the vast majority of baseball games today occur in the evenings. If it is desired to model a day game, the daytime factors can be modified. As with other stadium events, the parking ratio of employees is 0.01 spaces per seat. The arrivals for an evening baseball game will be more concentrated, occurring within 60 to 90 minutes. Baseball season extends from April through October.

Health Clubs

A wide variety of facilities can considered athletic or health clubs; ITE lists four separate categories:

■ Athletic clubs house indoor sports, including tennis, basketball, swimming, squash, and handball. Outdoor courts may also be provided, except in downtown environments. One distinguishing characteristic is that access is limited to members; another is there may be more social facilities, such as a high-quality restaurant, a moderately priced "grille," and banquet space. Some older urban athletic clubs include hotel facilities.

■ Racquet/tennis clubs are similar but do not have swimming pools and gymnasiums. These facilities are likely to have both outdoor and indoor courts.

■ Health clubs are focused on exercise and do not have swimming pools, courts, or gyms.

■ Recreational community centers are public facilities similar to athletic clubs, but they do not have the dining and banquet facilities of private clubs.

There are at least two subtypes of health clubs. The most common is the general workout facility; there are also some specialized clubs that are focused on exercise supervised one-on-one by personal trainers.

The health club is the type most commonly found in shared parking situations, although occasionally YMCA/ YWCA facilities and athletic clubs are located downtown without significant dedicated parking. The data regarding all of the four ITE categories are insufficient to develop shared parking recommendations except for health clubs. Although the *Parking Generation* database includes data from a separately published, detailed study, the results differ in some respects, as summarized in Table 4-11.

Several of the study team members had proprietary information on health club demand from several national chains. Because the consultant study referenced in Table 4-11 was a focused study of health clubs at the same time of year and collected additional data, including time-of-day variations, not reported in *Parking Generation*—as well as the fact that the team members considered the 85th percentile ratio used in the latter to be too high—this book's recommendations for base ratios and time-of-day adjustments are based on the consultant study. The weekday parking ratio is 7.0, with 0.4 of that demand being allocated to employees. The weekend ratio for health clubs (5.75 spaces/ksf), as well as monthly and hourly factors, are based on individual studies performed by team members. In each case, a different chain (each wishing to remain undisclosed) provided data on hourly and seasonal variations.

Table 4-11	Weekday Parking Generation at Health Clubs	
	Health/Fitness[1]	**Consultant Study[2]**
Sites	20	16
Peak Hour	6 p.m.	6 p.m.
Range (Spaces per ksf[3] GFA)	1.8–0.6	1.4–13.4
85th Percentile	8.27	6.9
Average Ratio	5.19	4.65
Employees/ksf	0.57	—

Notes
[1]ITE, *Parking Generation*, 3rd ed., Land Use Code 492.
[2]John Dorsett, "Parking Requirements for Health Clubs," *The Parking Professional*, April 2004, pp. 50–52.
[3]ksf = thousand sq. ft.

Convention Centers

Convention centers are often built in downtown and mixed-use settings by governmental entities to spur tourism and to support hotel, retail, and dining venues in the area. Evaluating the parking needed to serve these facilities is often difficult, because the parking demand of a convention center is unusually site-dependent and extremely variable from day to day. It is even more difficult to include these facilities in a shared parking analysis because little information has been published about the demand of these facilities for peak hours, much less by time of day or month of year. Therefore, additional research was conducted for this land use for this edition of *Shared Parking*. Information on booking and attendance has been provided by three convention centers located in Las Vegas, Indianapolis, and Anaheim, California.

The day-to-day programming of convention facilities is extremely variable, owing to the variety of events they commonly book. There are three main types of events, with several subcategories, all with distinctly different parking needs and characteristics, including modal split, persons per car, and turnover of parking spaces during the events (which translates to presence of attendees at peak hours): conventions and trade shows; consumer or public shows; and other events that do not require exhibition space.

Conventions and Trade Shows

Conventions are meetings of professional and special-interest groups that generally last for three to five days. Occurring in hotels or convention centers, conventions typically consist of multiple meetings and educational sessions with meals and social events. They sometimes include trade shows, which are exhibitions of products and new technology of interest to the attendees. Exhibition halls are generally not used while meetings occur during conventions; thus, the nominal attendance per square foot of space leased to a convention is lower than that which occurs in many other uses of the space. When trade shows are held independently of conventions, they use exhibit halls continuously through the show hours but generally without significant use of meeting rooms, although the trend today is toward more educational sessions. Trade shows and conventions typically operate on a registration basis.

Subcategories with differing parking characteristics are based on the market area of a particular show:

■ National events draw from a great enough distance that the majority of registrants will fly rather than drive. Registrants tend to be present for most of the scheduled hours. Typically, no more than 25 percent of the registrants drive and park at the convention center; most walk or take shuttle buses from hotels, even if they drive to attend the event.

■ National/local events are scheduled in areas where there is a large local base of potential delegates. For example, a convention of automotive engineers in Detroit would be considered a national/local convention, whereas the same group meeting in Las Vegas would be classified as a national event. As many as half the delegates may drive and park at the center, and there tends to be more turnover and less consistent attendance throughout the day.

■ Local events attract most of their registrants from the regional area, and thus 75 percent or more of the delegates drive and park. These events are also likely to have higher turnover.

Consumer/Public Shows

These exhibits and events are oriented to consumers and advertised to the general public. Typically only exhibitors and show organizers stay in hotels; nearly 100 percent of the attendees drive and park, and parking spaces usually turn over significantly throughout the day. Most consumer/public shows are scheduled on weekends, although they may have Friday hours as well. However, the largest consumer shows such as home and auto shows may run for up to two weeks. Attendance on weekdays (including Fridays) for such shows typically runs less than half that on week-ends. Certain types of public shows, such as job fairs, may occur only on weekdays.

Other Events

Several other event types typically are local in attendance, do not require exhibition space, and last one day or less. There are three subtypes:

■ Religious convocations, especially those termed "cru-sades," tend to have high rates of persons per car and may also draw busloads of people, resulting in a lower mode adjustment.

■ Business meetings and seminars generally have a high rate of arrival by private auto and typically will have little turnover.

■ Banquets and dances are usually evening events with a high modal split to private auto but also a relatively high number of persons per car. Luncheons and breakfasts, when not associated with another event, are more likely to be business-oriented, and thus have characteristics similar to meetings.

Conventions, trade shows, and consumer shows often require several days of setup and breakdown during which little or no parking demand is generated. As of late January 2004, the Las Vegas Convention Center had at least part of its facility booked (including move-in and move-out) for 338 days in 2004, but those events generated attendees on 181 days, roughly half the days of the year.

A more typical condition is to have two different events in progress, with setup and breakdown of one or two others occurring on the same day and some of the space not booked. Because it is difficult to find events that precisely fit the gaps between shows already booked, the maximum practical booked occupancy for conventions and trade shows is about 70 percent of the available exhibit space.[14] Certainly there are occasions when the entire facility is booked, but that condition is above the 85th percentile

design day and is not sustainable from week to week. Only three of the Las Vegas Convention Center's 261 events in 2004 booked the entire facility.

Other factors, not the least of which is event type, make the parking needs of similar-sized events markedly different. The percentage of attendees who drive and park and the pro-portion of nominal attendees present at any one time not only are different for conventions and trade shows, but also differ according to what percentage of the registrants come from local, regional, and national markets. Regional popula-tion and availability of competitive exhibition facilities will affect the bookings (and in turn parking generated) by con-sumer shows, and local hotel meeting and banquet spaces also compete for bookings.

The key concern of a convention center from a parking planning and management perspective is what amount of available parking (whether controlled by the convention cen-ter or not) will be required to achieve a successful calendar of bookings. Because most publicly owned facilities are built to spur hotel, dining, and miscellaneous tourist expenditures in the community, the first booking priority is usually national and national/local conventions. In turn, the design day is typ-ically a weekday convention of roughly 85th percentile mag-nitude in its parking needs.

A convention center will then try to fill as many of the spots in its calendar as possible between conventions and trade shows. Parking needs for these other activities still exist, even if it is not a critical issue in determining how much parking the center or other party provides specifically to serve the facility. In fact, peak-parking demand typically occurs during public shows (auto, boat, garden, home, and the like) because the attendance is local and nearly everyone (vendors and attendees) drives and parks. When the con-vention center is located downtown or in mixed-use settings, there is often a good fit for shared parking for public shows, especially on weekends.

The demand for parking will also depend on the setting and on what uses share parking. The Indiana Convention Center (ICC) is located in the heart of the Indianapolis CBD and adjacent to an adequate number of hotel rooms and commercial parking facilities; it thus needs few spaces and can share parking with multiple uses in a dynamic downtown. By contrast, McCormick Place in Chicago and the Los Angeles Convention Center are both located relatively far from the bulk of supporting hotel rooms and thus must maintain proportionately more parking on site as well as dedicated shuttles to hotels, managed on an event-by-event basis. The Anaheim Convention Center (ACC) is located across the street from Disneyland and shares parking and hotel rooms with the theme park.

To better understand the mix of events and their effect on parking needs, the *Shared Parking* study team evaluated the event calendars and other available data for the convention centers in Anaheim, Indianapolis, and Las Vegas. Table 4-12 summarizes the event data derived from the calendars of the three centers.

In terms of annual attendance per square foot of leasable space, the Indianapolis Convention Center is the most densely used facility, primarily because it books significantly more locally oriented small events at the same time as its exhibit halls are booked for conventions, trade shows, and consumer shows. Anaheim Convention Center, in turn, is more densely used than Las Vegas, which is generally only booked for relatively large conventions and trade shows.

Table 4-12 Use Statistics from Sample Convention Centers

	Anaheim	Indiana	Las Vegas
Calendar Year	2002	2001	2004
Exhibit Hall (sq. ft.)	841,750	395,000	1,984,755
Meeting Rooms (sq. ft.)	119,500	141,925	243,000
Total Gross Leasable Area (sq. ft.)	961,250	536,925	2,227,755
Events per Year	205	327	91
Event Days per Year*	672	915	261
Days with Bookings*	334	359	338
Days with Attendance	not available	not available	181
Annual Attendance	1,058,000	844,939	1,674,160
Annual Attendance/ksf[1]	1,101	1,574	744
Maximum Event	76,434	50,000	130,000
Average Event	5,161	2,584	18,397

Notes
*Includes setup and breakdown days.
[1] ksf = thousand sq. ft.

Sources: Anaheim Convention Center, Indiana Convention Center, and Las Vegas Convention Center.

Anaheim Convention Center

ACC is among those U.S. convention centers that has adequate parking for most days, and it monitors parked vehicles by event and day. The center has an arena that hosts family shows and sporting events, as well as seated convocations, and the floor also is used as exhibit space. For the purpose of this analysis, family shows and sporting events in the arena have been omitted as a factor in convention center demand, but the square footage of the area's "flat floor" is included in its exhibit area.

In 1993, a detailed study of parking demand was conducted for the facility. Figure 4-13 graphs the parked vehicles on selected peak-activity days over a four-year period, demonstrating the generation of vehicles by single and multiple events. Note, however, that this figure represents total vehicles parked, not peak-hour demand. Most days have significantly lower numbers of parkers, and the demand in any one hour is even lower. Estimates of parking needs on the peak days are presented in Figure 4-14 for purposes of comparison with the total attendance on those days.

The nominal attendance on the busiest days reached about 35 attendees per square foot of exhibit space but, due to turnover, far fewer were present at any one time and meeting space was not heavily used on those days. The ACC study was conducted because the center was going to be expanded. It lacked meeting space appropriate for conventions and also was unable to hold multiple events because of its inability to segment exhibit halls. Thus, it was by no means an underused facility.

Figure 4-13 Selected Peak Parking Days at Anaheim Convention Center, 1988–1992

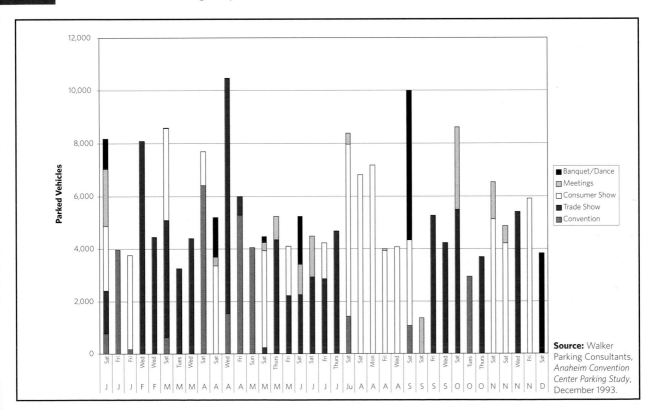

Source: Walker Parking Consultants, *Anaheim Convention Center Parking Study*, December 1993.

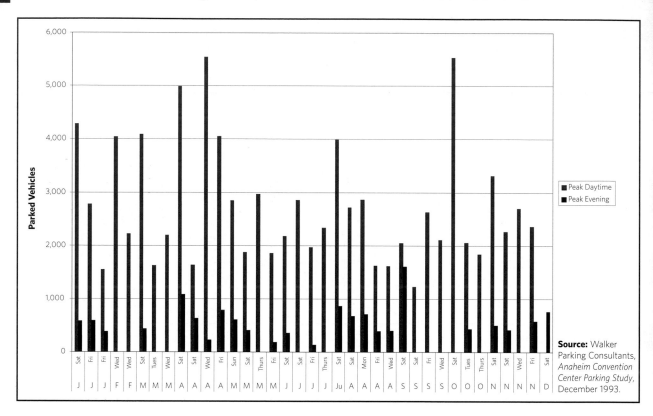

Source: Walker Parking Consultants, *Anaheim Convention Center Parking Study*, December 1993.

At the time of the study, the convention center had 3,130 parking spaces on site, and it had access to several thousand additional spaces for overflow. Figure 4-14 illustrates the parking needs on selected busy days throughout the year. In the peak month of August (which includes an annual home show with as many as 65,000 attendees over a 16-day run), demand exceeded on-site supply three or four days in each of the four years studied. The design day (approximating the 85th percentile day for the year) was then determined to be one that essentially fills the on-site parking. With 531,000 square feet of exhibit space and 78,000 square feet of meeting rooms, the parking need of 3,130 spaces is 5.1 spaces/ksf. This figure is significantly below the recommended ratio for convention space in the first edition of *Shared Parking*. Those factors (of 0.5 spaces per seat for conference rooms and 30

spaces per ksf of convention space) were intended for convention facilities in hotels, but they have since been applied to convention centers in mixed-use settings as well. Obviously, they significantly overstate the parking needs of larger convention centers that serve multiple, overlapping events.

The Anaheim Convention Center was subsequently expanded, and in 2002 it had 841,750 square feet of exhibition space and 119,500 square feet of meeting/ballroom space. Parking and attendance data by event were provided by ACC for 2002 but were not broken down by day. Only the booked days (including setup and breakdown days), rather than the days with event attendance, are reported in the calendar. Although an analysis similar to that conducted in 1993 was not possible, Figure 4-15 summarizes the seasonality of attendance and parked vehicles. In 2002, the

Figure 4-15   Seasonality of Attendance and Parked Vehicles, Anaheim Convention Center, 2002

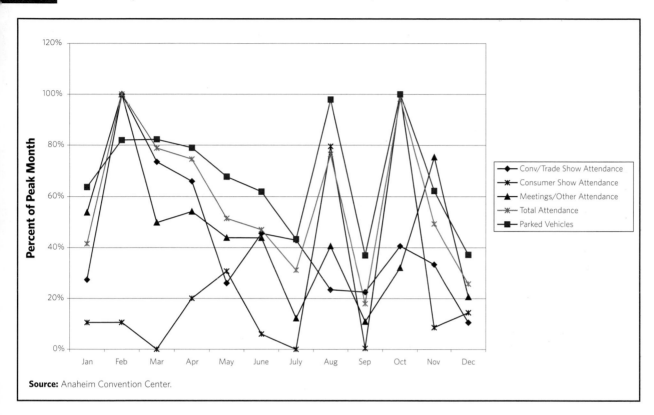

Source: Anaheim Convention Center.

month of October exceeded August (the peak month in the 1988–92 study) in total attendance and parked vehicles, largely because the expanded facility hosted a major auto show that month, with attendance exceeding 75,000 over a five-day run.

The data on attendance and parking by event for 2002 are presented in Table 4-13. Remember that "parked vehicles" is not the peak accumulation of vehicles and that the same vehicle may be parked several different times over the course of a multiday event. Also note that it is not always possible to accurately ascertain the vehicles parked for particular events.

Because the calendar reports booked days for each event rather than show days, it is impossible to determine the 85th percentile day for this facility. The study team reviewed larger

individual events to check the parking generation rates in 2002 against those in 1988–92. The largest convention, for the state dental association, was open to registrants for four days (according to its organizer's Web site). The estimated peak accumulation of vehicles on any one day, based on parking generation factors for the same group in the 1993 study, is about 3,000 vehicles. The estimated peak-hour parking accumulation ratio is thus about 3.1 spaces/ksf.

The largest trade show (so classified by ACC) had a six-day technical conference and a three-day trade show and thus is not representative of typical trade shows. The second largest trade show, which was also the 85th percentile show, had 25,680 persons over a three-day run, with 10,700 parked vehicles. There were no other events in the facility during its run. The estimated peak accumulation of vehicles

Table 4-13 Attendance by Event Type at Anaheim Convention Center, 2002

	Convention	Trade Show	Consumer Show	Banquets/ Dance	Meeting/ Other
Events	56	12	21	16	92
Booked Days	317	108	82	16	148
Maximum Attendance	38,000	32,000	76,434	10,269	16,878
Parked Vehicles	1,403	13,358	27,267	3,045	5,884
85th Percentile Event	8,235	25,680	21,142	7,744	2,772
Parked Vehicles	3,807	10,708	10,114	2,214	396
Average Event	6,106	12,887	12,101	3,455	1,605
Parked Vehicles	2,147	6,475	5,268	1,465	642

Source: Anaheim Convention Center.

for this show was about 3,500 vehicles, and the estimated peak-hour accumulation ratio is thus 3.6 spaces/ksf. The 5.5 spaces/ksf ratio from the 1993 study certainly encompasses that demand.

In 2002 the month of October exceeded August in total attendance and parked vehicles, largely because the expanded facility hosted a major auto show that month, with attendance exceeding 75,000 over a five-day run. The average attendance was thus about 15,300 persons/day. Several other smaller events were running at various times during this show. An estimated 5,000 vehicles were present at the peak hour, and thus the parking generation ratio on that day would have been about 5.2 spaces/ksf, quite similar to the design-day parking generation determined by the study of the 1988–92 data.

The peak attendance by event types other than trade shows at ACC has not increased in proportion to the increase in square feet of exhibit halls and meeting rooms. Rather, the additional meeting rooms have increased the number of smaller events, and there are significantly more overlapping events.

Based on the analysis of ACC's data from before and after the expansion, the study team determined that one ratio should be applied to the combined square footage of exhibit halls and meeting rooms for convention centers. Regarding evening parking demand, the size of banquets and dances at ACC in 1988–92 were similar to those in 2002, even though significantly more space was available in 2002. In other words, the parking needs in the evenings did not increase in proportion to the additional space. There is thus no meaningful way to estimate the demand on evenings relative to the square feet of available space in a large convention center. Conversely, ACC has less than ten large banquets and dances per year, which would not be considered frequent enough to qualify as "typical," much less as a design day for planning shared parking.

Indiana Convention Center

The Indiana Convention Center was selected for comparison with Anaheim because it does not have the resort reputation of Anaheim or Las Vegas, and it also lacks the mild winter weather of the other two. It is, however, a busy facility that generates both national and local events. Its competitive advantages over other facilities include the proximity of hotels, vibrant restaurants, and evening activity, as well as

Table 4-14 Attendance by Event Type at the Indiana Convention Center, 2001

	Conventions	Trade Shows	Consumer Shows	Banquets	Meetings/Other
Events	103	19	36	67	98
Total Attendance	350,111	113,973	287,198	50,288	43,369
Maximum Attendance	42,016	32,600	50,000	3,300	7,800
85th Percentile	3,300	12,304	13,391	1,500	800
Average Attendance	3,399	5,999	7,978	751	443

Source: Indiana Convention Center.

Circle Center (a downtown retail/dining/entertainment development), all within walking distance. The RCA Dome is also available for seated convocations. Data on attendance at the Indiana Convention Center for 2000 through 2002 were reviewed by the study team. The convention center has no dedicated parking supply, although it is connected to several municipal and commercial facilities via a skybridge system.

Table 4-14 shows the ICC attendance figures by event type for 2001. The center has 300,000 square feet of exhibit halls and uses the stadium's floor to add another 95,000 square feet for a total of 395,000 square feet of exhibit space. There are 74,323 square feet of ballrooms and 67,602 square feet of meeting rooms for a total of 141,925 square feet. It thus has about 15 percent more meeting and banquet space than ACC but less than half the exhibit space. It tends to host more events in each event type, but most are smaller. Although its largest convention and trade show events are equal to or larger than those at ACC, its average events are less than half as large. Its largest consumer show is about two-thirds the size of Anaheim's largest. There are about ten events a year that rent all of the available exhibit space.

The top five conventions at ICC all had over 20,000 attendees; the next five all had over 10,000. ACC, with more than twice the exhibit space but roughly half as many conventions, had four conventions attracting between 20,000 and 40,000 attendees but only two additional conventions with over 10,000 attendees.

ICC's 85th percentile convention is smaller than its average convention. This is because of its large number of small regional and local conventions, some of which are really multiday meetings with no trade-show component. A more realistic appraisal of the maximum use of ICC for a large convention would focus on two national conventions that each had about 15,000 attendees. There were only a few small unrelated banquets and meetings during each of these conventions. The nominal density of this size of convention would be 28 persons/ksf; factoring in the unrelated meetings, the overall density was less than 30 persons/ksf. With 70 percent registrant presence, a 25 percent auto modal split, and 1.2 persons per car, the parking generation rate of this size of event would be under 4 spaces/ksf. Therefore, the recommended visitor ratio of 5.5 spaces/ksf developed from analysis of the ACC parking data appears reasonable, if not conservative, for a design weekday at this facility.

The largest trade show at ICC, which occurs every year in early December, is oriented to the motor sports industry. A number of motor sports teams and suppliers are headquartered in Indianapolis, and therefore the show would be considered a national/local event. It lasts three days, and the average attendance per day is about 10,900 persons.

Reportedly, the show needs more exhibit space; the maximum trade show this facility can handle is about 20 nominal attendees per day per 1,000 square feet. With 50 percent of the registrants present at any one time, a 50 percent modal split to auto, and 1.2 persons per car, the maximum parking generation rate would be about 4.2 spaces/ksf. Because this is the largest trade show in this facility each year, it is not an 85th percentile event.

ICC is not dark in Late December; it regularly hosts a regional convention for the Fellowship of Christian Athletes between Christmas and New Year's Day. During same week, it also presents the largest consumer show of the year, the Indianapolis Auto Show, which typically runs seven days. Attendance at the auto show over the three-year data period ranged from 40,000 to 52,000 attendees. It is estimated that more than 10,000 persons attended the combination of activities on the peak Saturday. With 40 percent present at the peak hour, a 100 percent modal split to auto, and 2.0 persons per car, the parking generation of this event would be under 2,000 spaces, and the parking generation ratio would be under 4.0 visitor spaces/ksf.

ICC hosts large numbers of meetings and banquets, including a dozen high school proms in April and May each year. Up to 20 percent of the banquets and 10 percent of the meetings are associated with events in the adjacent domed stadium, such as pre-or postgame parties as well as hospitality suites for such events as marching band competitions. Some meetings and conventions are also related to RCA Dome events; for example, while the NCAA Final Four Basketball Tournament was staged at the dome, the college basketball coaches held their annual convention at ICC. The frequency of meetings and banquets results in relatively few days when there is not some event generating visitors at the convention center.

Las Vegas Convention Center

This facility was selected to represent a nearly "pure" calendar of national conventions and trade shows and thus to provide insight into the seasonality of those markets. According to the city's visitors and convention bureau Web site, Las Vegas offers 128,000 hotel rooms and over 9 million square feet of convention/meeting space. Because of the number of other facilities with exhibition, meeting, and banquet facilities, the Las Vegas Convention Center has a negligible number of meetings and banquets, as well as relatively few consumer shows. This facility focuses on hosting the largest of the large national conventions and trade shows. That is not to say that it does not host smaller conventions and trade shows, but its specialty is the megashow.

The Las Vegas Convention Center has almost 2 million square feet of exhibit hall space and nearly 250,000 square feet of meeting rooms. At the time of the *Shared Parking* study team's analysis, the 2004 calendar included 91 events on 181 days (not including setup and breakdown days). Therefore, for roughly half the days of the year, there was no active event at the convention center. Including setup and breakdown days, at least some portion of the facility was booked 338 days a year.

Two events in 2004 had 130,000 attendees, and five more ranged from 82,000 to 92,000 in attendance. The 85th percentile event had 32,000 attendees. There were three events of this size, two of which overlapped other large events (30,000 and 52,000 attendees). The 85th percentile day (including days with no events) in 2004 was expected to attract a total of 36,000 registrants. It must also be remembered that not all of this attendance is present at any one time. If the attendance at the peak hour is 50 percent of the nominal attendance, or 18,000, and 25 percent drive with 1.2 persons per car, the parking demand for this event would be less than 2.0 spaces/ksf. The convention center controls 5,500 parking spaces, or about 2.5 spaces/ksf. The total projected attendance for the 2004 calendar was about 1,675,000 persons, and the average attendance was about 18,400 persons per event. This facility thus serves about 60 percent more annual attendees than Anaheim and about twice as many as Indianapolis.

An unusual event at this facility is the NFR Cowboy Christmas Gift Show, a free consumer/trade show associated with the National Finals Rodeo (sometimes referred to as "the Superbowl of the rodeo circuit"). NFR is held in the arena on the campus of University of Nevada, Las Vegas, in early December. More than 140,000 persons attend the multiday rodeo every year, many of whom are either professional or amateur rodeo cowboys; most are expected to visit the gift show during its ten-day run. It is as much a trade show as a consumer show, although it is open to the general public. This event also skews the analysis of attendance by month, showing a higher percent of peak month in December than one would find in most other facilities.

A parking ratio of 5.5 spaces/ksf for attendees is recommended for both weekday and weekend conditions at convention centers. This ratio was derived from the Anaheim Convention Center parking data; however, data from the other two facilities indicate that this ratio is reasonable, if not conservatively high. The Indiana Convention Center has significantly more events, event days, and days with bookings, and its peak days are as busy if not busier than Anaheim's, but more of its events are significantly smaller. The Las Vegas Convention Center has a significantly lower parking demand due to its almost exclusive use by national conventions and trade shows. However, the seasonality of its use is valuable in

gure 4-16 Seasonality of Convention Center Attendance

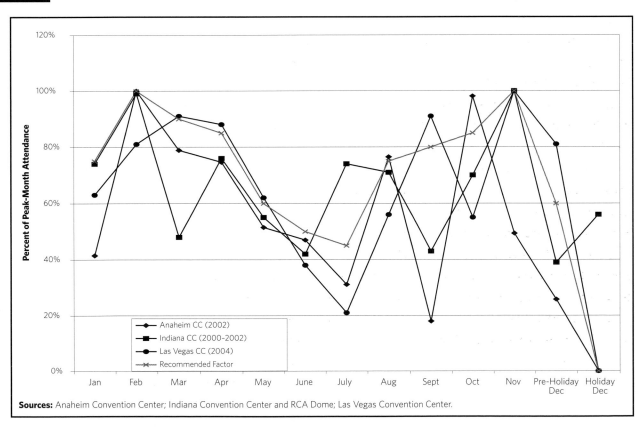

Sources: Anaheim Convention Center; Indiana Convention Center and RCA Dome; Las Vegas Convention Center.

understanding the general seasonality of conventions and trade shows.

Employees present at the peak hour on design days range from 1.5 percent to 5 percent;[15] 2.5 percent of the nominal attendance on the design day has been used for this book. With 1.2 persons per car and a small effective supply factor, the recommended ratio for employees is 0.5 spaces/ksf. The overall ratio for convention centers (both exhibition space and meeting rooms) is therefore 6.0 spaces/ksf.

Figure 4-16 presents the seasonality of attendance for all three facilities. One key conclusion is that the seasonality of convention center parking demand will vary and is especially driven by when annual consumer shows are scheduled. If an existing convention center is a key driver of activity in a shared parking analysis, its calendar should be evaluated for seasonality. In the absence of any reliable data, recommended monthly factors based on the seasonality of these three facilities are shown in the graph.

Hotels

Parking Generation has summarized observed parking generation on a per-guest-room basis for five different hotel types. One of the unfortunate limitations of the data, however, is that there are relatively small samples in some subcategories, as well as wide variations in the proportions of guest rooms, restaurants, and meeting/banquet and conference space within each type. As shown in Table 4-15, one of the significant differences noted in the data is that hotels in resort locations had peak parking needs during the daytime on weekdays rather than late at night. Some of the hotels in the full-service category apparently also had peak parking accumulations in the daytime. It is not known, however, whether the ITE data points for those sites were only collected in the daytime, and thus whether the peak hour for each site truly occurred in the daytime.

Land use 310 "hotel" as defined by *Parking Generation* is a full-service establishment with restaurants and cocktail

Table 4-15	Parked Vehicles per Hotel Guest Room				
	Hotel (310)	**Business (312)**		**Motels (320)**	**Resort (330)**
	Weekdays	**Weekdays**	**Saturdays**	**Weekdays**	**Weekdays**
Sites	14	3	3	5	3
Peak Hour	Varies	11 p.m.	Midnight	Varies	Daytime
Range	0.6-1.9	0.57-0.74	0.58-0.75	0.76-1.1	0.95-2.16
85th Percentile	1.14	0.71	0.72	1.02	1.86
Average	0.91	0.6	0.66	0.9	1.42

Source: ITE, *Parking Generation*, 3rd ed.

lounges as well as meeting/banquet/convention space. However, the quantities of the auxiliary spaces are not reported. Resort hotels typically have facilities similar to those of full-service hotels, but they are oriented to leisure travelers and have distinctly different time-of-day activity patterns. Given that the 85th percentile peak accumulation of parked vehicles for resort hotels was 1.9 spaces per occupied room in the daytime, it appears likely that factors other than occupied rooms are generating peak parking needs in the daytime. It is more likely that guests at resort hotels try to maximize their length of stay, checking out and storing luggage but remaining at the hotel to enjoy the facilities until after new guests arrive. This phenomenon also occurs for overnight guests generated by convention and meeting facilities. It is also possible that some attendees at convention hotels are local or decide to stay in lower-priced hotels that are distant enough to require driving. Thus, some daytime demand generated by large-scale convention facilities is not captive from hotel guest rooms.

Motels have traditionally been oriented to automobile travelers, have free parking, and offer little or no restaurant or meeting space. Business hotels as defined by ITE have limited restaurant and meeting facilities compared with full-service hotels. Examples include the Residence Inns, Marriott Courtyards, Fairfield Inns, and Hampton Inns. This classification reflects a significant change in hotel products since the publication of the first edition of *Shared Parking*. In the past, most hotels (except those clearly oriented to budget travelers) featured relatively large full-service restaurants and lounges. All of the business hotels defined by ITE have been designed to provide limited, if any, food service. Some hotels partner with "branded" casual dining restaurants to provide a venue that is attractive to both guests and locals. Others rely on casual restaurant choices nearby. Only upscale and resort hotels are likely to maintain the competitive position in terms of quality and pricing to attract local diners, and even then it

might primarily be for Sunday brunch, which is not generally a concern in shared parking planning.

In the ITE category of all-suites hotels, only two weekdays have been studied at two different hotels, along with one weekend day at one of the locations. One location was urban, the other suburban. Because of these differences, parking statistics were not reported in terms of range, average, or 85th percentile.

A detailed 1988 study of hotel parking needs published in *Urban Land* by one of the team members provides some assistance in determining parking needs and adjustment factors.[16] The 90th percentile values from detailed assessments (head counts in restaurants and meeting rooms, interviews and surveys of patrons and staff, and historical data on room occupancy, restaurant, and banquet sales) at four luxury hotels within the same chain were used to formulate those recommendations. The design days were selected as the 90th percentile days. All four of the hotels would be considered full-service hotels under the ITE codes.

Table 4-16 summarizes the various factors found in the 1988 study, with conversion to appropriate terminology/ methodology for this publication indicated in italics. Parking ratios similar to those in the first edition are recommended with some adjustments based on additional information gleaned from the above references. These factors, however, represent worst-case scenarios. As with other land uses, the recommended parking ratios assume a 100 percent modal split to private auto. The parking ratios must then be significantly reduced by mode adjustment and noncaptive factors to accurately reflect hotel parking needs in most mixed-use settings. For example, many hotels operate airport shuttles; taxis and public transportation also contribute to significantly reduced parking needs for registered guests at many locations. It is easier to make these adjustments if the base ratio assumes 100 percent auto use, even though it is rare that hotels considered in shared parking analysis actually experience 100 percent auto arrival by overnight guests.

	Office Park		**Airport**	
	Weekdays	**Weekends**	**Weekdays**	**Weekends**
Guest Rooms				
Percent Occupancy	100%	90%	100%	90%
Number of Guests per Occupied Room	1.2	1.7	1.2	1.3
Percent Drivers	55%	45%	45%	45%
Equivalent Mode Adjustment per Room	*66%*	*77%*	*54%*	*59%*
Employees				
Peak Number Present per Occupied Room	0.33	0.25	0.33	0.25
Percent Drivers	75%	70%	75%	70%
Equivalent Parking Accumulation, Spaces per Room	*0.25*	*0.18*	*0.25*	*0.18*
Restaurant Patrons				
Number per Guest Room	1.15	1.20	1.15	1.20
Percent Dining at Peak Hour	11.5%	9.0%	11.5%	9.0%
Diners per Guest Room at Peak Hour of Restaurant	*0.16*	*0.17*	*0.16*	*0.13*
Approximate Peak Diners per Sq. Ft. of Restaurant	*4.13*	*4.30*	*4.13*	*3.29*
Percent Nonguest (Noncaptive Ratio)	90%	30%	90%	70%
Percent Nonguest Drivers	70%	60%	80%	80%
If 100% Modal Split to Auto, Equivalent Persons per Car	*1.43*	*1.67*	*1.25*	*1.25*
Spaces/ksf[1] before Application of Noncaptive Ratio	*2.9*	*2.6*	*3.3*	*2.6*
Spaces/ksf after Application of Noncaptive Ratio	*2.6*	*0.8*	*3.0*	*1.8*
Equivalent Noncaptive Ratio for Ten Spaces/ksf	*26%*	*8%*	*30%*	*18%*
Meeting Attendees				
Number per ksf of Meeting Space	40	40	20	29
Percent Nonguest (Noncaptive Ratio)	60%	70%	90%	90%
Percent Nonguest Drivers	75%	75%	90%	40%
If 100% Modal Split to Auto, Equivalent Persons per Car	*1.3*	*1.3*	*1.1*	*2.5*
Spaces/ksf before Application of Noncaptive Ratio	*30.8*	*30.8*	*18.2*	*11.6*
Spaces/ksf after Application of Noncaptive Ratio	*18.5*	*21.6*	*20.2*	*12.9*

Table 4-16 Mode and Noncaptive Adjustments for Office Park and Airport Hotels

Notes
Default values are based on 90th percentile design values.
[1] ksf = thousand sq. ft.

Source: Barton-Aschman Associates, Inc.

The following discussion highlights issues for each component use that should be considered in evaluating parking demand at hotels.

Guest Rooms

While a business-oriented hotel typically has a higher parking ratio per guest room on weekdays than weekends, a resort hotel has just the opposite pattern. Monthly and time-of-day factors for resort hotels will be distinctly different than for business and airport hotels, as previously discussed. Therefore, separate ratios and monthly and time-of-day factors are provided in this edition of *Shared Parking* for leisure hotels and business hotels. The ratios assume that 100 percent of the parties that occupy guest rooms will arrive by car, or one space/guest room. Per the 1988 study, the parking ratio reflects 100 percent of rooms occupied on the design day for weekdays at business hotels and on weekends at leisure hotels, with 90 percent occupancy of rooms on weekends at business hotels and on weekdays at leisure hotels. The 1988 study's values for the percentage of drivers among hotel guests provide guidance for mode adjustment for at least the two subtypes of airport and office park hotels; however, they must be converted to mode adjustments that can be applied to the parking ratio, which is stated on a per room basis. Not surprisingly, the mode adjustment appropriate for an airport-based hotel is lower than that for a business park location. The weekend mode adjustment found in the 1988 study was lower than the weekday ratio for business hotels and the same as the weekend ratio for airport hotels.

Restaurants

The 1988 study tied parking ratios for restaurants/lounges to guest rooms rather than square feet of restaurant space (as in *Shared Parking*). The four hotels studied had a wide range of 0.47 to 0.98 seats per guest room, with an average of 0.74. The 90th percentile peak-hour occupancy of the restaurant/lounge (by guests and nonguests) was significantly lower: 0.13 to 0.17 diners per guest room. Thus, it would appear that these hotels had a significant overcapacity of restaurant space. Presenting the data as spaces per guest room minimized the impact of the excess restaurant/lounge seats or square feet at all four hotels. The hotels in this study had as much as 90 percent patronage by nonguests, but overall very low use per square foot.

Rather than creating more categories of hotels with an assumption of typical ratios of restaurant capacity per guest room, and providing separate time-of-day factors appropriate to each subtype based on assumptions related to its restaurant use, the study team has recommended a separate parking ratio for hotel restaurant/lounge areas. Ratios of 0.75 seats per guest room and 35 square feet per seat have been used to convert the 1988 study's recommended restaurant peak patrons per guest room to a peak presence of diners/ksf. (According to a special sort of the *Parking Generation* database, the ratio of building area per seat at restaurants appears to be about 33 square feet per seat for fine dining restaurants, with 35 square feet per seat at high turnover restaurants.) The square-feet-per-seat figures include the kitchen area; thus, it would be important to make sure that the square feet of restaurant/lounge space at a hotel used with the default factors recommended in this book include the kitchen space. The calculated parking ratio before application of the recommended noncaptive and mode adjustments ranges from 2.6 to 3.3 spaces/ksf.

It is difficult to justify recommending a ratio of under 4.0 parking spaces per square foot of restaurant/lounge space in hotels based on a single study, albeit highly detailed, of four hotels. Given the limited scope of that study, the parking ratio from the first edition of *Shared Parking* is still recommended for restaurants that are integral to the hotel (rather than being an attached branded restaurant). The ratio, ten spaces/ksf, is roughly half those for casual and fine dining restaurants. This ratio is intended to represent 85th percentile design-day conditions, with 100 percent arrivals by auto and no captive market adjustment already factored in. With this ratio, however, the noncaptive ratios observed in the 1988 study should be significantly reduced to the 10 to 30 percent range shown in Table 4-16.

Meeting/Banquet Rooms

Generally, hotels provide meeting rooms and conference centers in order to generate overnight guests. Once they have the facilities, however, they will fill the calendar with any event that generates revenue, including wedding receptions and other events that may not generate many overnight guests. Many business hotels (such as the Courtyard Marriotts) do not have any significant banquet space and offer only one or two meeting rooms. Without banquet capability and large conference support, these hotels rarely book events that generate significant parking demand in the evenings and on weekends.

Based on analysis of the detailed data in the ITE *Parking Generation* database, as well as the 1988 consultant study, there appears to be a breaking point in the amount of meeting/conference space provided at about 20 square feet per room. Below that amount, the meeting space is incidental to the hotel and does not create significant parking demand. When there is less than 20 square feet of meeting space per guest room, meeting space need not be considered in a shared parking analysis.

Evidence also suggests that above about 50 square feet per guest room, there could be significant usage of the space for conferences or banquets that would affect parking needs on weekdays and weekends. That type of space is hereafter called "conference/banquet." The meeting space in the hotels in the 1988 study fell into the conference/banquet category, albeit at the smaller end of the spectrum. The 90th percentile event was found to have a density of 40 persons per 1,000 square feet, with about 1.3 persons per car for nonguest attendees. Because the analysis used a higher design day, the resulting ratio of 30.8 spaces/ksf was rounded down to 30 spaces/ksf, the same figure recommended for conference space in the first edition of *Shared Parking*. It is recommended that a 60 percent noncaptive ratio be considered the starting point for this type of use on weekdays. Note that the design-day events on both weekends and weekdays at the airport hotels generated significantly lower parking ratios.

A number of convention hotels can accommodate all events associated with conventions of 1,000 persons or more. In such cases, there may be a significant local attendance, as well as some attendees who choose to stay in more economical hotels. The larger the facility, the less likely it is that its design day will reach the density observed in the 1988 studies. As noted previously, the recommended parking ratio of full-scale convention centers is 5.5 spaces/ksf (excluding employees), 20 percent of that recommended for smaller facilities. In the absence of any further available data, ratios of 20 spaces/ksf for daytime needs and ten spaces/ksf for weekend needs are recommended for facilities with over 50 square feet/room.

Employees

The recommended parking ratio for employees is 0.25 spaces per room on weekdays and 0.18 on weekends. These ratios reflect the assumption that hotel employees are somewhat more likely to take transit or to carpool than other employees. The mode adjustment factor of 75 percent on weekdays is equivalent to 1.33 persons per car with a 100 percent mode split, slightly higher than the persons per car for employee parking at most other land uses.

Monthly factors for guest rooms are based on the average hotel occupancy data presented in *Parking Generation*, which are based on seasonal variations of all hotels. Those factors should be modified for resort hotels, which have distinct tourist seasons. Suggested factors for hotels in climates that attract winter tourists are provided for resort hotels, but these may not be suitable for resorts in northern climes that only have summer seasons. Monthly factors for restaurants are the same as those for non–hotel-based restaurants, because the parking need is based on nonguest patronage. The monthly factors for hotel convention centers are the same as those for freestanding convention centers.

The time-of-day factors developed in the 1988 study have been used for each component, with an additional set of factors for guest rooms at resort hotels to reflect the greater presence of vehicles there during the daytime. The time-of-day figures in *Parking Generation* reflect overall parking occupancy. To check the reasonableness of these factors, projections of parking accumulation for the average size of each component in each ITE subtype are shown in Table 4-17. Meeting and convention space where reported by seats rather than square feet were converted using 40 seats/ksf.

Table 4-17 | Hotel Parking Needs Projections Using Recommended Default Values

	Office Park		Full-Service		Airport		Business		Resort	
	WD	WE	WD	WE	WD	WE	WD	WE	WD	WE
	Salzman	Salzman	ITE Avg.	ITE Avg.	Salzman	Salzman	Suburban	Suburban	Resort	Resort
Rooms	300	300	350	350	300	300	130	130	450	450
Guest Room Mode Adjustment	66%	77%	66%	77%	54%	59%	66%	77%	66%	77%
Restaurant ksf[1]	7,350	7,350	8,575	8,575	7,350	7,350	1,050	1,050	13,125	13,125
Percent Noncaptive	90%	30%	90%	30%	90%	30%	90%	30%	30%	30%
Mode Adjustment	70%	60%	70%	60%	70%	60%	70%	60%	60%	60%
Meeting Room ksf	7,000	7,000	—	—	7,000	7,000	1,310	1,310	—	—
Percent Noncaptive	60%	70%	60%	70%	60%	70%	60%	70%	60%	70%
Mode Adjustment	75%	75%	75%	75%	75%	75%	75%	75%	75%	75%
Convention ksf	—	—	20,400	20,400	—	—	—	—	31,175	31,175
Percent Noncaptive	25%	25%	25%	25%	25%	25%	25%	25%	25%	25%
Mode Adjustment	75%	75%	75%	75%	75%	75%	75%	75%	75%	75%
Estimated Peak-Hour Demand	304	252	322	289	264	210	105	97	470	393
Peak Hour	9 p.m.	9 p.m.	Noon	9 a.m.	5 p.m.	9 p.m.	8 a.m.	8 a.m.	Noon	8 a.m.
Overall Ratio: Spaces per Room	1.0	0.8	0.9	0.8	0.9	0.7	0.8	0.7	1.0	0.9
ITE 85th Percentile	1.1	0.9	1.1	—	—	—	0.7	0.7	1.86	—

Notes
[1] ksf = thousand sq. ft.
WD = Weekdays
WE = Weekends

Residential

One of the most significant development trends at the turn of the millennium is the development of residential uses in downtowns and other mixed-use settings. Creating live/work/play environments is one of the key goals of smart growth development, as is developing residential units near transit, in order to facilitate commuting without generating car trips and vehicles parked at transit stations.

Auto ownership per household increased over the period from 1960 to 2000 to an average of 1.75 vehicle per household. Some evidence indicates that the point of saturation may be near, since today there are more vehicles registered in the United States than there are licensed drivers. As discussed in *Parking Generation*, 2000 census data for Portland, Oregon, were evaluated by DKS Associates to determine patterns in the ratios of vehicles per household by location, as shown in Table 4-18.

Recognizing this trend, ITE's *Parking Generation* has separated residential uses into a number of different categories. An unfortunate side effect of the stratification is that the number of data points in any one category is relatively small, as illustrated in Table 4-19.

This book's recommended parking ratios for residents in suburban locations are 1.5 spaces/unit for rental units and 1.7 spaces/unit for owned units. It appears that an adjustment of about 80 percent to reflect auto ownership is appropriate for locations that are not downtown but well served by transit, reducing the former to 1.2 and the latter to 1.4. Adjustments as low as 50 percent appear to be appropriate for urban CBD locations, reducing the ratios to 0.75 spaces/rental unit and 0.85 spaces/owned unit. Although not technically mode adjustments, these values may be input into the mode adjustment cells in the *Shared Parking* model.

It should be recognized in shared parking analysis that at least some of the residential demand will likely be for reserved parking, with all time-of-day and seasonal factors at 100 percent. For default purposes, it is recommended that at least the first parked vehicle per unit be allocated as reserved. The remaining peak-hour values would be considered as resident parking that can be shared with other uses. For visitor parking, 0.15 spaces per unit have been added to each ratio.

The time-of-day factors are based on the factors found in the ITE database for low-rise apartments. Although some seasonality of residential parking needs is likely, no published source of data is available. Therefore, no adjustments for seasonality are recommended.

Table 4-18 Vehicles per Household, Portland, Oregon

Location	Owner-Occupied	Rental
Suburban	2	1.4
Central City, Not Downtown	1.8	1.2
CBD	1.6	0.7
Near Light-Rail Stations	—	—
More Than Ten Miles from CBD	1.9-2.0	1.0-1.3
Less Than Ten Miles from CBD	1.6-1.8	0.8-1.2

Source: DKS Associates, Portland, Oregon.

Peak-Hour Parking Accumulations at Residential Land Uses (Spaces/Dwelling Unit)

Location	Single-Family Detached (210)	Rental Townhouse (224)	Condominiums	Low-Rise Apartment (221)		High-Rise Apartment (222)
	Suburban	Suburban	Suburban	Suburban	Urban	Urban
Sites	6	3	5	19	12	7
Range	1.3-2.2	1.67-1.82	1.04-1.96	0.68-1.94	0.66-1.43	1.15-1.52
85th Percentile	2.14	1.78	1.68	1.46	1.17	1.52
Average Ratio	1.83	1.73	1.46	1.20	1.00	1.37

Source: ITE, *Parking Generation*, 3rd ed.

Vehicle Ownership at AvalonBay Projects

Parking is a challenging issue for AvalonBay, a developer of urban apartments in high-barrier-to-entry markets. One of the attractions of their locations—in cities such as San Francisco, New York, and Washington, D.C.—is that they are generally well served by public transit. However, while their tenants like being near transit, they also like their cars. A survey of renters at 41 properties found few locations where the average number of vehicles per unit was less than one, and several approached two. When the vehicle ownership was calculated by size of bedroom, the 85th percentile ratio averaged about one parking space per bedroom, which is a standard rule of thumb for residential parking.

The ratios by size of unit were: efficiency apartment, 1.0; one-bedroom apartment, 1.3; two-bedroom apartment, 1.0; and three-bedroom apartment, 0.75.

To create comparable data for different projects with varying mixes of unit size, a synthetic average parking ratio was calculated. This adjusted parking ratio used the average vehicle ownership reported for each unit size at a project and then combined to reflect the same mix of efficiencies and one-, two-, and three-bedroom units as for all developments in the AvalonBay portfolio. A comparison of these adjusted parking ratios for each development found only 14 properties with an average auto ownership of less than one per unit, and only two projects with 0.5 or less—both in major cities. These were urban projects, for which the 85th percentile adjusted ratio was 0.92 vehicles owned, and there was a narrow range. Twelve of the 14 projects had adjusted parking ratios of from 0.71 to 0.94 vehicles per unit. These ratios, which reflect auto ownership only and do not include additional visitor parking, suggest that such urban projects could get by with about one space per unit on average, and a little less in some extreme cases.

The more suburban projects reported adjusted parking ratios from 0.95 to about two per unit. The 85th percentile of these had an average of 1.5 vehicles per unit, which matches the ratio of 1.5, based on Institute of Transportation Engineers data, selected in this book for rental residential uses, at least as far as the residents' own parking needs are concerned. AvalonBay reports that visitor parking at its projects is a scarce commodity, since simply providing sufficient space for residents is a challenge. Decisions about visitor parking need to be part of the management strategy for each developer, and eventually each individual project.

The experiences for this developer must be interpreted within the context of its own management philosophy and market. Its renters are higher-income households willing to pay higher rents for urban locations and able to afford more cars. On the other hand, because parking is also more expensive in such locations, they may forego multiple vehicles or even prefer to get by without a car because of the available alternatives. Determining parking requirements for higher-density residential projects, owned or rented, requires close attention to consumer preferences and market realities.

Lyn Lansdale, vice president for strategic business services at AvalonBay Communities, points out the conflicts for an apartment developer. Many parking programs are designed with the expectation of generating additional income for the owner/developer. However, the ability to charge for parking is site-specific and may depend upon the practices of local competition, customer expectations in the submarket, parking constraints, parking alternatives for renters unwilling to pay, and other considerations. The least desirable situation for both owners and renters is empty parking spaces in a space-constrained property because of residents' unwillingness to pay the parking fees. This type of circumstance exacerbates an already difficult parking situation for the owners and incurs resentment from their customers.

Table 4-20 Office Parking Generation (Spaces per ksf[1] GFA)

| | Suburban | | Urban | Medical/Dental | Credit-Card Processing |
	Weekday	Saturday	Weekday	Weekday	Weekday
Sites	173	14	12	51	2
Range	0.86–5.58	0.2–1.0	1.46–3.43	1.5–5.3	5.5–5.6
85th Percentile	3.44	—	2.97	4	—
Average Ratio	2.84	0.5	2.4	3.1	5.6

Note
[1] ksf = thousand sq. ft.

Source: ITE, *Parking Generation*, 3rd ed.

Office

ITE has separated office uses into a number of categories as follows:

- 710: General Office Building
- 714: Corporate Headquarters
- 715: Single-Tenant Office Building
- 720: Medical/Dental Office Building
- 750: Office Park
- 760: Research and Development Center

Analysis of data in the nongovernmental categories for general office uses (excluding medical/dental offices and credit-card processing centers) indicates no statistically significant differences in parking accumulation. Therefore, categories 710, 714, 715, 750, and 760 have all been reported in a single group, coded as "701: Office Building." The sole data point in the credit-card processing category indicated significantly higher demand (5.57 spaces/ksf GFA). A separate code of 720 and tabulation of data are maintained for medical/dental offices. In addition, three governmental office uses are included in the 730 series: Governmental Offices, U.S. Post Office, and Courthouse/Jails/Corrections. A limited number of data points are available for these governmental uses, with significant variation in the demand. It is therefore recommended that a site-specific study of the parking needs of a governmental building be conducted before including it in a shared parking analysis.

The data for general office uses in *Parking Generation* indicate a statistically significant difference in the peak accumulation of parked vehicles observed for suburban office uses from those in urban areas (see Table 4-20). By breaking out the latter uses from those in suburban settings, the 85th percentile of peak accumulations observed for suburban offices is higher than the data found in the second edition of *Parking Generation*, while the 85th percentile of the urban sites is lower. The *Parking Generation* text further notes that several studies conducted in downtown areas with paid parking and high-quality transit options found parking ratios of between 1.0 and 2.0 spaces/ksf GFA.

In the ITE database, the parking ratio declines as the size of the building increases, as demonstrated by the fact that the fitted curve diverges from the average rate as GFA increases. The fitted curve is equivalent to average ratios, however. Therefore, a special sort of the ITE database was conducted. Flat ratios below 25,000 square feet and above 500,000 square feet appear to be appropriate. The slope of the fitted curve is steeper below 100,000 square feet than over that figure. Thus, a four-segment ratio is recommended: 3.8 spaces/ksf below 25,000 square feet, scaling down to 3.4 spaces/ksf at 100,000 square feet, and scaling to 2.8 spaces/ksf at 500,000 square feet.

Trends in Office Employment Density

Employers	Workers per ksf[1]		
	1985	**1995**	**2003**
Government	3.9	4.0	3.8
Private Downtown	3.9	3.5	3.7
Private Suburban	3.7	3.4	3.6

Note
[1] ksf = thousand sq. ft.

Source: Building Owners and Managers Association International, *BOMA Experience Exchange Reports* (New York: BOMA International, 1996 and 2004).

---

able 4-22 Land Use 701: Office Building

Time of Parking Demand Study	Average Weekday Peak Period Parking Demand Ratio (Parked Vehicles per ksf[1] GFA)	Parking Demand Studies within Time Period	
		Number of Study Sites	**Percentage of Entire Data Set**
1970–1976	2.8	7	4
1978–1979	3.2	14	8
1981	2.8	18	10
1982	2.8	27	15
1983	2.7	21	11
1984	2.6	32	17
1985–1986	2.9	20	11
1987–1990	3.0	16	9
1991	2.7	17	9
1994–1996	2.8	7	4
Total	2.8	179	100

Note
[1] ksf = thousand sq. ft.

Source: ITE, *Parking Generation*, 3rd ed.

Parking Generation reports that one study conducted by King County Metro in Seattle, Washington, found that 6.5 percent of the peak parking accumulation at general office buildings is for visitor parking. This statistic is consistent with a general rule of thumb reported by the study team that visitor parking accounts for 5 to 7 percent of office parking on a per space basis. The recommended ratios are actually between 7 and 8 percent visitor parking because of rounding effects.

It appears that a mode adjustment of about 0.85 is appropriate for urban parking situations with higher-density development and some transit availability, while a mode adjustment of 0.3 to 0.6 is appropriate for downtown office space in areas with paid parking and high-quality transit service.

The ITE information included only two studies of weekend parking needs, with widely varying results. A Saturday study found 10 percent of the weekday demand, while a Sunday study found 90 percent of the weekday demand. The latter point appears to reflect a unique use. This book's recommended ratio for Saturday demand is 10 percent of the weekday ratio, which thus varies from 0.38 spaces/ksf for smaller buildings to 0.28 spaces/ksf for large office complexes, somewhat lower than the 0.5 ratio suggested in the first edition of Shared Parking.

In recent years, some developers have argued that parking demand is increasing and that parking supply ratios should be higher than recommended above. Others have argued that a ratio of 3.0 spaces/ksf is excessive given that the average occupancy in a relatively large database is below 3.0 spaces/ksf. One means of understanding the ratios as well as trends over time is to review the density of employees per square foot. The Building Owners and Managers Association International (BOMA) conducts nationwide benchmarking surveys every year. The averages for specific types of space in 1985, 1995, and 2003 are shown in Table 4-21. While employment density in privately owned buildings in 2003 was 5 to 6 percent greater than it was in 1995, it remains less than it was in 1985. The overall occupancy (that is, the percent of leased space) of privately developed office space in 2003 was the lowest in five years.

The average ratios in the ITE database have varied slightly year to year, but there is no consistent trend overall, as illustrated in the summary of average parking ratios in Table 4-22.

In sum, no statistical data indicate that office worker density in general is increasing significantly. Conversely, it is recognized that offices that involve significant data processing or telemarketing will generate higher worker densities, as much as six or seven employees per ksf, and in turn higher parking ratios. For that reason, a separate category has been developed for data processing.

In some cases, leasing agreements require reserved parking for some tenants. The provisions vary, from senior management parking in a dedicated area to large numbers of spaces being reserved around-the-clock for tenant employees. Another factor to be considered in a shared parking analysis is the specific type of reserved space. If the space is reserved 24 hours a day, the time-of-day and monthly factors should be counted as 100 percent for all conditions. If spaces are to be reserved for more limited periods, the factors should be adjusted accordingly. Another variation in reserved-space approaches is by space or by area. A space reserved for one individual merits a 100 percent factor. If a group of employees is allowed access to the area but may park in any spot, the number of spaces within the area may reflect some presence factor between free access by all parkers (often considered to be 85 percent) and 100 percent for individually reserved spaces.

Seasonal variation of office parking is not very significant. Parking Generation does not provide any data on seasonality of demand. The previously mentioned Patton Harris Rust & Associates shared parking study for the Peterson Companies included an evaluation of traffic and parking needs at two office complexes in Virginia during Late December.[17] It found an average reduction in daily link volumes of 42 percent for the period in 2000 as compared with two weeks later in January 2001. Hourly occupancy studies were also conducted. It was concluded that there is at least a 20 percent reduction in parking needs in Late December. This book also recommends reductions of 5 percent for July and August.

The ITE database includes one survey of demand at a credit-card processing center, with an observed accumulation of 5.6 vehicles/ksf. This result is consistent with the study team's experience with office uses that have higher densities of employees per square foot. These tend to be "back-of-house" operations for processing large amounts of information, call centers, telemarketing, and so on. In some cases, they may also operate with multiple shifts. A ratio of 6.0 spaces/ksf is suggested as a starting point for such data processing office operations. The same time-of-day and seasonal adjustments for offices may be applied, except when it is known that the processing center will operate with multiple shifts.

Most medical and dental offices require a higher level of utilities, particularly water, and they often interact closely with outpatient operations such as laboratory services and radiology. Therefore, medical and dental offices often are concentrated in specially designed buildings. These tenancies require more visitor parking than a general office building. The ITE database on medical/dental offices is relatively small (18 sites), but it indicates an 85th percentile accumulation of 4.3 spaces/ksf. The recommended *Shared Parking* ratios are 3.0 patient spaces and 1.5 employee spaces/ksf. The operation of medical offices on Saturdays is highly variable according to the practices of the tenants; family practices, pediatricians, immediate care centers, dentists, and others oriented to routine care of adults and children are more likely to operate on Saturdays than specialty practices.

Another use that requires more visitor parking than general office tenancies is a bank. The drive-in bank category in *Parking Generation* found an 85th percentile ratio of 4.6 vehicles/ksf among 12 data points in suburban locations. There were 49 sites for banks with drive-ins in urban locations, with an observed ratio of 4.1 vehicles/ksf. Owing to the small sample and questions about the results, the walk-in bank category has been ignored in this book. Where headquarters banks are provided, a general office ratio would appear to be more appropriate.

The study team also reviewed a study comparing 40 days of parking in Seattle banks in 1990. It found an average ratio of 2.47 and an 85th percentile ratio of 3.66 spaces/ksf GFA. The recommended ratios for branch banks with drive-ins are 4.6 spaces/ksf. It appears that a mode adjustment of about 85 percent would be appropriate for urban branch locations. Suburban banks are far more likely to be open on Saturday mornings than central city banks; suburban banks can be quite busy on Saturday mornings, and thus the recommended ratio is the same as for weekdays.

Notes

1. *Parking Generation*, 7th ed. (Washington, D.C.: Institute of Transportation Engineers, 2004); ULI–the Urban Land Institute and the International Council of Shopping Centers, *Parking Requirements for Shopping Centers*, 2nd ed. (Washington, D.C.: ULI–the Urban Land Institute, 1999).

2. Gerald Salzman, "Hotel Parking: How Much Is Enough?" *Urban Land*, January 1988, pp. 14–17.

3. U.S. Census Bureau, "Unadjusted and Adjusted Estimates of Monthly Retail and Food Services Sales by Kinds of Business" for years 1999, 2000, 2001, and 2002. Available at www.census.gov/mrts/www/data/html/nsal02.html.

4. Walker Parking Consultants, restaurant parking data collected nationally, 2001–2003.

5. Robin Londner, "Wannado Moves DC-9 to Sawgrass," *South Florida Business Journal*, www.bizjournals.com/southflorida/stories/2003/07/28/story6.html?GP= OTC-MJ1752087487 (July 28, 2003).

6. "Meadowlands Xanadu Unveils First Wave of Major Tenants, Consumer Brands, and Entertainment Experiences," press release, www.meadowlandsmills.com (October 5, 2004).

7. Raymond Braun, "Exploring the Urban Entertainment Center Universe," *Urban Land Supplement*, August 1995, pp. 11–12.

8. Lesley Hensel, "Finding New Uses for Old Theatres," *Realty Times*, April 4, 2001.

9. Various statistical reports, www.natoonline.org/statisticsadmissions.htm (January 2005).

10. "Q & A—John Fithian: A Conversation with the President of NATO," *Digital Cinema Report*, www.digitalcinemareport.com/qajohnfithian.html (February 2003).

11. Patton Harris Rust & Associates, *Fairfax Corner Shared Parking Study*, including addendum 2, February 2001.

12. Wilbur Smith Associates, unpublished study of movie theater parking patterns, Pigeon Forge, Tennessee, June 2001.

13. Broadway statistics posted at www.livebroadway.com/bwygrosses (Fall 2004).

14. David C. Petersen, *Developing Sports, Convention, and Performing Arts Centers*, 3rd ed. (Washington D.C.: ULI–the Urban Land Institute, 2001), p. 31.

15. Mary Smith, "Parking," in *Transportation Planning Handbook*, 2nd ed., ed. John D. Edwards, Jr. (Washington D.C.: Institute of Transportation Engineers, 1999), p. 513.

16. Salzman, "Hotel Parking."

17. Patton Harris Rust & Associates, *Fairfax Corner Shared Parking Study*.

Chapter 5

Analysis of Mixed Uses and Shared Parking Case Studies

A series of case studies was conducted in July and August 2003 to check the reasonableness of the *Shared Parking* retail, cineplex, and restaurant parking ratios and factors, since these have been significantly changed for this edition. The days of the occupancy counts were randomly selected. Note that no reserved parking has been considered unless otherwise noted in the case study. These sites comprise the first seven case studies in this chapter.

The remaining case studies (including two at different stages of development at the same site) were derived from analyses previously conducted by the study team, during which occupancy counts were collected for various mixed-use projects. In many of these cases, the land uses were originally tabulated using the categories in the first edition of *Shared Parking*; it was not possible to retabulate the uses existing at the time of field occupancy studies according to the more refined breakdown recommended in this edition. However, it is useful to compare observed occupancies to the parking required using the modified time-of-day and monthly factors now recommended in this book.

Some case studies included occupancy counts over multiple days; overall, there were 32 comparisons of projections by the shared parking model with occupancy counts for that time of day and season. Figure 5-1 summarizes the land uses included in the case studies, showing the proportion of GLA in each category. Case study 5.10 also had a hotel, but no information was available to convert it to GLA.

5.1   Puente Hills Mall

This super regional mall with nearly 1.2 million square feet is located in City of Industry, California, a Los Angeles suburb. One of the largest centers in Los Angeles County, it is anchored by Sears and Robinsons-May. It includes just over 1 million square feet of retail space, a 4,100-seat cineplex, and over 50,000 square feet of restaurants/food service. Car counts were taken on a Saturday in mid-July 2003.

Figure 5-1 Land Uses Represented by Case Studies

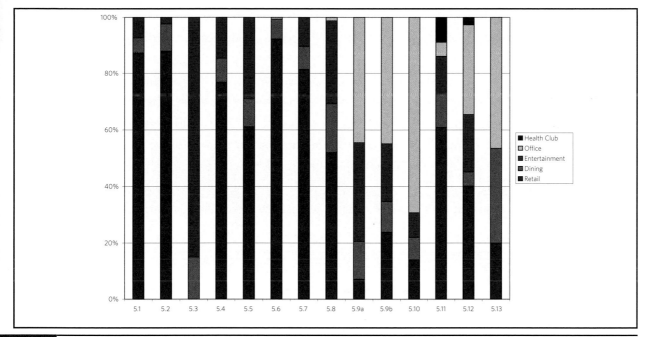

Table 5-1 Unadjusted Parking Requirements for Each Land Use, Case Study 5.1

| Land Use | Quantity | WEEKDAYS | | | WEEKENDS | | |
		Base Ratio	Units	Unadjusted Parking Spaces	Base Ratio	Units	Unadjusted Parking Spaces
Super Regional Shopping Center (>600,000 sq. ft.)	1,029,432	3.20	/ksf[1] GLA	3,326	3.60	/ksf GLA	3,742
Employee		0.80		832	0.90		935
Fine/Casual Dining	20,905	15.75	/ksf GLA	319	17.50	/ksf GLA	355
Employee		2.25		57	2.50		63
Family Restaurant	26,676	9.00	/ksf GLA	240	12.75	/ksf GLA	340
Employee		1.50		40	2.25		60
Fast Food	16,570	13.25	/ksf GLA	211	13.25	/ksf GLA	190
Employee		1.75		37	1.75		33
Cineplex	4,100	0.19	/seat	779	0.26	/seat	1,066
Employee		0.01		41	0.01		41
Subtotal: Customer/Guest Spaces				4,875			5,702
Subtotal: Employee/Resident Spaces				1,007			1,132
Subtotal: Reserved Spaces				—			—
Total Parking Spaces				5,882			6,834

Note
[1]/ksf = per 1,000 sq. ft.

At this center, the parking needs of the retail uses dwarf those of the dining uses and cineplex. Thus, parking needs will peak at 2 p.m. on a weekend in December. The study team also projected the parking need in July for comparison with the observed car counts.

Selecting noncaptive ratios for each use is an iterative and intuitive process that begins with quick estimations of the potential for captive patronage. Parking spaces required for each use can be used without adjusting for persons per car in this process. For weekend afternoon conditions at this project, the unadjusted parking demand for retail visitors is 3,742 parkers. With a need for about 1,132 employee spaces,

there is thus a pool of about 3,742 + 1,132 = 4,875 potential spaces that might be shared through captive patronage. If the dining and entertainment demand totals 1,671 spaces in the evening, and afternoon demand is roughly half of the evening, then there is an unadjusted demand of perhaps 900 parked vehicles in the afternoon. It seems reasonable to assume that the casual dining, family restaurants, and cinema categories each have 10 percent captive patronage, thus reducing parking requirements in the peak hour by roughly 90 spaces. If desired, one could test those assumptions more carefully for each land use by using the actual time-of-day adjustments. For fine/casual dining restaurants, the after-

Table 5-2 Estimated Weekend Shared Parking Requirements, Case Study 5.1

Land Use	Unadjusted Demand	Month Adjustment December	Peak-Hour Adjustment 2 p.m.	Noncaptive Adjustment Daytime	Mode Adjustment Daytime	December 2 p.m.	July 2 p.m.	July 8 p.m.
Super Regional Shopping Center	3,742	100%	100%	100%	100%	3,742	2,403	1,562
Employee	935	100%	100%	100%	100%	935	748	561
Fine/Casual Dining	355	100%	45%	90%	100%	144	141	348
Employee	63	100%	75%	100%	100%	47	47	63
Family Restaurant	340	100%	65%	90%	100%	199	195	217
Employee	60	100%	100%	100%	100%	60	60	57
Fast Food	199	100%	90%	50%	100%	89	90	50
Employee	33	100%	95%	100%	100%	31	31	20
Cineplex	1,066	67%	55%	90%	100%	354	485	981
Employee	41	80%	60%	100%	100%	20	25	41
Subtotal: Customer/Guest Spaces	5,702					4,528	3,314	3,158
Subtotal: Employee/Resident Spaces	1,132					1,093	911	742
Subtotal: Reserved Spaces	—					—	—	—
Total Parking Spaces	6,834					5,621	4,225	3,900
Reduction in Parking Required[1]	18%				vs. Observed		3,821	3,574
					Estimated/Observed		1.11	1.09

Note

[1] The reduction in parking spaces required due to shared parking analysis is presented as a percentage of the sum of the unadjusted demand for each land use. To the right, the projected need for spaces is compared with the observed accumulation from the car counts, and a ratio of estimated to observed spaces is calculated, to gauge the reasonableness of the shared parking analysis. This format is also employed for all subsequent tables summarizing the shared parking analyses in this chapter.

noon demand would be reduced by 355 x .45 x 10% = 16 spaces. Family restaurants have faster service and are even more attractive to mall employees, but their 2 p.m. demand is about 65 percent of peak noontime demand. Therefore, a 90 percent noncaptive adjustment (10 percent reduction) would reduce the family restaurant parking spaces at 2 p.m. by about 340 x .65 x 10% = 22 vehicles. For the cineplex, a 90 percent noncaptive adjustment would result in 1,066 x .55 x 10% = 59 less vehicles parked for the cineplex, presumably a result of children going to the movies while parents shop. The total reduction for the three uses is actually 97 spaces, as compared with the rough estimate of 90 spaces. Similarly, the fast-food uses (which include ice cream and other stores that attract customers between meals and thus are relatively busy at 2 p.m.) are reduced by a 50 percent noncaptive factor, or about 100 vehicles less than would otherwise be parked.

On weekdays, there are fewer family visits in which parties arriving in one vehicle split up and visit multiple venues than on weekends, even in the summer. Thus, the 10 percent assumption is halved to 5 percent (95 percent noncaptive), except that the same 50 percent reduction is used for fast-food uses. In the evening, no noncaptive adjustments are assumed for the cinema and restaurants except for the fast-food uses, which are assumed to be 50 percent noncaptive. No mode adjustment was made for this center.

At the peak hour of 2 p.m. in December, 5,621 parking spaces would be recommended for this center, a reduction of 18 percent as compared with the sum of 6,834 spaces calculated without shared parking. The observed peak-hour accumulation on a Saturday afternoon in July was 3,821 spaces. The projected demand of 4,178 spaces for an afternoon in July exceeds this observed accumulation by about 11 percent. The estimated parking need for a Saturday evening in July at 8 p.m. is 3,880 spaces, as compared with the observed accumulation of 3,574 spaces, a differential of about 9 percent. If one were doing a shared parking analysis for an existing cen-

ter and had the occupancy counts in hand, one might first try to change the 90 percent noncaptive ratios to 80 percent on weekends, and the 95 percent noncaptive ratios on weekdays to 90 percent. However, that would only reduce the overall daytime demand on weekends by another 97 spaces, or 3 percent. When, as in this case, one use predominates (retail accounts for two-thirds of the unadjusted customer demand on a weekday, and more than 80 percent of the customer demand after the noncaptive ratios are applied), tinkering with noncaptive ratios does not make a significant change in the bottom-line estimate of required parking spaces.

Although with this mix of uses it is obvious that weekend demand will exceed weekday demand, a weekday analysis is presented in Table 5-3. Note that on weekdays in July, the cineplex and restaurants swing the peak hour to the evening.

About 12 percent of this center is occupied by nonretail uses. According to the guidelines of ULI's *Parking Requirements for Shopping Centers*, the parking ratio of 4.5 spaces/ksf (per thousand square feet) for a super regional center should be increased by 0.03 spaces/ksf for each percentage of nonretail space over 10 percent. (The guidelines recommend shared parking methodology for those centers with over 20 percent of GLA in nonretail uses.) Thus, a single ratio of 4.56 spaces/ksf could be applied to the total square footage of all uses: 1,179,927 square feet. The estimated peak-hour spaces using this methodology would be 5,380 spaces. The unitary shared parking ratio—the total spaces estimated by shared parking analysis divided by the total GLA (with the cinema converted to its square footage)—would be about 4.72 spaces/ksf. The shared parking analysis using this book's recommended factors results in a number of spaces about 4.5 percent higher than that using all square footage at a single rate, per *Parking Requirements for Shopping Centers*. Either methodology justifies less parking than is now provided at the center, which is 6,347 spaces, a ratio of 5.4 spaces/ksf.

Land Use	Unadjusted Demand	Month Adjustment December	Peak-Hour Adjustment 1 p.m.	Noncaptive Adjustment Daytime	Mode Adjustment Daytime	December 1 p.m.	July 1 p.m.	July 7 p.m.
Super Regional Shopping Center	3326	100%	100%	100%	100%	3,326	2,136	2,029
Employee	832	100%	100%	100%	100%	832	666	632
Fine/Casual Dining	319	100%	75%	95%	100%	227	223	297
Employee	57	100%	90%	100%	100%	51	51	57
Family Restaurant	240	100%	90%	95%	100%	205	201	188
Employee	40	100%	100%	100%	100%	40	40	38
Fast Food	211	100%	100%	50%	100%	105	106	84
Employee	37	100%	100%	100%	100%	37	37	33
Cineplex	779	23%	45%	95%	100%	77	183	343
Employee	41	50%	60%	100%	100%	12	18	31
Subtotal: Customer/Guest Spaces	4,875					3,940	2,849	2,941
Subtotal: Employee/Resident Spaces	1,007					972	812	791
Total Parking Spaces	5,882					4,912	3,661	3,732
Reduction	16%							

5.2 Fashion Island

This project is an upscale super regional shopping center with almost 1.2 million square feet of GLA in affluent Newport Beach, California. It overlooks the Pacific Ocean and hosts many community events throughout the year. It first opened in 1967 and later underwent a five-year renovation that was completed in 1989. Another enhancement project featuring a carousel was completed in 2003. Anchor tenants include Bloomingdale's, Macy's, and Neiman Marcus. The center also includes a 1,634-seat cineplex and various restaurant tenants. Compared with Puente Hills, which also has about 1.2 million square feet, Fashion Island has about the same retail GLA, a significantly smaller cineplex, but more space in the restaurant categories.

As with Puente Hills, the peak parking need for this center is clearly driven by the retail uses; thus, parking peaks in

December. For this analysis, the noncaptive ratios used for Puente Hills were modified by increasing the noncaptive ratio for Fashion Island's considerably larger quantity of fine/casual dining restaurants from 90 to 95 percent. The noncaptive ratios for cinema and family restaurants were not modified from those assumed for Puente Hills.

The peak hour was again 2 p.m. in December. July was also modeled for comparison with the occupancy counts.

Compared with Puente Hills, this center has the same retail GLA, more fine/casual dining, and less cinema and family restaurant uses. While the afternoon in December remains the overall peak, the analysis projects that the demand will peak at 6 p.m. on a weekend when retail demand is still relatively high and the restaurants are getting busy. However, the occupancy counts found a clear peak in the afternoon. The model in fact underestimated afternoon

Table 5-4 Unadjusted Parking Requirements for Each Land Use, Case Study 5.2

Land Use	Quantity	WEEKDAYS			WEEKENDS		
		Base Ratio	Units	Unadjusted Parking Spaces	Base Ratio	Units	Unadjusted Parking Spaces
Super Regional Shopping Center	1,032,160	3.20	/ksf[1] GLA	3,303	3.60	/ksf GLA	3,716
Employee		0.80		826	0.90		929
Fine/Casual Dining	70,009	15.75	/ksf GLA	1,101	17.50	/ksf GLA	1,327
Employee		2.25		215	2.50		234
Family Restaurant	4,700	9.00	/ksf GLA	42	12.75	/ksf GLA	60
Employee		1.50		7	2.25		11
Fast Food	32,060	13.25	/ksf GLA	409	13.25	/ksf GLA	385
Employee		1.75		72	1.75		64
Cineplex	1,634	0.19	/seat	310	0.26	/seat	425
Employee		0.01		16	0.01		16
Subtotal: Customer/Guest Spaces				5,255			5,913
Subtotal: Employee/Resident Spaces				1,136			1,254
Total Parking Spaces				6,391			7,167

Note
[1]/ksf = per 1,000 sq. ft.

Table 5-5 Estimated Weekend Shared Parking Requirements, Case Study 5.2

Land Use	Unadjusted Demand	Month Adjustment December	Peak-Hour Adjustment 2 p.m.	Noncaptive Adjustment Daytime	Mode Adjustment Daytime	December 2 p.m.	July 2 p.m.	July 6 p.m.
Super Regional Shopping Center	3,716	100%	100%	100%	100%	3,716	2,387	1,909
Employee	929	100%	100%	100%	100%	929	743	632
Fine/Casual Dining	1,327	100%	45%	95%	100%	567	556	1,171
Employee	234	100%	75%	100%	100%	176	176	234
Family Restaurant	60	100%	65%	90%	100%	35	34	41
Employee	11	100%	100%	100%	100%	11	11	10
Fast Food	385	100%	90%	50%	100%	173	173	164
Employee	64	100%	95%	100%	100%	61	61	58
Cineplex	425	67%	55%	90%	100%	141	194	235
Employee	16	80%	60%	100%	100%	8	10	16
Subtotal: Customer/Guest Spaces	5,913					4,632	3,344	3,520
Subtotal: Employee/Resident Spaces	1,254					1,185	1,001	950
Subtotal: Reserved Spaces	—					—	—	—
Total Parking Spaces	7,167					5,817	4,345	4,470
Reduction	19%				vs. Observed		4,524	4,218
					Estimated/Observed		0.96	1.06

demand by 4 percent and overestimated evening demand by 6 percent, compared with the occupancy counts.

A reduction of about 19 percent in the estimated number of spaces is required using the recommended shared parking methodology, compared with the sum of the unadjusted spaces of each use. The nonretail uses comprise about 12 percent of the total 1,174,489 square feet (the cineplex occupies 27,500 square feet); therefore, the recommended parking ratio according to *Parking Requirements for Shopping Centers* would be 4.56 spaces/ksf or 5,356 spaces, almost 8 percent less than projected by using shared parking methodology. The unitary ratio resulting from the shared parking analysis is 4.96 spaces/ksf; the parking supply at Fashion Island is 5,803 spaces, or about 4.94 spaces/ksf. Given that the shared parking model itself appeared to underestimate the afternoon demand by far less that the ratio per *Parking Requirements for Shopping Centers*, it would appear that it is more reliable to use the shared parking model than the formula in *Parking Requirements* for this type of center.

5.3 Veterans Plaza

This project, located in Tampa, Florida, in a suburban area with little or no public transit, contains a 24-screen cineplex and several restaurants. It also includes an ice cream store and Starbucks, which are considered fast-food uses. Overall, Veterans Plaza has about 121,500 square feet of GLA. It was selected for this analysis because it has no traditional retail uses such as fashion. Parking counts were taken in July 2003 on a Saturday evening.

Clearly, the peak parking for this center is driven by the cineplexes. The parking model indicates that parking requirements would peak in Late December on a Saturday evening. Because visits to the sit-down restaurants and cineplex would be sequential, a noncaptive adjustment was applied only to the fast-food uses. July projections are also shown for comparison with parking observations.

The observed peak accumulation of vehicles was 1,433; the projected parking spaces exceeded the observed accumulation by 12 percent. A 15- to 30-minute wait was noted

| **Table 5-6** | Unadjusted Parking Requirements for Each Land Use, Case Study 5.3 |

Land Use	Quantity	WEEKDAYS Base Ratio	Units	Unadjusted Parking Spaces	WEEKENDS Base Ratio	Units	Unadjusted Parking Spaces
Fine/Casual Dining	23,210	15.25	/ksf[1] GLA	354	17.00	/ksf GLA	395
Employee		2.75		64	3.00		70
Fast Food	3,949	12.75	/ksf GLA	50	12.00	/ksf GLA	47
Employee		2.25		9	2.00		8
Cineplex	4,564	0.19	/seat	867	0.26	/seat	1,187
Employee		0.01		46	0.01		46
Subtotal: Customer/Guest Spaces				1,271			1,629
Subtotal: Employee/Resident Spaces				119			124
Total Parking Spaces				1,390			1,753

Note
[1] /ksf = per 1,000 sq. ft.

Table 5-7 Estimated Weekend Shared Parking Requirements, Case Study 5.3

Land Use	Unadjusted Demand	Month Adjustment Late December	Peak-Hour Adjustment 8 p.m.	Noncaptive Adjustment Evening	Mode Adjustment Evening	Late December 8 p.m.	July 8 p.m.
Fine/Casual Dining	395	95%	100%	100%	100%	375	387
Employee	70	100%	100%	100%	100%	70	70
Fast Food	47	95%	50%	50%	100%	11	12
Employee	8	100%	60%	100%	100%	5	5
Cineplex	1,187	100%	100%	100%	100%	1,187	1,092
Employee	46	100%	100%	100%	100%	46	46
Subtotal: Customer/Guest Spaces	1,629					1,573	1,491
Subtotal: Employee/Resident Spaces	124					121	121
Total Parking Spaces	1,753					1,694	1,612
Reduction	3%				vs. Observed		1,433
					Estimated/Observed		1.12

for seating at the restaurants at 8 p.m.; therefore, the monthly adjustment for July might have been increased to 100 percent. Even without this adjustment, however, the model projection exceeds the observed accumulation and thus would be considered conservative. Although there is only a 4 percent reduction in the estimated parking need due to shared parking, the methodology remains a reasonable means of determining the appropriate parking supply for this type of project.

The projected peak parking ratio for this project is approximately 13.9 spaces/ksf (with the cineplex converted to square feet); 2,004 spaces, equaling about 16.5 spaces/ksf, are provided at the center. The parking needed for this center is thus at least three times that calculated using the ratio of 4.0 spaces/ksf for a shopping center with less than 400,000 square feet. Obviously, *Parking Requirements for Shopping Centers* does not recommend such a practice with this combination of uses, but many zoning ordinances call shopping centers commercial space and apply a single ratio for shopping, restaurants, cinema, and office. This concern is further discussed in chapter 6's recommendations for zoning ordinances.

5.4 Long Beach Towne Center

This outdoor shopping center qualifies as a power center by virtue of its tenancies and its super regional size. It was developed in 1998 on the site of a former naval hospital at the intersection of the 605 Freeway and Carson Street in Long Beach, California. It has a discount orientation, and its anchors are two "big boxes" (Sam's Club and Lowe's Home Improvement) and a 5,000-seat cineplex, which combined occupy more than 45 percent of the GLA. It also has a car wash, a gas station, three fast-food units with drive-throughs on outlots, and an entertainment arcade of over 11,000 square feet. Although the center totals over 832,000 square feet of GLA, only about 372,000 square feet of typical shopping uses remain after the big boxes, restaurants, and cinema uses are deducted. The tenants in the shopping category are more typically found in community/power centers. This center has 4,428 spaces, for a ratio of 5.32 spaces/ksf (using the cineplex's GLA in square feet). Also located on part of the property is an Auto Nation used-car dealership, but that use's parking operates independently from the remainder of the site and therefore was not included in the shared parking analysis.

The nonretail uses occupy about 23 percent of the total square footage; therefore, *Parking Requirements for Shopping Centers* would recommend use of the shared parking methodology rather than an adjusted unitary ratio. The parking required for Sam's Club was projected using *Parking Generation*'s discount superstore category; the weekday ratio is 4.1 spaces/ksf, and the weekend ratio is 5.5 spaces/ksf. Similarly, the garden/building supply information in *Parking Generation* was used for the Lowe's store. The 85th percentile

Table 5-8 Unadjusted Parking Requirements for Each Land Use, Case Study 5.4

Land Use	Quantity	WEEKDAYS Base Ratio	Units	Unadjusted Parking Spaces	WEEKENDS Base Ratio	Units	Unadjusted Parking Spaces
Community Shopping Center	372,570	2.90	/ksf[1] GLA	1,080	3.20	/ksf GLA	1,192
Employee		0.70		261	0.80		298
Discount Superstore	128,000	3.25	/ksf GLA	416	4.40	/ksf GLA	563
Employee		0.85		109	1.10		141
Convenience Retail	3,800	4.90	/ksf GLA	19	4.00	/ksf GLA	15
Employee		1.20		5	1.00		4
Home Improvement Store	135,197	2.10	/ksf GLA	284	3.60	/ksf GLA	487
Employee		0.50		68	0.90		122
Fine/Casual Dining	31,281	15.25	/ksf GLA	477	17.00	/ksf GLA	532
Employee		2.75		86	3.00		94
Family Restaurant	16,253	9.00	/ksf GLA	146	12.75	/ksf GLA	207
Employee		1.50		24	2.25		37
Fast Food	23,744	12.75	/ksf GLA	303	12.00	/ksf GLA	285
Employee		2.25		53	2.00		47
Active Entertainment	11,616	4.20	/ksf GLA	49	6.50	/ksf GLA	76
Employee		0.40		5	0.50		6
Cineplex	5,000	0.19	/seat	950	0.26	/seat	1,300
Employee		0.01		50	0.01		50
Subtotal: Customer/Guest Spaces				3,724			4,657
Subtotal: Employee/Resident Spaces				661			799
Total Parking Spaces				4,385			5,456

Note
[1] /ksf = per 1,000 sq. ft.

parking generation rates are 2.6 spaces/ksf on weekdays and 4.5 spaces/ksf on weekends. The monthly adjustment for Lowe's was based on the U.S. Census Bureau's data for garden and home improvement stores, and the time-of-day adjustments were based on those for retail stores. The gas station includes a convenience store, and therefore its square footage was so classified. The parking required for the car wash was not included in the analysis, as it might add only ten spaces at peak hours, which is less than 0.1 percent of the total need for parking.

There is about 40 percent less retail space at Long Beach Towne Center than at Fashion Island or Puente Hills, with about the same restaurant GLA and cinema seats as at Puente Hills but considerably fewer restaurant and more cinema seats than at Fashion Island. Therefore, the weekend daytime noncaptive ratios are 95 percent for the fine/casual dining and cinema and 90 percent for the family restaurants. No captive market adjustments were employed for those three uses in the evening. The fast-food uses were assumed to be 50 percent noncaptive for both daytime and

Table 5-9 Estimated Weekend Shared Parking Requirements, Case Study 5.4

Land Use	Unadjusted Demand	Month Adjustment Late December	Peak-Hour Adjustment 2 p.m.	Noncaptive Adjustment Daytime	Mode Adjustment Daytime	Late December 2 p.m.	July 2 p.m.	July 7 p.m.
Community Shopping Center	1,192	80%	100%	100%	100%	954	766	574
Employee	298	90%	100%	100%	100%	268	238	191
Discount Superstore	563	80%	100%	100%	100%	450	362	271
Employee	141	90%	100%	100%	100%	127	113	90
Convenience Retail	15	95%	65%	100%	100%	9	9	14
Employee	4	100%	100%	100%	100%	4	4	4
Home Improvement Store	487	70%	95%	100%	100%	324	411	216
Employee	122	90%	100%	100%	100%	110	122	92
Fine/Casual Dining	532	95%	45%	95%	100%	216	223	495
Employee	94	100%	75%	100%	100%	71	71	94
Family Restaurant	207	95%	65%	95%	100%	121	125	142
Employee	37	100%	100%	100%	100%	37	37	35
Fast Food	285	95%	90%	50%	100%	122	128	114
Employee	47	100%	95%	100%	100%	45	45	42
Active Entertainment	76	100%	100%	90%	100%	68	63	56
Employee	6	100%	100%	100%	100%	6	6	5
Cineplex	1,300	100%	75%	95%	100%	926	625	957
Employee	50	100%	60%	100%	100%	30	30	50
Subtotal: Customer/Guest Spaces	4,657					3,190	2,712	2,839
Subtotal: Employee/Resident Spaces	799					698	666	603
Total Parking Spaces	5,456					3,888	3,378	3,442
Reduction	29%				vs. Observed		2,736	2,095
					Estimated/Observed		1.23	1.64

evening. The active entertainment was assumed to be 90 percent noncaptive in the daytime and 95 percent noncaptive in the evening.

Preliminary analysis indicates that 2 p.m. on a Saturday in Late December is the overall peak time period, but the December 2 p.m. projection is only 35 spaces less than Late December's. In the summer, with the cinema busy and lower retail activity, the projected peak hour shifts to the evening. This shift toward entertainment peaks reflects similar amounts of dining uses and a slightly larger cinema than Puente Hills, but only about two-thirds as much retail space.

The observed peak accumulation of vehicles in July 2003 was 2,736 spaces at 2 p.m.; the projected peak parking need thus exceeded the observed accumulation by about 10 percent. The July 2003 occupancy study found 2,095 spaces occupied

at 8 p.m.; the projected peak parking need significantly exceeded the observed accumulation by about 60 percent.

A second analysis was then undertaken to calculate parking demand for the retail components with the single ratio that is recommended by *Parking Requirements for Shopping Centers*. (This was an intermediate step, and so a table showing the analysis is not provided here.) All the retail was thereby placed in the super regional category at 4.5 spaces/ksf. This adjustment increased the peak demand projection to 4,044 spaces on a Saturday afternoon in December, with 3,092 spaces estimated for an afternoon in July. The afternoon demand in December using the single ratio of 4.5 spaces/ksf is higher than the projection using the shared parking methodology above but less than the projection for July (due to differences in monthly factors for retail

Table 5-10 Revised Estimated Weekend Shared Parking Requirements, Case Study 5.4

Land Use	Unadjusted Demand	Month Adjustment December	Peak-Hour Adjustment 2 p.m.	Noncaptive Adjustment Daytime	Mode Adjustment Daytime	December 2 p.m.	July 2 p.m.	July 8 p.m.
Community Shopping Center	2,047	100%	100%	100%	100%	2,047	1,315	855
Employee	512	100%	100%	100%	100%	512	410	307
Fine/Casual Dining	532	100%	45%	90%	100%	215	211	521
Employee	94	100%	75%	100%	100%	71	71	94
Family Restaurant	207	100%	65%	85%	100%	114	112	132
Employee	37	100%	100%	100%	100%	37	37	35
Fast Food	285	100%	90%	50%	100%	128	128	71
Employee	47	100%	95%	100%	100%	45	45	28
Active Entertainment	76	67%	100%	90%	100%	46	63	60
Employee	6	80%	100%	100%	100%	5	6	5
Cineplex	1,300	67%	55%	90%	100%	431	592	1,196
Employee	50	80%	60%	100%	100%	24	30	50
Subtotal: Customer/Guest Spaces	4,447					2,981	2,421	2,835
Subtotal: Employee/Resident Spaces	746					694	599	519
Total Parking Spaces	5,193					3,675	3,020	3,354
Reduction	29%				vs. Observed		2,736	2,095
					Estimated/Observed		1.10	1.60

and the other uses). A third check used the community shopping center ratio, despite the size of the Long Beach center. This adjustment changed the peak month to December, while reducing the projected peak demand in December to 3,675, the afternoon demand in July to 3,020, and the evening demand in July to 3,354 spaces. This revised shared parking analysis for the site is summarized in Table 5-10.

In sum, using the basic ratio for all retail rather than individualized ratios for the big boxes did not materially change the estimated evening parking requirement (23 percent over that observed in both cases), but it significantly lowered the overestimate of demand in the daytime, from 64 percent in Table 5-9 to 44 percent in Table 5-10.

Not only does this case study demonstrate that it is better to use one ratio for retail, rather than separating out big box uses, but the community shopping center (<400,000 square feet) parking ratio appears to be more appropriate for this particular power center, even though Long Beach Towne Center has over 600,000 square feet of retail space. It is certainly true that this type of center does not experience as much browsing from store to store, and the length of stay is considerably shorter than in a traditional super regional shopping center with fashion retail. However, a subsequent case study suggests that the appropriate ratio for the size of the center should generally be used for power centers.

The Long Beach center's cineplex occupies 110,000 square feet. The unitary parking ratio of this project using shared parking analysis is approximately 4.86 spaces/ksf. Shared parking in fact reduces the parking requirement calculation by 29 percent compared with the sum of the uses, but it still overestimates the July parking needs by 44 percent in the daytime and by 23 percent in the evening.

5.5   Covina Town Square

This power center provides about 400,000 square feet of GLA in a community nestled at the base of the San Gabriel Mountains, 20 miles east of Los Angeles. Its major tenants include a 30-screen cinema (which at one point was the largest in Los Angeles County), Home Depot, Michael's, PetSmart, and Staples. It is similar to but considerably smaller than Long Beach Towne Center. About 36 percent of this center is allocated to nonretail uses, making shared parking analysis the appropriate approach to calculating parking needs. The center has 2,209 parking spaces, providing a ratio of 6.0 spaces/ksf (using the cineplex's GLA).

Instead of separating out the big-box retailers, which appeared to overstate the parking need at Long Beach, the community retail category was employed for all the retail uses in this case study. With considerably less retail but a cinema similar to Long Beach's, the recommended number of parking spaces was calculated for 8 p.m. for July, December, and Late December. Owing to the dominance of the entertainment uses, a noncaptive ratio of 90 percent was used for the retail uses in the evening.

The peak demand was projected to occur at 8 p.m. in Late December at 2,131 spaces. Although not shown in Table 5-12, December demand at 8 p.m. was considerably lower at 1,900 spaces; the 2 p.m. requirement in December was 1,751 spaces. Thus, evening parking need is higher than in the daytime even in that month. In this center, though, July demand is greater than in December and only 5 percent less than in Late December.

The observed occupancy at 8 p.m. in July 2003 was 1,920 spaces, 6 percent less than projected by the shared parking methodology. According to the city of Covina's economic development Web site, the cinema in this center ranked 28th in the nation in attendance in 1999, and its amenities are unparalleled in the eastern San Gabriel valley. Even with this highly successful cinema, the shared parking model, using a single ratio for all retail uses, projects a reasonable result.

Table 5-11 Unadjusted Parking Requirements for Each Land Use, Case Study 5.5

Land Use	Quantity	WEEKDAYS			WEEKENDS		
		Base Ratio	Units	Unadjusted Parking Spaces	Base Ratio	Units	Unadjusted Parking Spaces
Community Shopping Center	232,753	2.90	/ksf[1] GLA	675	3.20	/ksf GLA	745
Employee		0.70		163	0.80		186
Fine/Casual Dining	10,000	15.25	/ksf GLA	153	17.00	/ksf GLA	170
Employee		2.75		28	3.00		30
Family Restaurant	17,302	9.00	/ksf GLA	156	12.75	/ksf GLA	221
Employee		1.50		26	2.25		39
Fast Food	10,527	12.75	/ksf GLA	134	12.00	/ksf GLA	126
Employee		2.25		24	2.00		21
Cineplex	4,922	0.19	/seat	935	0.26	/seat	1,280
Employee		0.01		49	0.01		49
Subtotal: Customer/Guest Spaces				2,053			2,542
Subtotal: Employee/Resident Spaces				290			325
Total Parking Spaces				2,343			2,867

Note
[1]/ksf = per 1,000 sq. ft.

Table 5-12 Estimated Weekend Shared Parking Requirements, Case Study 5.5

Land Use	Unadjusted Demand	Month Adjustment Late December	Peak-Hour Adjustment 8 p.m.	Noncaptive Adjustment Evening	Mode Adjustment Evening	Late December 8 p.m.	July 8 p.m.	July 2 p.m.
Community Shopping Center	745	80%	50%	90%	100%	268	280	478
Employee	186	90%	75%	100%	100%	126	112	149
Fine/Casual Dining	170	95%	100%	100%	100%	162	167	69
Employee	30	100%	100%	100%	100%	30	30	23
Family Restaurant	221	95%	65%	100%	100%	136	141	120
Employee	39	100%	95%	100%	100%	37	37	39
Fast Food	126	95%	50%	50%	100%	30	32	57
Employee	21	100%	60%	100%	100%	13	13	20
Cineplex	1,280	100%	100%	100%	100%	1,280	1,178	583
Employee	49	100%	100%	100%	100%	49	49	29
Subtotal: Customer/Guest Spaces	2,542					1,876	1,798	1,307
Subtotal: Employee/Resident Spaces	325					255	241	260
Total Parking Spaces	2,867					2,131	2,039	1,567
Reduction	26%				vs. Observed		1,920	
					Estimated/Observed		1.06	

5.6   Burbank Empire

This project is yet another newer power center in the Los Angeles metropolitan area, located in Burbank at the intersection of Empire Avenue and the Golden State Freeway. At the time of the data collection, it had about 600,000 square feet of GLA, anchored by a 150,000-square-foot Target and a 135,000-square-foot Lowe's. There were three fast-food restaurants with drive-throughs, an Olive Garden, and an Outback Steakhouse. There was also a 4,000-square-foot lending agency office in a storefront, but it is not a full-service bank. Since the completion of the field survey, a Costco Wholesale Club has been added, and the GLA has been increased to about 900,000 square feet. No cineplex is located at this site. The estimated need for spaces using shared parking analysis is shown in Table 5-13.

With a predominance of retail uses, an afternoon in December is expected to generate the peak parking need. A noncaptive adjustment was not applied to the retail uses in the evening, but 95 percent factors were applied to the restaurants in the daytime on weekends, and the same 50 percent noncaptive factor was employed for fast-food uses as in the other case studies. The observed occupancy in the afternoon in July was 1,968 spaces, about 4 percent less than the projected parking demand of 2,052 spaces in July.

The unitary ratio of this center is approximately 4.71 spaces/ksf. At the time of the field study, 92 percent of this center's GLA was allocated to retail uses. *Parking Requirements for Shopping Centers* recommends simply using the super regional center parking ratio of 4.5 spaces/ksf against the center's total square footage. This would result in a peak-hour

Table 5-13 Unadjusted Parking Requirements for Each Land Use, Case Study 5.6

Land Use	Quantity	WEEKDAYS			WEEKENDS		
		Base Ratio	Units	Unadjusted Parking Spaces	Base Ratio	Units	Unadjusted Parking Spaces
Regional Shopping Center	566,059	3.15	/ksf[1] GLA	1,783	3.53	/ksf GLA	1,999
Employee		0.78		443	0.88		500
Fine/Casual Dining	23,426	15.25	/ksf GLA	357	17.00	/ksf GLA	398
Employee		2.75		64	3.00		70
Fast Food	20,226	12.75	/ksf GLA	258	12.00	/ksf GLA	243
Employee		2.25		46	2.00		40
Office	4,000	0.30	/ksf GFA	1	0.03	/ksf GFA	—
Employee		3.50		14	0.35		1
Subtotal: Customer/Guest Spaces				2,399			2,640
Subtotal: Employee/Resident Spaces				567			611
Total Parking Spaces				2,966			3,251

Note
[1] /ksf = per 1,000 sq. ft.

Land Use	Unadjusted Demand	Month Adjustment December	Peak-Hour Adjustment 2 p.m.	Noncaptive Adjustment Daytime	Mode Adjustment Daytime	December 2 p.m.	July 2 p.m.
Regional Shopping Center	1,999	100%	100%	100%	100%	1,999	1,284
Employee	500	100%	100%	100%	100%	500	400
Fine/Casual Dining	398	100%	45%	95%	100%	170	167
Employee	70	100%	75%	100%	100%	53	53
Fast Food	243	100%	90%	50%	100%	109	109
Employee	40	100%	95%	100%	100%	38	38
Office	—	100%	60%	100%	100%	—	—
Employee	1	100%	60%	100%	100%	1	1
Subtotal: Customer/Guest Spaces	2,640					2,278	1,560
Subtotal: Employee/Resident Spaces	611					592	492
Total Parking Spaces	3,251					2,870	2,052
Reduction	12%				vs. Observed		1,968
					Estimated/Observed		1.04

need for 3,190 spaces for the design day/hour of shopping centers, a Saturday afternoon in December. Shared parking methodology would reduce the required spaces by about 12 percent as compared with the super regional ratio but would still appear to produce a reasonable parking supply.

In the Long Beach Towne Center case study, it was determined that a power center might be better modeled with community shopping center ratios, even though the GLA would otherwise suggest using regional shopping center ratios. A check was performed of the recommended parking spaces using the community shopping center ratio of 4.0, instead of one scaled closer to 4.5 because of the GLA in retail uses. This projection resulted in a peak need of 2,628 spaces at 2 p.m. in December as compared with 2,870 spaces using the higher retail ratio, and 1,887 spaces at 2 p.m. in July. In this case, therefore, the community shopping center ratio would underestimate demand in July by about 100 spaces, or about 5 percent. Although this is not a very significant deviation, it is therefore recommended that

power centers employ the appropriate ratios for the retail GLA as recommended in *Parking Requirements for Shopping Centers*.

Burbank Empire has about 2,800 spaces, a ratio of about 4.64 spaces/ksf. Separating out its storefront office space was not necessary, given that it is only a small component of the overall parking need. In this case, the office use represents less than 1 percent of the total GLA.

5.7   Westfield Promenade

This regional shopping center, located in Woodland Hills, California, serves the western end of the San Fernando Valley market. In 2000, the owners commenced a $35 million redevelopment to transform the center from a well-located but weak high-end specialty center into an entertainment/retail center by redesigning the lower level and adding new destination tenants and restaurants. The second level was also redesigned and remerchandized to complement the new lower-level tenants and the existing, highly successful AMC Theatre.

Upon completion in fall 2001, the new retail venues included a Barnes & Noble superstore, Chick's Sporting Goods, Maggiano's Little Italy, and the Corner Bakery. The GLA in August 2003, when the occupancy studies were conducted, was approximately 546,200 square feet. With the cinema occupying 56,675 square feet, nonretail uses occupy about 19 percent of the GLA. For that level of dining/entertainment uses, *Parking Requirements for Shopping Centers* recommends using a single adjusted ratio instead of shared parking methodology. The adjusted ratio would therefore be 4.36 (scaled between 4 and 4.5 according to the GLA), plus .03 x 9 percent excess dining/entertainment, or a ratio of 4.63 spaces/ksf. The parking requirement would then be 2,529 spaces.

The combination of the fine/casual dining restaurants with the cineplex's parking requirements roughly equals the retail parking need at this center, which makes it more difficult to guess whether retail or entertainment uses control demand. To start the process, the same noncaptive adjustments used for Long Beach Towne Center were employed. The test run indicated that the peak hour for parking will be 7 p.m. in December. Even though the GLA is less entertainment- and dining-oriented than at Long Beach (19 versus 23 percent), the peak parking need swings to the evening in December, rather than in the daytime as at Long Beach. This pattern is due to higher monthly factors for restaurants than cinema in December. Proportionately, there is about the same concentration of restaurants in the GLA at Westfield Promenade, but there is less cinema than at Long Beach. For these reasons, the study team decided to assume a 95 percent noncaptive adjustment of retail parking needs in the evening.

Table 5-15 Unadjusted Parking Requirements for Each Land Use, Case Study 5.7

| Land Use | Quantity | WEEKDAYS | | | WEEKENDS | | |
		Base Ratio	Units	Unadjusted Parking Spaces	Base Ratio	Units	Unadjusted Parking Spaces
Regional Shopping Center	444,566	2.97	/ksf[1] GLA	1,319	3.29	/ksf GLA	1,462
Employee		0.72		321	0.82		366
Fine/Casual Dining	43,724	15.25	/ksf GLA	667	17.00	/ksf GLA	743
Employee		2.75		120	3.00		131
Fast Food	1,225	12.75	/ksf GLA	16	12.00	/ksf GLA	15
Employee		2.25		3	2.00		2
Cineplex	2,841	0.19	/seat	540	0.26	/seat	739
Employee		0.01		28	0.01		28
Subtotal: Customer/Guest Spaces				2,542			2,959
Subtotal: Employee/Resident Spaces				472			527
Total Parking Spaces				3,014			3,486

Note

[1] /ksf = per 1,000 sq. ft.

Table 5-16 Estimated Weekend Shared Parking Requirements, Case Study 5.7

Land Use	Unadjusted Demand	Month Adjustment December	Peak-Hour Adjustment 7 p.m.	Noncaptive Adjustment Evening	Mode Adjustment Evening	December 7 p.m.	August 8 p.m.	August 2 p.m.
Regional Shopping Center	1,462	100%	75%	95%	100%	1,042	623	1,009
Employee	366	100%	80%	100%	100%	293	220	293
Fine/Casual Dining	743	100%	95%	100%	100%	706	737	315
Employee	131	100%	100%	100%	100%	131	131	98
Fast Food	15	100%	80%	50%	100%	6	4	7
Employee	2	100%	90%	100%	100%	2	1	2
Cineplex	739	67%	80%	100%	100%	396	554	290
Employee	28	80%	100%	100%	100%	22	25	15
Subtotal: Customer/Guest Spaces	2,959					2,150	1,918	1,621
Subtotal: Employee/Resident Spaces	527					448	377	408
Subtotal: Reserved Spaces	—					—	—	—
Total Parking Spaces	3,486					2,598	2,295	2,029
Reduction	25%				vs. Observed		2,217	
					Estimated/Observed		1.04	

The observed parking occupancy at 8 p.m. in August 2003 was 2,217 spaces. The shared parking estimate exceeds the observed demand by 4 percent. Shared parking analysis would recommend 2,598 spaces for the peak hour in December, about 3 percent more than the calculation using the formula in *Parking Requirements per Shopping Centers*. Shared parking analysis thus would provide for a little better margin of error for a center that is still in the process of transformation.

5.8 Ahwatukee Foothills Towne Center

This shared parking study was conducted in 1997, between phases of development.[1] At the time of data collection, this community center consisted of over 300,000 square feet of GLA, with 46,000 square feet of restaurant space. There was also a 4,180-seat cineplex, a 4,000-square-foot bank branch, and 8,951 square feet of fast food. The center is located within the city of Phoenix in the foothills of the South Mountains and is conveniently accessible via I-10. Virtually all traffic to the site is by private automobile. A total of 2,758 parking spaces existed at the time of the study.

The center opened in late 1996, and Phase I was 100 percent occupied by the summer of 1997. Tenants at the time of the study included Barnes & Noble, an AMC cineplex, Petco, and Men's Wearhouse. The restaurants included Ruby Tuesday, On the Border, Macaroni Grill, Cucina Cucina, Oscar's Rock Bottom, and El Paso. AMC reported that the cineplex was the 11th busiest in the nation at that time. The 24-screen cineplex was the first with stadium-style seating in the metropolitan Phoenix area. Reportedly, patrons were driving long distances to visit the cineplex, and the percentage of parents willing to drive and drop off nondriving teens was believed to be lower than normal because of their journeys' extent. These factors suggest that the cineplex may have been in a honeymoon stage at the time of the occupancy counts.

The first step was to evaluate the parking required by the individual land uses. Table 5-17 summarizes the parking generated by each land use according to the parking ratios on weekdays and weekends. Clearly, the restaurants and cineplex were driving peak-hour parking requirements, since they accounted for over three-quarters of the peak parking requirement that would be generated if these uses were independently located. The weekend need was 19 percent more than the weekday need. Evenings in July and late December resulted in the peak overall accumulation of parked vehicles.

Because of the predominance of entertainment/dining activities, a 90 percent noncaptive adjustment was used in the evening. The design-day parking requirement using this book's model is thus estimated to be 2,329 parking spaces on a weekend evening in Late December, which is an 18 percent reduction compared with the unadjusted maximum demand of each land use.

Occupancy counts were conducted on a Friday and a Saturday evening in October. The observed parking occupancy on the Saturday in October was 2,537 parking spaces, while 2,179 vehicles were observed parking at the peak hour on the Friday evening. The Friday evening count was considered a weekend condition. The shared parking analysis appeared to underestimate (by 24 percent) the need for spaces at this center; in fact, the observed occupancy in October was greater (by almost 8 percent) than projected for the design day in late December. The research team noted that the estimated parking ratio for the cinema was 0.33 spaces per seat in October; at the time, however, the cineplex was unique in the market. Other facilities are likely to enter the market and compete with this facility, making its parking needs more typical.

| Table 5-17 | Unadjusted Parking Requirements for Each Land Use, Case Study 5.8 |

Land Use	Quantity	WEEKDAYS Base Ratio	Units	Unadjusted Parking Spaces	WEEKENDS Base Ratio	Units	Unadjusted Parking Spaces
Community Shopping Center	165,708	2.90	/ksf[1] GLA	481	3.20	/ksf GLA	530
Employee		0.70		116	0.80		133
Fine/Casual Dining	46,099	15.25	/ksf GLA	703	17.00	/ksf GLA	784
Employee		2.75		127	3.00		138
Fast Food	8,951	12.75	/ksf GLA	114	12.00	/ksf GLA	107
Employee		2.25		20	2.00		18
Cineplex	4,180	0.19	/seat	794	0.26	/seat	1,087
Employee		0.01		42	0.01		42
Bank	4,000	3.00	/ksf GFA	12	3.00	/ksf GFA	12
Employee		1.60		6	1.60		6
Subtotal: Customer/Guest Spaces				2,104			2,520
Subtotal: Employee/Resident Spaces				311			337
Total Parking Spaces				2,415			2,857

Note
[1] /ksf = per 1,000 sq. ft.

Table 5-18 Estimated Weekend Shared Parking Requirements, Case Study 5.8

Land Use	Unadjusted Demand	Month Adjustment Late December	Peak-Hour Adjustment 8 p.m.	Noncaptive Adjustment Evening	Mode Adjustment Evening	Late December 8 p.m.	October 8 p.m.	October 2 p.m.
Community Shopping Center	530	80%	50%	90%	100%	191	205	350
Employee	133	90%	75%	100%	100%	90	80	106
Fine/Casual Dining	784	95%	100%	100%	100%	745	751	321
Employee	138	100%	100%	100%	100%	138	138	104
Fast Food	107	95%	50%	50%	100%	25	26	47
Employee	18	100%	60%	100%	100%	11	11	17
Cineplex	1,087	100%	100%	100%	100%	1,087	674	352
Employee	42	100%	100%	100%	100%	42	34	20
Bank	12	80%	—	100%	100%	—	—	—
Employee	6	80%	—	100%	100%	—	—	—
Subtotal: Customer/Guest Spaces	2,520					2,048	1,656	1,070
Subtotal: Employee/Resident Spaces	337					281	263	247
Total Parking Spaces	2,857					2,329	1,919	1,317
Reduction	18%				vs. Observed	2,537		
					Estimated/Observed	0.76		

Ahwatukee Foothills Towne Center offers little more than 52 percent retail space. Given that parking demand was underestimated, possible adjustments in the noncaptive ratio would be to eliminate the 10 percent reduction for retail and the 50 percent reduction for fast food. The former adjustment would add 19 spaces to the evening demand and the latter would add 13, for a total increase of 32 spaces. This would only change the parking requirement in Late December by 1.4 percent, however, and clearly would not close the gap with the observed occupancy.

5.9 Irvine Spectrum

Irvine Spectrum is a premier entertainment center in southern California. Opened in 1995, it has since been expanded in several phases to encompass more than 1 million square feet of retail/dining/entertainment uses. It includes a 6,400-seat cineplex, an IMAX 3-D theater, and other entertainment uses such as a Dave & Buster's nightclub, Sega City, and a NASCAR Silicon Motor Speedway. It also shares parking with an adjacent office complex. However, the center has only 56,800 square feet of retail. Clearly, this is an entertainment destination rather than a shopping venue. The center has become a prime attraction for both residents and tourists. Car counts were conducted in July 2002 and late April 2003 on Wednesday, Friday, and Saturday, between phases of the project's expansion.[2] Projections of peak-hour parking were made for weekends and weekdays in those two months for comparison with the parking occupancy data. (At first blush, weekday demand seemed about equal to the weekend demand, due to the office component.)

The parking ratio for active entertainment was developed by the consultant who performed this study. The monthly factors used for this analysis were set to equal those of cinema uses, which reflect school schedules and other demand

Table 5-19 Unadjusted Parking Requirements for Each Land Use (2002 GLA), Case Study 5.9

Land Use	Quantity	WEEKDAYS Base Ratio	WEEKDAYS Units	WEEKDAYS Unadjusted Parking Spaces	WEEKENDS Base Ratio	WEEKENDS Units	WEEKENDS Unadjusted Parking Spaces
Community Shopping Center	56,800	2.90	/ksf[1] GLA	165	3.20	/ksf GLA	182
Employee		0.70		40	0.80		45
Fine/Casual Dining	95,300	15.25	/ksf GLA	1,453	17.00	/ksf GLA	1,620
Employee		2.75		262	3.00		286
Fast Food	12,000	12.75	/ksf GLA	153	12.00	/ksf GLA	144
Employee		2.25		27	2.00		24
Nightclub	83,900	15.25	/ksf GLA	1,279	17.00	/ksf GLA	1,426
Employee		1.25		105	1.50		126
Active Entertainment	71,000	4.20	/ksf GLA	298	6.50	/ksf GLA	462
Employee		0.40		28	0.50		36
Cineplex	6,400	0.19	/seat	1,216	0.26	/seat	1,664
Employee		0.01		64	0.01		64
Office	355,000	0.22	/ksf GFA	77	0.02	/ksf GFA	8
Employee		2.77		982	0.28		98
Subtotal: Customer/Guest Spaces				4,641			5,506
Subtotal: Employee/Resident Spaces				1,508			679
Total Parking Spaces				6,149			6,185

Note
[1] /ksf = per 1,000 sq. ft.

factors. Because of the center's entertainment orientation, the retail uses were assumed to be 75 percent noncaptive. The food court was considered to be 50 percent noncaptive, while active entertainment (which is oriented to children and young adults) was considered to be 90 percent noncaptive in the daytime and 95 percent noncaptive in the evening. The cinema was also assumed to be 95 percent noncaptive on weekday afternoons. The restaurants were assumed to be 95 percent noncaptive (due to the office buildings) in the daytime on weekdays.

The center has easy access from three major interstates and a strong connection to nearby affluent residential communities. Transit service is available to virtually all of Orange County, and a number of hotels run complimentary shuttle buses to the site for guests. Young adults are frequently dropped off at the center by parents. Given these factors, the mode adjustments were 90 percent in the daytime and 95 percent in the evening for employees and visitors.

Evening in Late December is still the peak period for weekdays, despite the lower office demand in that month. The peak hour is later than in other case studies, owing to the size of the cinema and the large nightclub component. July at 9 p.m. and 1 p.m. (the peaks for afternoon and evening) were also evaluated. Note that the recommended spaces on

Table 5-20 Estimated Weekday Shared Parking Requirements (2002 GLA), Case Study 5.9

Land Use	Unadjusted Demand	Month Adjustment Late December	Peak-Hour Adjustment 9 p.m.	Noncaptive Adjustment Evening	Mode Adjustment Evening	Late December 9 p.m.	July 9 p.m.	July 1 p.m.
Community Shopping Center	165	80%	25%	75%	95%	24	38	59
Employee	40	90%	75%	100%	95%	26	23	27
Fine/Casual Dining	1,453	95%	100%	100%	95%	1,311	1,218	913
Employee	262	100%	100%	100%	95%	249	236	212
Fast Food	153	95%	30%	50%	95%	21	22	69
Employee	27	100%	40%	100%	95%	10	10	24
Nightclub	1,279	95%	100%	100%	95%	1,154	1,139	—
Employee	105	100%	100%	100%	95%	100	100	9
Active Entertainment	298	100%	50%	95%	95%	134	124	222
Employee	28	100%	40%	100%	95%	11	11	25
Cineplex	1,216	100%	100%	100%	95%	1,155	635	271
Employee	64	100%	100%	100%	95%	61	46	26
Office	77	80%	—	100%	95%	—	—	30
Employee	982	80%	3%	100%	95%	22	27	756
Subtotal: Customer/Guest Spaces	4,641					3,799	3,176	1,564
Subtotal: Employee/Resident Spaces	1,508					479	453	1,079
Total Parking Spaces	6,149					4,278	3,629	2,643
Reduction	30%				vs. Observed		2,797	2,225
					Estimated/Observed		1.30	1.19

weekdays are 30 percent less than the sum of the unadjusted demands for each land use.

The observed occupancy at 1 p.m. on a weekday in July was 2,225 spaces; the observed occupancy at 8 p.m. was 2,797 spaces. The model thus overestimated the daytime need on weekdays in July by about 19 percent and the evening need by about 30 percent, even with the mode and noncaptive adjustments. One might therefore assume that there may be fewer arrivals by private vehicle (due both to shuttles and to parental drop-offs in the evening) as well as even more captive demand at some land uses.

The weekend demand was also projected to peak in Late December, with 122 spaces (2.4 percent) less demand in July. The peak parking in the afternoon on a Saturday in July was estimated to be 2,222 spaces, compared with an observed occupancy of 1,935 spaces. The daytime demand for July was thus overprojected by about 15 percent. At 9 p.m., the projected parking requirement was 5,005 spaces, compared with a peak observed occupancy of 5,221 spaces. Thus, the assumptions for ratios and time-of-day, noncaptive, and mode adjustments overestimated the demand for all conditions except on weekend evenings, when they underestimated the demand by about 4 percent.

Between July 2002 and April 2003, the retail and office space was significantly increased and some tenants changed, resulting in minor changes in restaurant, nightclub,

Table 5-21 Estimated Weekend Shared Parking Requirements (2002 GLA), Case Study 5.9

Land Use	Unadjusted Demand	Month Adjustment Late December	Peak-Hour Adjustment 9 p.m.	Noncaptive Adjustment Evening	Mode Adjustment Evening	Late December 9 p.m.	July 9 p.m.	July 2 p.m.
Community Shopping Center	182	80%	30%	75%	95%	31	42	79
Employee	45	90%	65%	100%	95%	25	22	32
Fine/Casual Dining	1,620	95%	90%	100%	95%	1,316	1,358	643
Employee	286	100%	100%	100%	95%	272	272	193
Fast Food	144	95%	30%	50%	95%	19	21	58
Employee	24	100%	40%	100%	95%	9	9	21
Nightclub	1,426	95%	100%	100%	95%	1,287	1,270	0
Employee	126	100%	100%	100%	95%	120	120	11
Active Entertainment	462	100%	90%	95%	95%	375	345	344
Employee	36	100%	90%	100%	95%	31	31	32
Cineplex	1,664	100%	100%	100%	95%	1,581	1,454	720
Employee	64	100%	100%	100%	95%	61	61	35
Office	8	80%	—	100%	95%	—	—	4
Employee	98	80%	—	100%	95%	—	—	50
Subtotal: Customer/Guest Spaces	5,506					4,609	4,490	1,848
Subtotal: Employee/Resident Spaces	679					518	515	374
Total Parking Spaces	6,185					5,127	5,005	2,222
Reduction	17%				vs. Observed		5,221	1,935
					Estimated/Observed		0.96	1.15

and active entertainment uses. The unadjusted demand of the individual components increased almost 29 percent.

Because the retail uses significantly increased without an overall increase in the dining/entertainment uses, the 2003 retail patronage was considered to be 90 percent noncaptive in both daytime and evening, rather than the 75 percent estimate used for the 2002 projection.

With the additional office and retail uses, the daytime demand in April 2003 was projected to be slightly higher than the evening demand. The observed occupancy on a weekday in April at 2 p.m. was 3,084 spaces; the observed occupancy at 8 p.m. was 2,493 spaces. Therefore, the shared parking model, even with the mode and noncaptive adjust-

ments, still overprojected daytime demand by 19 percent (the same as the projection for 2002) and evening demand by 46 percent (more than 2002's 30 percent). It would have been appropriate to assume more captive patronage of the retail, even though there was five times as much retail as in 2002. However, we retained the 90 percent noncaptive patronage ratio for weekend evening projections because the model had previously underestimated the evening demand. Occupancy was observed on the weekend in early May, and therefore weekend demand was modeled.

The recommended number of spaces per these assumptions for the peak period of an evening in Late December increased from 5,127 to 5,726, an increase of only 12 percent,

Table 5-22 Unadjusted Parking Requirements for Each Land Use (2003 GLA), Case Study 5.9

Land Use	Quantity	WEEKDAYS			WEEKENDS		
		Base Ratio	Units	Unadjusted Parking Spaces	Base Ratio	Units	Unadjusted Parking Spaces
Community Shopping Center	303,200	2.90	/ksf[1] GLA	879	3.20	/ksf GLA	970
Employee		0.70		212	0.80		243
Fine/Casual Dining	127,800	15.25	/ksf GLA	1,949	17.00	/ksf GLA	2,173
Employee		2.75		351	3.00		383
Fast Food	12,000	12.75	/ksf GLA	153	12.00	/ksf GLA	144
Employee		2.25		27	2.00		24
Nightclub	66,700	15.25	/ksf GLA	1,017	17.00	/ksf GLA	1,134
Employee		1.25		83	1.50		100
Active Entertainment	63,500	4.20	/ksf GLA	267	6.50	/ksf GLA	413
Employee		0.40		25	0.50		32
Cineplex	6,400	0.19	/seat	1,216	0.26	/seat	1,664
Employee		0.01		64	0.01		64
Office	572,400	0.20	/ksf GFA	114	0.02	/ksf GFA	11
Employee		2.60		1,488	0.26		149
Subtotal: Customer/Guest Spaces				5,595			6,509
Subtotal: Employee/Resident Spaces				2,250			995
Total Parking Spaces				7,845			7,504

Note
[1] /ksf = per 1,000 sq. ft.

Table 5-23 Estimated Weekday Shared Parking Requirements (2003 GLA), Case Study 5.9

Land Use	Unadjusted Demand	Month Adjustment Late December	Peak-Hour Adjustment 8 p.m.	Noncaptive Adjustment Evening	Mode Adjustment Evening	Late December 8 p.m.	May 8 p.m.	May 2 p.m.
Community Shopping Center	879	80%	40%	90%	95%	240	379	426
Employee	212	90%	90%	100%	95%	163	145	153
Fine/Casual Dining	1,949	95%	100%	100%	95%	1,759	1,538	1,000
Employee	351	100%	100%	100%	95%	333	316	284
Fast Food	153	95%	50%	50%	95%	35	34	58
Employee	27	100%	60%	100%	95%	15	15	23
Nightclub	1,017	95%	75%	100%	95%	688	653	—
Employee	83	100%	100%	100%	95%	79	79	7
Active Entertainment	267	100%	90%	95%	95%	217	126	119
Employee	25	100%	60%	100%	95%	14	11	17
Cineplex	1,216	100%	100%	100%	95%	1,155	219	114
Employee	64	100%	100%	100%	95%	61	30	17
Office	114	80%	1%	100%	95%	1	1	103
Employee	1,488	80%	7%	100%	95%	79	99	1,339
Subtotal: Customer/Guest Spaces	5,595					4,095	2,950	1,820
Subtotal: Employee/Resident Spaces	2,250					744	695	1,840
Total Parking Spaces	7,845					4,839	3,645	3,660
Reduction	38%				vs. Observed		2,493	3,084
					Estimated/Observed		1.46	1.19

Table 5-24 Estimated Weekend Shared Parking Requirements (2003 GLA), Case Study 5.9

Land Use	Unadjusted Demand	Month Adjustment Late December	Peak-Hour Adjustment 8 p.m.	Noncaptive Adjustment Evening	Mode Adjustment Evening	Late December 8 p.m.	May 9 p.m.	May 2 p.m.
Community Shopping Center	970	80%	50%	90%	95%	332	276	522
Employee	243	90%	75%	100%	95%	156	120	175
Fine/Casual Dining	2,173	95%	100%	100%	95%	1961	1,781	844
Employee	383	100%	100%	100%	95%	364	364	259
Fast Food	144	95%	50%	50%	95%	32	20	57
Employee	24	100%	60%	100%	95%	14	9	21
Nightclub	1,134	95%	75%	100%	95%	768	971	—
Employee	100	100%	100%	100%	95%	95	95	9
Active Entertainment	413	100%	90%	95%	95%	335	238	238
Employee	32	100%	90%	100%	95%	27	22	23
Cineplex	1,664	100%	100%	100%	95%	1581	1,122	556
Employee	64	100%	100%	100%	95%	61	49	28
Office	11	80%	—	100%	95%	—	—	—
Employee	149	80%	—	100%	95%	—	—	—
Subtotal: Customer/Guest Spaces	6,509					5,009	4,408	2,223
Subtotal: Employee/Resident Spaces	995					717	659	595
Total Parking Spaces	7,504					5,726	5,067	2,818
Reduction	24%				vs. Observed		6,169	3,074
					Estimated/Observed		0.82	0.92

despite the addition of 471,600 square feet, which increased the total GLA more than 50 percent from about 800,000 square feet to nearly 1.3 million. That is because the uses added tended to generate daytime demand rather than evening demand, making better use of the existing spaces. The shared parking model underestimated evening demand more significantly than for 2002 (18 percent versus 4 percent); the observed occupancy at 9 p.m. in early May was greater than the projection for a peak hour in Late December. The model also underestimated parking requirements for weekend afternoons by 8 percent, whereas previously it had overestimated demand for weekday afternoons by 15 percent.

5.10 Reston Town Center

Reston Town Center is the downtown area of the planned community of Reston, Virginia. Since development of the Town Center began in 1990, it has won 23 national and regional awards for quality in planning, design, construction, and operation, including the prestigious American Institute of Architects Award for Excellence in Urban Design.

Phase I included two Class A office towers and a Hyatt Regency Hotel. At the street level there are retail shops, restaurants, and entertainment, including a 13-screen cinema with 2,918 seats. The centerpiece of Phase I is Fountain Square, an open civic plaza with a fountain sculpture

Figure 5-2 Reston Town Center

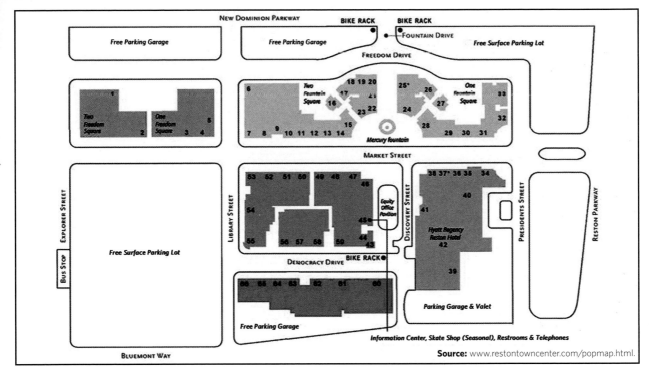

Source: www.restontowncenter.com/popmap.html.

designed by Brazilian-born sculptor Saint Clair Cemin. Phase II included two additional office towers known as Freedom Square. Two low-rise buildings are planned to the south of the Phase II to include office, retail, and restaurants. The open-air pavilion is the scene of year-round events and festivals; from November to mid-March, the pavilion is converted to an ice skating pavilion.

A shared parking study was conducted in 1999 prior to Phase II.[3] The GLA for the restaurants then present was estimated from the number of seats using a ratio of 30 square feet per seat. With over half a million square feet of office space and less than 200,000 square feet of retail/dining/entertainment space, Reston Town Center's parking needs peaked on a weekday afternoon. Occupancy counts were conducted on a Thursday in May.

Transit service is available, and some employees of tenants may live within walking distance; therefore a 5 percent reduction in car use was assumed for daytime employees, but no mode adjustment was made for evenings. It was assumed that the retail patronage was 90 percent noncaptive in the daytime and evenings. The restaurants were assumed to be 95 percent noncaptive in the daytime on weekdays due to both the hotel and office uses, but 100 percent noncaptive in the evenings and weekends. The dominance of the office uses reflected in Table 5-25 caused parking to peak on weekdays in December.

The peak accumulation of vehicles was 2,538 spaces at 2:30 p.m. in May. The shared parking analysis projected about 4 percent more demand at 2 p.m. in May. Shared parking analysis reduced the design-day parking spaces in December by 33 percent.

Table 5-25 Unadjusted Parking Requirements for Each Land Use, Case Study 5.10

Land Use	Quantity	WEEKDAYS Base Ratio	Units	Unadjusted Parking Spaces	WEEKENDS Base Ratio	Units	Unadjusted Parking Spaces
Community Shopping Center	105,267	2.90	/ksf[1] GLA	305	3.20	/ksf GLA	337
Employee		0.70		74	0.80		84
Fine/Casual Dining	60,000	15.25	/ksf GLA	915	17.00	/ksf GLA	1,020
Employee		2.75		165	3.00		180
Cineplex	2,918	0.19	/seat	554	0.26	/seat	759
Employee		0.01		29	0.01		29
Hotel-Business	515	1.00	/room	515	0.90	/room	464
Employee	515	0.25	/room	131	0.18	/room	93
Office	520,723	0.20	/ksf GFA	104	0.02	/ksf GFA	10
Employee		2.60		1,354	0.26		135
Subtotal: Customer/Guest Spaces				2,393			2,590
Subtotal: Employee/Resident Spaces				1,753			521
Total Parking Spaces				4,146			3,111

Note
[1]/ksf = per 1,000 sq. ft.

Table 5-26 Estimated Weekday Shared Parking Requirements, Case Study 5.10

Land Use	Unadjusted Demand	Month Adjustment December	Peak-Hour Adjustment 2 p.m.	Noncaptive Adjustment Daytime	Mode Adjustment Daytime	December 2 p.m.	May 2 p.m.	May 8 p.m.
Community Shopping Center	305	100%	100%	90%	100%	275	164	146
Employee	74	100%	100%	100%	95%	70	56	53
Fine/Casual Dining	915	100%	65%	95%	100%	565	522	833
Employee	165	100%	90%	100%	95%	141	141	157
Cineplex	554	23%	55%	100%	100%	70	58	150
Employee	29	50%	60%	100%	95%	8	8	15
Hotel-Business	515	67%	60%	100%	66%	137	184	250
Employee	131	100%	100%	100%	95%	124	124	26
Office >500,000 sq. ft.	104	100%	100%	100%	100%	104	104	1
Employee	1354	100%	100%	100%	95%	1,286	1,286	95
Subtotal: Customer/Guest Spaces	2,393					1,151	1,032	1,380
Subtotal: Employee/Resident Spaces	1,753					1,629	1,615	346
Total Parking Spaces	4,146					2,780	2,647	1,726
Reduction	33%				vs. Observed		2,538	
					Estimated/Observed		1.04	

5.11 Easton Town Center

This super regional center in Columbus, Ohio, includes about 600,000 square feet of retail, plus large restaurant, cineplex, and health club components as well as 50,000 square feet of office space. Approximately 61 percent of the nearly 1 million square feet of GLA is retail. The cinema seats were estimated from the 134,000 square feet of the cinema's GLA, using a ratio of 22.5 square feet per seat, which is average for these venues. Occupancy counts were taken from 11 a.m. to 10 p.m. on a Thursday, Friday, and Saturday in mid-November 2002.[4]

With 986,900 total square feet of GLA, the observed parking ratio in mid-November was just over 6 spaces/ksf, while the shared parking analysis projected a peak ratio of 5.4 spaces/ksf in December. With office space being such a minor use, parking peaks on weekends. Preliminary runs found that an evening in December was the peak period. The shared parking model was then also run for afternoon and evening in November. After a preliminary run using adjustments similar to those employed for Ahwatukee Foothills Towne Center found that demand was underestimated, the model was rerun with no captive market adjustments. There was no breakout of the restaurants between fine/casual dining, family, and fast food, since that was not recommended by the shared parking methodology at the time of this case study.

able 5-27 Unadjusted Parking Requirements for Each Land Use, Case Study 5.11

Land Use	Quantity	WEEKDAYS			WEEKENDS		
		Base Ratio	Units	Unadjusted Parking Spaces	Base Ratio	Units	Unadjusted Parking Spaces
Super Regional Shopping Center (>600k)	600,194	3.20	/ksf[1] GLA	1,921	3.60	/ksf GLA	2,161
Employee		0.80		480	0.90		540
Fine/Casual Dining	115,038	15.25	/ksf GLA	1,754	17.00	/ksf GLA	1,956
Employee		2.75		316	3.00		345
Employee		0.40		—	0.50		—
Cineplex	5,956	0.19	/seat	1,132	0.26	/seat	1,549
Employee		0.01		60	0.01		60
Health Club	87,671	6.60	/ksf GLA	579	5.50	/ksf GLA	482
Employee		0.40		35	0.25		22
Office (25,000 to 100,000 sq. ft.)	50,000	0.30	/ksf GFA	15	0.03	/ksf GFA	2
Employee		3.37		168	0.34		17
Subtotal: Customer/Guest Spaces				5,401			6,150
Subtotal: Employee/Resident Spaces				1,059			984
Total Parking Spaces				6,460			7,134

Note
[1] /ksf = per 1,000 sq. ft.

Table 5-28 Estimated Weekend Shared Parking Requirements, Case Study 5.11

Land Use	Unadjusted Demand	Month Adjustment December	Peak-Hour Adjustment 7 p.m.	Noncaptive Adjustment Evening	Mode Adjustment Evening	December 7 p.m.	November 8 p.m.	November 3 p.m.
Super Regional Shopping Center	2,161	100%	75%	100%	100%	1,621	1,011	1,556
Employee	540	100%	80%	100%	100%	432	365	462
Fine/Casual Dining	1,956	100%	95%	100%	100%	1,858	1,819	819
Employee	345	100%	100%	100%	100%	345	345	246
Cineplex	1,549	67%	80%	100%	100%	830	1,208	631
Employee	60	80%	100%	100%	100%	48	48	34
Health Club	482	90%	60%	100%	100%	260	123	117
Employee	22	100%	75%	100%	100%	17	10	10
Office	2	100%	—	100%	100%	—	—	1
Employee	17	100%	—	100%	100%	—	—	6
Subtotal: Customer/Guest Spaces	6,150					4,569	4,161	3,124
Subtotal: Employee/Resident Spaces	984					842	768	758
Total Parking Spaces	7,134					5,411	4,929	3,882
Reduction	24%				vs. Observed		5,616	5,965
					Estimated/Observed		0.88	0.65

While parking occupancy did peak strongly, with 5,616 vehicles observed at 8 p.m. on Friday (considered a weekend), the peak on a Saturday in November was observed to be 5,965 spaces at 3 p.m. The occupancy counts were stopped at 8 p.m. on Saturday, with 5,408 vehicles observed. However, the Friday evening counts were generally higher than the Saturday evening counts. Both afternoon and evening parking requirements were underestimated by 35 percent and 12 percent, respectively. Since the peak spaces needed for the entire center using shared parking methodology (5,367) were less than the peak occupancy observed on a Saturday afternoon in mid-November, the model clearly underestimated the need for parking at this center. Therefore, one must conclude that this center performs well above the norm for shopping centers.

Counts were also taken on Thursday and Friday. Parking requirements on a weekday were modeled per Table 5-29.

With no noncaptive adjustments (as in the weekend analysis), the peak weekday parking need was projected to occur at 6 p.m. in Late December.

The Friday afternoon count (considered as weekday demand) was 3,513 at 1 p.m. and counted to rise throughout the afternoon and evening until the 9 p.m. count noted in Table 5-29 (defined as a weekend count). On Thursday, the parking occupancy peaked at 3,071 spaces at 1 p.m., declined to 2,645 by 5 p.m., then climbed back up to almost 4,200 spaces at 7 p.m. Both afternoon and evening parking demand were overestimated on weekdays (with no captive reductions assumed) by 5 percent and 12 percent, respectively. The model worked well for the weekdays, but the center clearly performs well above normal on weekends in mid-November.

Table 5-29	Estimated Weekday Shared Parking Requirements, Case Study 5.11							
Land Use	**Unadjusted Demand**	**Month Adjustment Late December**	**Peak-Hour Adjustment 6 p.m.**	**Noncaptive Adjustment Evening**	**Mode Adjustment Evening**	**Late December 6 p.m.**	**November 7 p.m.**	**November 1 p.m.**
Super Regional Shopping Center	1,921	80%	70%	100%	100%	1,076	1,314	1,383
Employee	480	90%	95%	100%	100%	410	410	410
Fine/Casual Dining	1,754	95%	95%	100%	100%	1,583	1,631	1,223
Employee	316	100%	100%	100%	100%	316	300	270
Cineplex	1,132	100%	70%	100%	100%	792	226	127
Employee	60	100%	100%	100%	100%	60	30	17
Health Club	579	95%	100%	100%	100%	550	443	327
Employee	35	100%	100%	100%	100%	35	25	24
Office	15	80%	5%	100%	100%	1	—	7
Employee	168	80%	25%	100%	100%	34	17	144
Subtotal: Customer/Guest Spaces	5,401					4,002	3,614	3,067
Subtotal: Employee/Resident Spaces	1,059					855	782	865
Subtotal: Reserved Spaces	—					—	—	—
Total Parking Spaces	6,460					4,857	4,396	3,932
Reduction	25%				vs. Observed		4,197	3,513
					Estimated/Observed		1.05	1.12

5.12 Block at Orange

Located in Orange, California, this center has approximately 800,000 square feet of GLA but is roughly 50 percent entertainment. It has a Dave & Buster's adult entertainment venue and a Vans Skatepark active entertainment facility. Parking occupancy counts were conducted from 9 a.m. to 10 p.m. on a Thursday, Friday, and Saturday in February 2002 as part of a shared parking analysis for a proposed expansion.[5] In addition, a patron survey was conducted in the summer of 1999 that provided information on noncaptive ratios at that time.

This center has many similarities to and competes with Irvine Spectrum and a third dining/entertainment destination (Downtown Disney) in Orange County, California. Like Irvine Spectrum after its 2002 expansion, the Block at Orange has achieved a nearly ideal balance between weekday and weekend demand, with the office space comple-menting the retail and entertainment uses. This analysis used the same mode and noncaptive adjustments as for Irvine Spectrum's 2003 GLA, with the additional assumption that 90 percent of the health club patrons are noncaptive in the daytime on weekdays.

The peak accumulation on the Thursday in February was 3,391 spaces at 8:30 p.m. (Counts were taken at 30-minute intervals, but the model only projects parking need on an hourly basis.) The model underestimated the shared parking requirement by about 24 percent. In the afternoon, the observed accumulation was 3,295 spaces; the model therefore underestimated the need by 17 percent. (Conversely, the same factors for the similar and directly competitive Irvine Spectrum overestimated the required parking on weekdays by 19 percent in the afternoon and 46 percent in the evening.) The study team's first change was to remove the

Table 5-30 Unadjusted Parking Requirements for Each Land Use, Case Study 5.12

Land Use	Quantity	WEEKDAYS Base Ratio	WEEKDAYS Units	WEEKDAYS Unadjusted Parking Spaces	WEEKENDS Base Ratio	WEEKENDS Units	WEEKENDS Unadjusted Parking Spaces
Regional Shopping Center	471,671	3.01	/ksf[1] GLA	1,419	3.34	/ksf GLA	1,577
Employee		0.74		347	0.84		394
Fine/Casual Dining	37,948	15.25	/ksf GLA	579	17.00	/ksf GLA	645
Employee		2.75		104	3.00		114
Fast Food	21,165	12.75	/ksf GLA	270	12.00	/ksf GLA	254
Employee		2.25		48	2.00		42
Nightclub	59,955	15.25	/ksf GLA	914	17.00	/ksf GLA	1,019
Employee		1.25		75	1.50		90
Active Entertainment	42,335	4.20	/ksf GLA	178	6.50	/ksf GLA	275
Employee		0.40		17	0.50		21
Cineplex	6,066	0.19	/seat	1,153	0.26	/seat	1,577
Employee		0.01		61	0.01		61
Health Club	31,144	6.60	/ksf GLA	206	5.50	/ksf GLA	171
Employee		0.40		12	0.25		8
Office	375,434	0.22	/ksf GFA	81	0.02	/ksf GFA	8
Employee		2.74		1,028	0.27		103
Subtotal: Customer/Guest Spaces				4,800			5,526
Subtotal: Employee/Resident Spaces				1,692			833
Total Parking Spaces				6,492			6,359

Note
[1] /ksf = per 1,000 sq. ft.

mode adjustments; this reduced the underestimation of demand to 9 percent in the daytime and 24 percent in the evening. (This intermediate step is not shown in a table.) Then we modified the noncaptive ratios for retail to 100 percent daytime and 95 percent evenings, and for active entertainment to 95 percent at all time periods. These noncaptive adjustment changes only slightly modified the underestimate of demand to 7 percent in the daytime and to 18 percent in the evening.

An occupancy of 5,389 spaces was observed on the Saturday night at 10 p.m. The model as discussed above underestimated demand on Saturdays by 46 percent in the evening, as compared to an underestimate of about 13 percent in the daytime.

This center clearly performs well above the 85th percentile, as its peak occupancy in February was 21 percent greater than the peak parking need projected for Late December. Indeed, the peak occupancy in February was only 19 percent less than the sum of the unadjusted parking spaces for each land use. The observed parking ratio for the retail/dining/entertainment components (i.e., ignoring office and health club uses) on Saturday night in February was 7.0

Table 5-31 Estimated Weekday Shared Parking Requirements, Case Study 5.12

Land Use	Unadjusted Demand	Month Adjustment Late December	Peak-Hour Adjustment 2 p.m.	Noncaptive Adjustment Daytime	Mode Adjustment Daytime	Late December 2 p.m.	February 2 p.m.	February 8 p.m.
Regional Shopping Center	1,419	80%	100%	95%	90%	971	657	553
Employee	347	90%	100%	100%	90%	281	250	237
Fine/Casual Dining	579	95%	65%	95%	90%	306	276	425
Employee	104	100%	90%	100%	90%	84	80	89
Fast Food	270	95%	90%	50%	90%	104	92	54
Employee	48	100%	95%	100%	90%	41	39	26
Nightclub	914	95%	—	100%	90%	—	—	557
Employee	75	100%	10%	100%	90%	7	6	64
Active Entertainment	178	100%	95%	90%	90%	137	81	85
Employee	17	100%	95%	100%	90%	15	12	8
Cineplex	1,153	100%	75%	100%	90%	778	120	230
Employee	61	100%	60%	100%	90%	33	16	29
Health Club	206	95%	70%	90%	90%	111	111	149
Employee	12	100%	75%	100%	90%	8	8	6
Office	81	80%	100%	100%	90%	58	73	1
Employee	1,028	80%	100%	100%	90%	740	925	68
Subtotal: Customer/Guest Spaces	4,800					2,465	1,410	2,054
Subtotal: Employee/Resident Spaces	1,692					1,209	1,336	527
Total Parking Spaces	6,492					3,674	2,746	2,581
Reduction	43%				vs. Observed		3,295	3,391
					Estimated/Observed		0.83	0.76

spaces/ksf. The study team believes that the monthly variations at this center are significantly lower than normal. The February shared parking demand is 22 percent less than the Late December projection. It is estimated, however, that the parking ratio in Late December would be closer to 8 spaces/ksf than the ratio of 8.5 spaces/ksf that would result if the Late December demand were 22 percent greater than the February demand. In other words, the "valleys" in the monthly variation of parking demand seem less deep than those commonly seen.

Table 5-32 Revised Estimated Weekday Shared Parking Requirements, Case Study 5.12

Land Use	Unadjusted Demand	Month Adjustment Late December	Peak-Hour Adjustment 2 p.m.	Noncaptive Adjustment Daytime	Mode Adjustment Daytime	Late December 2 p.m.	February 2 p.m.	February 8 p.m.
Regional Shopping Center	1,419	80%	100%	100%	100%	1,135	768	615
Employee	347	90%	100%	100%	100%	312	278	250
Fine/Casual Dining	579	95%	65%	95%	100%	340	307	473
Employee	104	100%	90%	100%	100%	94	89	99
Fast Food	270	95%	90%	50%	100%	115	102	57
Employee	48	100%	95%	100%	100%	46	43	27
Nightclub	914	95%	—	100%	100%	—	—	587
Employee	75	100%	10%	100%	100%	8	7	68
Active Entertainment	178	100%	95%	95%	100%	161	95	90
Employee	17	100%	95%	100%	100%	16	13	8
Cineplex	1,153	100%	75%	95%	100%	822	127	242
Employee	61	100%	60%	100%	100%	37	18	31
Health Club	206	95%	70%	95%	100%	130	130	157
Employee	12	100%	75%	100%	100%	9	9	6
Office	81	80%	100%	100%	100%	65	81	1
Employee	1,028	80%	100%	100%	100%	822	1,028	72
Subtotal: Customer/Guest Spaces	4,800					2,768	1,610	2,222
Subtotal: Employee/Resident Spaces	1,692					1,344	1,485	561
Total Parking Spaces	6,492					4,112	3,095	2,783
Reduction	37%				vs. Observed		3,295	3,391
					Estimated/Observed		0.93	0.82

Land Use	Unadjusted Demand	Month Adjustment Late December	Peak-Hour Adjustment 8 p.m.	Noncaptive Adjustment Evening	Mode Adjustment Evening	Late December 8 p.m.	February 8 p.m.	February 2 p.m.
Regional Shopping Center	1,577	80%	50%	95%	100%	599	555	899
Employee	394	90%	75%	100%	100%	266	236	315
Fine/Casual Dining	645	95%	100%	100%	100%	613	554	237
Employee	114	100%	100%	100%	100%	114	108	81
Fast Food	254	95%	50%	50%	100%	60	53	96
Employee	42	100%	60%	100%	100%	25	24	38
Nightclub	1,019	95%	75%	100%	100%	726	654	—
Employee	90	100%	100%	100%	100%	90	81	8
Active Entertainment	275	100%	90%	95%	100%	235	139	154
Employee	21	100%	90%	100%	100%	19	15	17
Cineplex	1,577	100%	100%	100%	100%	1,577	930	486
Employee	61	100%	100%	100%	100%	61	49	29
Health Club	171	95%	30%	100%	100%	49	49	41
Employee	8	100%	50%	100%	100%	4	4	4
Office	8	80%	—	100%	100%	—	—	5
Employee	103	80%	—	100%	100%	—	—	62
Subtotal: Customer/Guest Spaces	5,526					3,859	2,934	1,918
Subtotal: Employee/Resident Spaces	833					579	517	554
Total Parking Spaces	6,359					4,438	3,451	2,472
Reduction	30%				vs. Observed		5,389	2,846
					Estimated/Observed		0.64	0.87

Table 5-34 Summary of Tenants and Parking Required at Time of Zoning Approval, Case Study 5.13

Shared Parking Class	Tenant	Business Type	GLA (Sq. Ft.)	Parking Ratio	Parking Required	Comments re Code
Bank	First Bank and Trust	Bank	4,308	1/250	17.23	Considered Retail
Family Restaurant	Bauducco's	Dining	683	1/45	15.18	
	Bauducco's	Kitchen/Service	6,037	1/250	24.15	
	Bauducco's	Office	340	1/250	1.36	
	Kaminari Sushi	Dining	313	1/45	6.96	
	Kaminari Sushi	Kitchen/Service	887	1/250	3.55	
Subtotal			8,260		51.19	
Fast Food	Popeye's Chicken	Dining	549	1/45	12.20	
	Popeye's Chicken	Kitchen/Service	891	1/250	3.56	
	Spudnuts Donuts	Dining	281	1/45	6.24	
	Spudnuts Donuts	Kitchen/Service	952	1/250	3.81	
	Subway	Dining	274	1/45	6.09	
	Subway	Kitchen/Service	812	1/250	3.25	
	Taco Bell	Dining	564	1/45	12.53	
	Taco Bell	Kitchen/Service	1,270	1/250	5.08	
	Baskin-Robbins	Takeout	960	1/250	3.84	
	Domino's Pizza	Takeout	1,432	1/250	5.73	
Subtotal			7,985		62.33	
Medical	Dr. Henteleff	Optometry	1,050	1/250	4.20	Approved at Office Ratio
Office	CBF	Physical Therapy	1,198	1/250	4.79	Approved at Office Ratio
	Complete Body Fitness	Physical Therapy	907	1/200	4.54	Approved as Medical Office
	Westlake Eye Surgery	Medical	2,754	1/200	13.77	Approved as Medical Office
Subtotal			5,909		27.3	
Office	Creative Partners International	Office	2,498	1/250	9.99	
	Drake Institute	Office	2,500	1/250	10.00	
	John Friedman	Office	840	1/250	3.36	
	Kumon Learning Center	Office	599	1/250	2.40	
	Leftfield Productions	Office	5,954	1/250	23.82	
Subtotal			12,391		49.56	
Retail	Center Stage	Retail	1,205	1/250	4.82	
	Cleopatra Day Spa	Retail	1,200	1/250	4.80	
	Jessica's Alterations	Retail	895	1/250	3.58	
	Postal Depot Plus	Retail	1,128	1/250	4.51	
	TP Nails	Retail	812	1/250	3.25	
	Village Glen Cleaners	Retail	854	1/250	3.42	
	Westlake Florist	Retail	1,294	1/250	5.18	
	Westlake Photo Lab	Retail	864	1/250	3.46	
	Westlake Sports Collectables	Retail	495	1/250	1.98	
	Management Office	Office	966	1/250	3.86	Counted as Office
Subtotal			9,713		38.85	
	Miscellaneous	—	379	1/250	1.52	Retail
	Corridors, Toilets, etc..	—	1,772	1/250	7.09	Counted as Office
Total			50,717		255.07	

Source: Kaku Associates.

Table 5-35 Unadjusted Parking Requirements for Each Land Use, Case Study 5.13

Land Use	Quantity	WEEKDAYS Base Ratio	Units	Unadjusted Parking Spaces	WEEKENDS Base Ratio	Units	Unadjusted Parking Spaces
Community Shopping Center	9,713	2.90	/ksf[1] GLA	28	3.20	/ksf GLA	31
Employee		0.70		7	0.80		8
Family Restaurant	8,260	9.00	/ksf GLA	74	12.75	/ksf GLA	105
Employee		1.50		12	2.25		19
Fast Food	7,985	12.75	/ksf GLA	102	12.00	/ksf GLA	96
Employee		2.25		18	2.00		16
Office	12,391	0.30	/ksf GFA	4	0.03	/ksf GFA	0
Employee		3.50		43	0.35		4
Medical/Dental Office	5,909	3.00	/ksf GFA	18	3.00	/ksf GFA	18
Employee		1.50		9	1.50		9
Bank (Drive-in Branch)	4,308	3.00	/ksf GFA	13	3.00	/ksf GFA	13
Employee		1.60		7	1.60		7
Subtotal: Customer/Guest Spaces				239			263
Subtotal: Employee/Resident Spaces				96			63
Total Parking Spaces				335			326

Note
[1] /ksf = per 1,000 sq. ft.

5.13 Village Glen Plaza

This small community center in Westlake Village, California, included a variety of uses in about 50,000 square feet of GLA at the time of the shared parking analysis. (Space that was vacant or proposed at the time of the occupancy studies was not included in the review.) This case study considers both the zoning requirements of the locality and the difficulties inherent in determining parking requirements before tenants of a shopping center are known. Table 5-34 summarizes the square footage by tenant type, as well as the local requirements for parking that were established at the time of approval, which in this case was issuance of the building permit for the construction of each building.

This center had less than 20 percent of the space leased to retail uses at the time of the study. Office, medical office, and bank uses represented 45 percent of the GLA, and family restaurants and fast food occupied almost one-third of the leased space.

The local ordinance uses the older convention of one space per a given number of square feet in their ordinance. Retail, general office, and bank uses all require the same ratio: one space per 250 square feet, or four spaces/ksf. Medical office uses require slightly more parking at one space per 200 square feet, or five spaces/ksf. The kitchen/service areas of any food service use also require one space per 250 square feet, but dining areas require one space per 45 square feet, which is equivalent to 22.22 spaces/ksf. The management office of a shopping center is generally considered part of the retail GLA and thus is classified as retail in accordance with *Parking Requirements for Shopping Centers*. However, cor-

Table 5-36 Estimated Weekday Shared Parking Requirements, Case Study 5.13

Land Use	Unadjusted Demand	Month Adjustment December	Peak-Hour Adjustment 1 p.m.	Noncaptive Adjustment Daytime	Mode Adjustment Daytime	December 1 p.m.	August 1 p.m.	August 6 p.m.
Community Shopping Center	28	100%	100%	90%	100%	25	17	18
Employee	7	100%	100%	100%	100%	7	6	5
Family Restaurant	74	100%	90%	95%	100%	63	63	57
Employee	12	100%	100%	100%	100%	12	12	11
Fast Food	102	100%	100%	50%	100%	51	50	43
Employee	18	100%	100%	100%	100%	18	18	16
Office < 25,000 sq. ft.	4	100%	45%	100%	100%	2	2	—
Employee	43	100%	90%	100%	100%	39	37	11
Medical/Dental Office	18	100%	90%	100%	100%	16	15	12
Employee	9	100%	100%	100%	100%	9	9	6
Bank (Drive-in Branch)	13	100%	50%	100%	100%	7	6	—
Employee	7	100%	100%	100%	100%	7	7	—
Subtotal: Customer/Guest Spaces	239					164	153	130
Subtotal: Employee/Resident Spaces	96					92	89	49
Total Parking Spaces	335					256	242	179
Reduction	24%				vs. Observed		222	107
					Estimated/Observed		1.09	1.67

ridors, toilets, and miscellaneous spaces are not part of the GLA and thus are not considered by this book to generate parking; the local ordinance in this case counted them as office or retail as noted.

Two of the four medical office uses were classified as office at the time of the building permit. The overall local parking requirement for the occupied space is 255 spaces, or 5.03 spaces/ksf, which is roughly one space per 200 square feet. Note that the calculation of required parking under the Thousand Oaks Ordinance did not consider shared parking.

Most of the retail tenants would be classified as convenience retail, including the alterations shop, mailing service, photo lab, and florist. However, in a typical situation, the community shopping center category would be used.

A review of monthly factors indicated that the peak need is in December, when all the monthly factors are 100 percent.

The peak time of day was found to be noon, which was consistent with the occupancy counts. Shared parking projections were then developed for both weekends and weekdays in December and August, which was the month of the occupancy counts. With far more office than other uses, the noncaptive adjustments for weekdays were assumed to be 90 percent for retail and 95 percent for family restaurants, with a 50 percent adjustment in fast-food parking needs.

Although there were minor differences in the individual calculations, the August parking requirement was roughly the same on both weekends (259 spaces) and weekdays (244 spaces). The projected parking required using shared parking analysis was slightly more than the zoning requirement (262 versus 259 spaces).

The peak parking accumulation on weekdays was 222 spaces on a Wednesday in August at noon, almost the same

Estimated Weekend Shared Parking Requirements, Case Study 5.13

Land Use	Unadjusted Demand	Month Adjustment December	Peak-Hour Adjustment Noon	Noncaptive Adjustment Daytime	Mode Adjustment Daytime	December Noon	August Noon	August 6 p.m.
Community Shopping Center	31	100%	85%	100%	100%	26	17	17
Employee	8	100%	100%	100%	100%	8	6	5
Family Restaurant	105	100%	100%	100%	100%	105	104	73
Employee	19	100%	100%	100%	100%	19	19	18
Fast Food	96	100%	100%	50%	100%	48	47	40
Employee	16	100%	100%	100%	100%	16	16	14
Office	—	100%	90%	100%	100%	—	—	—
Employee	4	100%	90%	100%	100%	4	3	—
Medical/Dental Office	18	100%	30%	100%	100%	5	5	—
Employee	9	100%	100%	100%	100%	9	9	—
Bank (Drive-in Branch)	13	100%	90%	100%	100%	12	11	—
Employee	7	100%	100%	100%	100%	7	7	—
Subtotal: Customer/Guest Spaces	263					196	184	130
Subtotal: Employee/Resident Spaces	63					63	60	37
Subtotal: Reserved Spaces	—					—	—	—
Total Parking Spaces	326					259	244	167
Reduction	21%				vs. Observed		78	70
					Estimated/Observed		3.13	2.13

Observed Parking Occupancies, Case Study 5.13

Time	Wednesday 8/27/03	Thursday 8/28/03	Friday 8/29/03	Saturday 8/30/03	Sunday 8/31/03	Maximum Observed
10 a.m.	116	136	111	60	23	136
12 noon	222	195	198	78	50	222
2 p.m.	152	152	145	—	—	155
4 p.m.	128	134	106	—	—	134
6 p.m.	107	111	115	70	47	115
8 p.m.	44	61	63	56	39	63

Source: Parking utilization surveys conducted by Baker Hogan Houx, as reported in *Parking Survey and Parking Analysis for Village Glen Plaza Shopping Center, Westlake Village, California,* September 2003.

Table 5-39

Summary of Case Studies

Case	Name	Total GLA	Retail	Dining	Entertainment	Office	Other	Shared Parking Reduction[1]	Estimated Demand/ Observed Occupancy			
									Weekday		Weekend	
									Day	Evening	Day	Evening
5.1	Puente Hills Mall	1,189,927	87%	5%	7%	—	—	18%	—	—	1.11	1.09
5.2	Fashion Island	1,174,489	88%	10%	2%	—	—	19%	—	—	.96	1.06
5.3	Veterans Plaza	121,500	—	15%	85%	—	—	3%	—	—		1.12
5.4	Long Beach Towne Center	832,461	77%	9%	15%	—	—	29%	—	—	1.44	1.23
5.5	Covina Town Square	381,325	61%	10%	29%	—	—	26%	—	—		1.06
5.6	Burbank Empire	613,711	92%	7%	—	1%	—	12%	—	—	1.04	—
5.7	Westfield Promenade	546,190	81%	8%	10%	—	—	25%	—	—	—	1.04
5.8	Ahwatukee Foothills Towne Center	318,808	52%	17%	30%	1%	—	18%	—	—	—	0.76
5.9	Irvine Spectrum											
	2002	796,700	7%	13%	35%	45%	—	17%	1.19	1.3	1.15	0.96
	2003	1,274,700	24%	11%	20%	45%	—	24%	1.19	1.46	0.92	0.82
5.10	Reston Town Center[2]	751,645	14%	8%	9%	69%	—	33%	1.04	—	—	—
5.11	Easton Town Center[3]	987,147	61%	12%	14%	5%	9%	24%	1.12	1.05	0.65	0.88
5.12	Block at Orange	1,175,147	40%	5%	20%	32%	3%	30%	0.93	0.82	0.87	0.64
5.13	Village Glen Plaza	48,566	20%	33%	—	47%	—	24%	1.09	1.67	—[4]	—[4]

Notes

[1] Estimated peak demand vs. sum of unadjusted peak demand for each land use.
[2] GLA excludes hotel.
[3] Other = health club.
[4] Counts were taken on Labor Day weekend and are deemed not representative.

as the projected 242 spaces needed on a weekday at noon. Although the ratio of estimated parking to observed is shown in Tables 5-36 and 5-37, the weekend observations may not be representative of August conditions generally, since the observation dates occurred over the Labor Day weekend. Note, however, the variation in observed accumulation from day to day.

Conclusions

Table 5-39 presents a summary of the case studies, indicating total GLA of the development, the percentage of GLA in various key categories, the amount of reduction achieved by the shared parking analysis, and the ratio of the estimated demand to the observed occupancy. It should be noted that the noncaptive adjustments were not manipulated to achieve a desired ratio of estimated demand. Rather, consistent assumptions were made across the case studies to identify trends.

Figure 5-3 further illustrates the amount of reduction achieved by shared parking analysis (versus the sum of the unadjusted peak parking requirement for each land use).

Figure 5-4 compares the observed occupancy with the estimated demand for particular times of day and days of the week. Clearly, four of the developments—Ahwatukee

Comparison of Estimated Shared Parking Requirements with Sum of Unadjusted Requirements

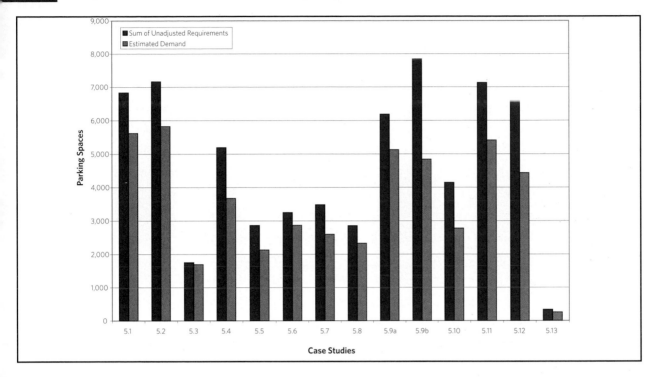

Comparison of Observed Occupancies with Estimated Shared Parking Requirements

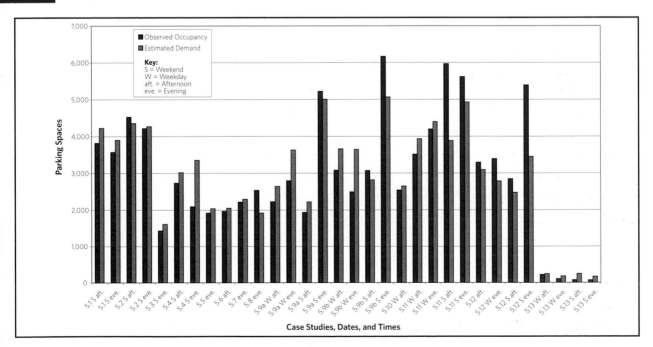

Analysis of Mixed Uses and Shared Parking Case Studies **133**

Foothills Towne Center, Easton Town Center, Irvine Spectrum, and the Block at Orange—must be performing significantly better than the design-day assumptions in the shared parking methodology's base demand ratios and/or monthly and hourly factors. (It is not surprising that shared parking studies were commissioned in anticipation of expansion in these four highly successful projects and thus that rather extensive data were collected on the existing parking occupancy.) All four had observed parking occupancies in "off months" that exceeded the projected parking requirements in the peak month for that center. Conversely, while in all of the four cases weekend evening parking requirements were underestimated, weekday daytime parking needs were overestimated for three of the four centers.

All four of these centers appear to be the type of developments that contribute parking occupancy data points above the 85th percentile on design days to a database like *Parking Generation*'s. Thus, the shared parking methodology and its default values appear to be reasonably reliable except at unusually successful projects, which should not be surprising given the generally accepted definition of design-day parking demand. Obviously, one should not design every parking supply to accommodate an exceptional level of success.

The following sections discuss some findings from the case studies in further detail.

Effect of Noncaptive Ratio Assumptions

The relatively small noncaptive adjustments assumed in this book (at least 90 percent noncaptive except for 50 percent noncaptive for fast-food tenancies) reasonably modeled conditions (46 percent maximum) in five (more than a third) of the case studies, and modifying the noncaptive adjustments proved unnecessary. In two cases where the deviation was around 10 percent, adjusting the noncaptive ratios made no material difference. In case study 5.1, adjusting noncaptive ratios was not effective in a situation where retail predomi-

nates (retail accounted for two-thirds of the unadjusted customer demand on a weekend and more than 80 percent of the customer demand after the noncaptive ratios were applied). At the other end of the spectrum, modifying the noncaptive adjustments at Ahwatukee Foothills Towne Center (case study 5.8), a project with little more than half its GLA in retail, did not materially close a 24 percent shortfall between the estimated parking requirement and the observed parking demand. In the cases where shared parking methodology significantly overestimated demand, attempts to tinker with the ratios would require significant increases in captive ratios to better model parking requirements. But those assumptions would be inconsistent with the assumptions in the five cases where shared parking analysis did model observed conditions well.

The study team believes that the variations in parking needs documented in this book are more indicative of the strength of tenants in a particular marketplace than of the effects of captive market assumptions.

Base Ratio Modifications

Case studies 5.4 (Long Beach Towne Center), 5.5 (Covina Town Square), and 5.6 (Burbank Empire) are all power centers with varying amounts of retail, dining, and entertainment. In all three cases, it was confirmed that it is more reliable to use one parking ratio for all retail uses (as recommended by *Parking Requirements for Shopping Centers*) than to use customized ratios for big-box and other particular retail tenants.

Unitary Ratios versus Shared Parking Analysis

Three cases—5.1, Puente Hills Mall; 5.2, Fashion Island; and 5.7, Westfield Promenade—lay within the 10–20 percent dining/entertainment range for which *Parking Requirements for Shopping Centers* would recommend an adjusted single ratio rather than shared parking methodology (see Table

Table 5-40	Comparison of Shared Parking Methodology with Unitary Ratios				
Case Study	Retail Uses (GLA)	Unitary Ratio[1] (spaces/ksf[2])	Unitary Ratio Estimated/Observed	Shared Parking Ratio (spaces/ksf)	Shared Parking Estimated/Observed
5.1: Puente Hills Mall	87%	4.56	1.07	4.72	1.11
5.2: Fashion Island	88%	4.56	0.88	4.95	0.96
5.7: Westfield Promenade	81%	4.63	1.01	4.76	1.04

Notes
[1] Per *Parking Requirements for Shopping Centers.*
[2] /ksf = per 1,000 sq. ft.

5-40). At Fashion Island, the shared parking analysis for a center with only 12 percent dining/entertainment uses underestimated demand in the peak hour observed by 4 percent, as compared with the 12 percent underestimated using the unitary ratio recommended by *Parking Requirements for Shopping Centers*. The main differences between the case studies were that the other two centers have fairly balanced cinema and restaurant GLAs, while Fashion Island is "unbalanced," with 10 percent restaurant and 2 percent cinema. Thus, while the adjusted unitary ratio per *Parking Requirements for Shopping Centers* is reasonably consistent (less than 4 percent variation between the two) with ratios developed by shared parking methodology, and either methodology may be reliably used for centers with over 10 percent dining/entertainment, the unitary ratio may not be as accurate with predominantly dining uses.

Overall Conclusion

The revised default factors in this second edition of *Shared Parking* are reasonably accurate for a wide variety of combinations of retail/dining/entertainment and office developments. By the very definition of "design day," there will be some projects that generate parking needs exceeding projections based on these default values. In some cases, this might only occur during a honeymoon period when, for example, a distinctively positioned new product enters the marketplace; however, over time other competitors will surely try to match if not exceed the success of such a venue. In other cases, a development may simply have compelling advantages in the marketplace that will never be duplicated.

Notes

1. Walker Parking Consultants, "Shared Parking Analysis: Ahwatukee Foothills Towne Center," 1997.

2. Kaku Associates, "Irvine Spectrum Center Shared Parking Study: Buildout Analysis."

3. Wells & Associates, LLC, 1999.

4. Wells & Associates, LLC, 2002.

5. Wells & Associates, LLC, "Shared Parking Analysis Update: The Block at Orange," 2003.

Design, Operation, and Management of Shared Parking

I mplementing shared parking successfully requires careful planning, but planning is not enough. Inadequate follow-through on management considerations will foil the best parking plan. This chapter discusses some of the key issues related to managing shared parking. Two particularly crucial issues are:

■ How can constraints be avoided in the areas of design, operations, and management that might otherwise preclude the effective implementation of shared parking?

■ What guidelines are appropriate for design, operation, and management of shared parking facilities?

Most management issues do not represent concerns unique to shared parking; they are usually general concerns that apply to all types of parking.

Types of Users

For shared parking purposes, parking spaces can be classified according to three categories: (1) spaces used by employees and residents, which generally experience low turnover, have longer stays, and serve regular users who are familiar with the parking system; (2) spaces used by patrons and visitors, which generally experience higher turnover, have shorter stays, and usually serve a mix of familiar and unfamiliar users; and (3) spaces reserved for use by individuals or particular user groups. These characteristics are not always mutually exclusive; hotel guests' vehicles, for example, may be parked for longer periods than those of hotel employees.

As with any type of parking facility, the design, management, and operation of shared parking facilities must recognize the different types of users to function efficiently. Keeping employees out of parking intended for customers is a common parking management problem, not only because of parking by employees of the project but also by employees from other destinations in a larger district or area.

This edition of *Shared Parking* has therefore provided separate parking ratios and recommended adjustment factors for employees/residents and customers/patrons in order to facilitate better design, management, and operation of parking facilities. Adapting a shared parking plan to the needs of different users is further discussed later in this chapter.

Walking Distances

Among the more critical issues for parking design, which in turn affects its ability to be shared and managed, is the walking distance from the parking area to the destination. As stated by one of the most widely quoted experts on pedestrian design, John J. Fruin, "there are indications that the tolerable limit of human walking distance is more situation-related than energy-related."[1] The tolerable walking distance for "a given design situation is related to such factors as the trip purpose of the individual, the available time, and the walking environment."

A 300-foot walking distance may be unacceptable to a customer wishing to pick up a single product at a drug or convenience store. A 2,000-foot walking distance from a parking facility is generally considered acceptable for theme parks and event facilities; event parkers wishing to avoid parking fees may trek even farther. The weather and available protection from precipitation will affect acceptable walking distances, as will the "friction" along the walking path of travel. Walking through areas perceived as unsafe will significantly reduce acceptable walking distances. Having to cross major streets, railroad tracks, or bridges across freeways also can be less desirable than a more direct, pedestrian-friendly route. Another key factor is the visibility of the ultimate destination along the path of travel. The walking distances from the farthest spaces at a regional shopping center are often significantly longer than those in downtowns or other activity centers, but being able to see a mall entry from the parking space can make the long distance more acceptable.

Table 6-1 presents acceptable walking distances, employing a level-of-service (LOS) approach similar to the traffic engineering profession's level-of-service classification system. The LOS classification can be used to gauge the acceptability of a design component to its potential users. LOS A is the best or ideal performance, LOS B is good, LOS C is average, and LOS D is below average but minimally acceptable.

Table 6-1 Level-of-Service (LOS) Conditions for Walking Distances from Parking

Maximum Walking Distance	LOS D	LOS C	LOS B	LOS A
Within Parking Facilities				
Surface Lot	1,400 ft.	1,050 ft.	700 ft.	350 ft.
Structure	1,200 ft.	900 ft.	600 ft.	300 ft.
From Parking to Destination				
Climate-controlled	5,200 ft.	3,800 ft.	2,400 ft.	1,000 ft.
Outdoors, Covered	2,000 ft.	1,500 ft.	1,000 ft.	500 ft.
Outdoors, Uncovered	1,600 ft.	1,200 ft.	800 ft.	400 ft.

Mary S. Smith and Thomas A. Butcher, "How Far Should Parkers Have to Walk?" *Parking*, September 1994.

Table 6-2 Factors Influencing Selection of Level of Service

LOS D	LOS C	LOS B	LOS A
Long Term			Short Term
Low Turnover			High Turnover
Familiar			Unfamiliar
Teenagers			Stress, Age, Disability
Just Glad to Find a Space			High Expectations
Urban			Rural
Speculative Office Building			Prestige Office Building

Table 6-2 suggests some factors for determining the appropriate level of service for a particular set of circumstances. For further discussion of the selection of an appropriate level of service, see *Parking Structures*.[2]

The level of service of the overall walking distance from a parking space to a destination's entry can be considered as the average of its parts. For example, if the walking distance from a parking space to an elevator tower is 600 feet or LOS B, and the walking distance from the pedestrian exit of the garage to the destination is 1,600 feet or LOS D, then the overall experience is LOS C.

Why More Parking Is Not Always Better

When parking is relatively inexpensive to develop and provided free to the users, most segments of the community (including residents who might be adversely affected by spillover parking, zoning staff and boards, lenders, and tenants) tend to believe that more is better. One has only to drive through suburban commercial areas to see that parking is generally oversupplied. The planning community has recognized that designing roadways for the peak-hour volume that may ever occur is not in the best interests of the community; this philosophy, however, is not nearly as widely accepted in parking planning. With free surface parking,

developers have less incentive to argue with requirements that commonly result in significantly more parking spaces provided than are reasonably necessary for a design day. They can always seek permission to develop something additional after the initial project is fully leased and operating, if the parking supply proves to be excessive.

Developers, tenants, and lenders sometimes express concern about the competitive edge that the appearance of ample parking may give a competing development if their own site has a lower parking ratio. Developers and business owners do on occasion advertise "abundant free parking" when they perceive that their competitors are not able to equal that claim.

An unintended end result of surface parking, especially in excessive amounts, is an inherently lower-density development, which in turn means it may be difficult to serve it economically by transit. When buildings are surrounded by parking lots, pedestrian trips between nearby establishments become difficult. Pedestrian connections between buildings are rarely well-developed, which encourages many to get into their cars and drive a block or two for lunch or errands.

Parking structures are more commonly found in denser developments and particularly on sites with higher land costs. Higher-cost structured parking is more likely to be charged back to parkers to help pay for it. Charging for parking also makes it easier to manage. There is less flexibility, however, to redevelop underused areas with structured parking, and therefore there is more incentive for developers, at least, to carefully consider how many spaces are truly required.

Ultimately, the important criterion is whether the parking supply is *adequate*. Vacant parking spaces in a fully leased project do not benefit anyone, while having a negative impact on the built environment. In today's economic climate, the key to a successful development is the provision of sufficient parking spaces to accommodate demand. The operating costs and rising land values associated with unused parking areas are encouraging many developers to seek additional compatible land uses to share the available parking supply.

According to a 1965 ULI/ICSC survey, regional shopping centers then averaged 7.0 parking spaces per 1,000 square feet of leasable floor area. In recent years, many developers have both infilled the periphery of such sites and redeveloped shopping centers with additional offices, movie theaters, restaurants, and other uses, aiming to take advantage of not only the oversupply of parking spaces but also the potential for shared parking. When properly planned and designed, these infill projects do not harm the existing uses; in fact, to the extent that the center's overall attractiveness is improved during less active retail hours, the existing businesses may be enhanced. But the community should encourage well-planned projects from day one, with flexibility for phasing and future market changes. One of the hottest trends in development is "lifestyle centers," with retail, dining, entertainment, office, and in some cases residential uses. Such projects may be proposed in suburban settings with surface parking, but they nonetheless would be better served by careful planning of sharing parking resources in the master plan. All too often there is nervousness, if not resistance, on the part of the community, lenders, and tenants to reducing parking requirements through shared parking.

If a community's buy-in to shared parking is to be significantly increased, the more-is-better public attitude regarding parking requirements must change. It is therefore important to better communicate the costs of land and parking, as discussed in the next section.

The Cost of Parking

Few outside the parking industry understand the magnitude of the cost of parking for a development. Even developers who have only dealt with surface parking in the past are often surprised if not shocked by the cost of structured parking.

Table 6-3 presents a comparison of the typical costs to own and operate surface-lot and structured parking spaces in the United States. This analysis is based largely on a more detailed discussion of the topic in ITE's *Transportation Planning Handbook*, with cost figures updated to 2004 dollars.[3] The assumed operating expenses also reflect a more recent survey of parking facility owners.[4] Obviously, numerous factors can significantly alter the costs of owning and operating parking; these figures are simply typical, illustrating the incremental costs for structured parking.

Where land is inexpensive, it is clearly more economical to build surface parking. In more urban settings, development is often actually redevelopment, and land values will reflect the buildings that are already present on the site and the potential future return on an investment to redevelop it. Of course, the developer's overall decision regarding redeveloping land in such circumstances will hinge on the overall rental/lease opportunities and return on investment. But a decision to use structured parking instead of surface parking will be driven primarily by the availability of land. And if it costs $300/space per year to collect parking fees for a 500-space facility, at least $25/space must be collected each month to make it worthwhile to charge for parking before one even begins to recover the increased capital costs of structured parking. When a developer can purchase land in

Table 6-3 The Costs of Owning and Operating Parking

	Surface Lot	Above-Grade Structure	Underground Structure
Capacity (spaces)	500	500	500
Levels	1	6	3
Footprint of Parking Area	240 x 660 ft.	120 x 240 ft.	240 x 240 ft.
Incremental Site Area (acres)	4.0	0.7	None
Construction Cost/Space	$3,000	$15,000	$30,000
Estimated Construction Cost	$1,500,000	$7,500,000	$15,000,000
Project Cost (Construction + 15%)	$1,725,000	$8,625,000	$17,250,000
Land Cost per Acre to Equal Total Underground Cost	$3,375,000	$10,803,571	
Land Cost per Acre to Equal Total Above-Grade Cost	$1,815,000		
Annual Cost to Own per Space Excluding Land	$277	$1,384	$2,768
Basic Operating Cost per Space	$75	$300	$365
Revenue Collection per Space	—	$300	$300
Security Cost per Space	$38	$75	$150
Total Cost to Own and Operate per Space per Year	$389	$2,059	$3,583
Monthly Revenue per Space Required to Break Even	$32	$178	$299
Total Cost to Own and Operate per Year	$194,668	$1,029,592	$1,791,685

Assumptions:

Underground structure is short-span (30x30-ft. column grid) owing to construction above. Above-grade structure is long-span (20–45 ft. x 50–60 ft.).

Surface lot size increased by 10% for landscaping, setbacks, access, etc., typical of suburban location; above-grade structure site increased by 5%; underground structure not increased.

Construction cost based on average design costs across United States in 2004.

Project costs increased 15% for design and other miscellaneous soft costs.

Term for financing: 20 years. Cost of funds: 5%. (These figures used to determine annualized cost to own the facility.)

Basic operating costs include utilities, insurance, supplies, routine and structural maintenance, snow removal, etc. Surface lot has lower utilities but six times the snow removal cost of above-grade structure. Below-grade structure has no snow removal but higher utilities for lighting and ventilation.

Surface lot assumed to be in suburban location with free parking and no security. Underground structure will have higher security than above-grade parking structure.

an undeveloped area for less than $50,000/acre ($1/square foot), it is obvious why free surface parking is the norm in suburban development. It does not reflect a conscious philosophy by the development community to design for automobiles rather than people, but rather simple economics.

Where land is expensive and property must be more densely developed to make a project economically viable, above-grade structured parking is the norm. When developers own and operate structured parking, which in Table 6-3 involve more than five times the costs of owning and operating surface parking, they have a much greater incentive to more carefully scrutinize how they plan, design, and manage the parking resource. In turn, those with structured parking are more likely to charge users for some or all of the costs of parking.

Underground parking is significantly more expensive, to the point where there is little economic incentive to choose it except in the most densely developed areas of the largest cities. These urban areas are strongly served by public transit, and thus there are natural market forces setting the price of parking, which in turn affect both commuter and consumer travel-mode decisions. That said, if underground parking is the only viable option, there is strong incentive to minimize its capacity while maximizing its use and revenues, all of which can be accomplished by shared parking analysis.

Numerous factors other than cost affect parking development decisions, not the least of which is how much property can be acquired and what lease rates can be obtained for the occupied space. Even where land costs are lower, sites of restricted size or shape may dictate structured parking. Ultimately, the potential return on investment in a project as a whole is what drives developers to choose to develop or not develop a particular site. For retail, restaurants, and service businesses, the potential return on investment also drives tenant decisions to locate in a particular project, whether or not parking will be surface or structured and paid or free to their employees and customers.

Encroachment from Without and Within a Project

Encroachment in a parking system is the use of spaces intended for one user group by parkers who should be using other spaces. It can result from a wide variety of factors, but most often encroachment by parkers from outside a project results either from a lack of adequate convenient parking to serve adjacent uses or from the relative pricing and convenience of parking facilities near a project. While the vast majority of U.S. shopping centers built in the second half of the last century had free parking, that does not work well if it is located in an area where parking for other users is paid. It can be a major change in mindset for a shopping center developer and potential tenants to accept that paid parking may be necessary to keep other users out of parking intended for shoppers.

Another encroachment situation can occur in projects with strong links to transit; the project's parking spaces, if free, can quickly become a de facto park-and-ride lot. Similarly, encroachment can come from within a project, most often when employees are asked to park in more distant spaces and to leave the more convenient ones for customers. The longer the walking distances to the available spaces, the more this strategy can become a problem. The size of the employment base is a significant factor. Managing employee parking for retail/dining/entertainment uses is one thing; employee demand at shopping centers is typically no more than 20 percent of the overall parking requirement. However, office employees in a large mixed-use project or commuter parking in a transit-oriented development can exponentially increase the challenges of achieving successful shared parking.

Although in an ideal shared parking situation any space is usable by a parker attracted by any tenant use, the reality is that developers, property owners, and tenants do have priorities. Those that rely on drawing customers and visitors for economic success will often want to have the most convenient spaces available for their customers. These spaces will turn over more often, and concentrating short-term users in one area will significantly reduce the time needed to search for a vacant parking space. Turnover is also a factor in the concern for more convenient parking; the shorter the stay, the shorter the acceptable walking distance. Office employees and other employment-based users are usually concerned with having an overall adequate supply as convenient as possible to the leasable space. When both of these types of uses are present in the same project and shared parking is proposed, potential conflicts in the design and management of parking must be resolved early in the project's planning.

Projects may also have a natural organization that may make sense from many perspectives but sometimes is not ideal for shared parking. In other words, if a project were designed solely from a parking perspective, it might look quite different than one designed considering multiple fac-

Figure 6-1 Site Plan for Shared Parking Analysis Example Project

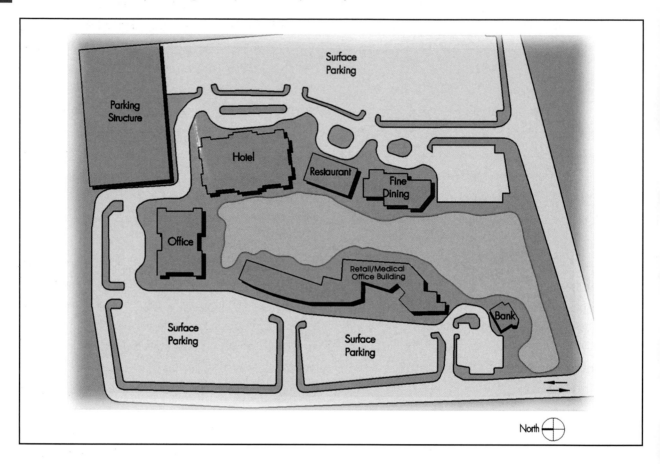

tors. The hypothetical project reviewed in chapter 3 is a case in point: its design placed buildings with strong pedestrian connections around a group of retention ponds (see Figure 6-1). The surface parking areas were thereby limited, owing to the overall size of the site, appropriate building design for the expected tenancies, and the shapes and sizes of the ponds. It was therefore recommended that all employees, including those of the retail/medical office building and restaurants, be required to park in the surface lots near the office building and in the parking structure at all times. Simply asking employees to park in the structure would not work; human nature (in the United States, at least) is to try to park as close as possible to one's destination.

From a parking planner's perspective, the ideal design of this project would be to place a large parking supply in the middle where the ponds are, so that all spaces would be equally convenient to all destinations. Parking management would then not be necessary. Obviously, the overall project is made more desirable by putting shared site amenities in that location instead, but it then requires parking management to make shared parking work. Use of the parking structure spaces by retail and restaurant patrons on weekends when office employees are not present may necessitate valet parking. Trying to keep the limited supply of convenient surface parking for customer use would be critical for the success of a shared parking plan on this site.

Similar challenges occurred with the Downtown Silver Spring project in Maryland, also discussed in chapter 3. That project relies on shared off-site parking for employees. Keeping the spaces within the project available for customers was absolutely necessary to retain the commitment of lenders and potential tenants.

Solutions to encroachment problems vary. They depend on the community in which the project is located and the community's parking policies. The character of the location (CBD, urban neighborhood, outlying suburban area) also is a determining factor in the solution to the problem. Ultimately, one of the best ways to control employee and commuter parking positively (as opposed to punitively through fines, towing, or even dismissal for violation of employer policy) is to price parking in such a way that employees are dissuaded from parking in areas intended for customers. Sometimes the concept of paid parking poses a significant psychological hurdle for interested parties. Therefore a few comments about the pros and cons of paid parking are appropriate at this juncture, before a more detailed discussion of alternate parking management strategies.

Using Parking Charges to Manage Parking

The three main reasons to charge for parking are (1) to recover some of parking's capital and operating costs; (2) to manage parking use; and (3) to manage transportation demand. The latter has already been touched on, but it is worth repeating that when employees are not charged for the full cost of parking, they are less likely to carpool or to take transit—public goals important to many cities.

In many cases, the primary reason for paid parking is to manage it. The concern is usually keeping employees out of more convenient spaces so that these spaces will be available to customers. This is the fundamental reason the parking meter was invented almost 75 years ago. Customers are

willing and able to pay a small amount for a short stay at a convenient space; employees (and other regular users) are presumed not to be willing to pay those rates all day long, every working day. Regular users are endlessly inventive, however, and with each new strategy to keep them out of the most convenient spaces, new tactics for avoiding penalties are developed. Such is the history of parking management in almost any setting. Universities, hospitals, shopping centers, and downtowns all struggle with managing who parks where.

Customer Parking Charges: Pros and Cons

Merchants and city officials in all but the most urban settings are often concerned over the cost of customer parking in a central business district or mixed-use development where paid parking is employed or contemplated. Where competition for patronage is strong, free parking does factor into patronage of a particular business if one can get the same goods or services at convenient locations without paying for parking, which is often the case at shopping centers. There is a strong consensus (81.4 percent) among shopping center executives that paid parking is a significant deterrent to drawing customer traffic, with a majority (58.1 percent) believing that it is an extreme deterrent.[5]

Conversely, free parking by itself does not guarantee the success of a retail or entertainment center. What caused the decline of retail shopping in American downtowns in the latter half of the 20th century was the availability of the same goods and services closer to the suburban homes where much of the middle-class population had migrated. What has turned the tide for the downtowns that are now thriving are distinctive retail/dining and entertainment destinations. That is not to say that chain stores or restaurants and the like cannot be successful downtown, but simply that any one chain store found in several locations throughout a metropolitan area will not be the sole generator of a trip downtown, with or without paid parking. No one would drive 20 miles solely to get to a Starbucks or T.G.I. Friday's, but many people will patronize such businesses while downtown for another reason.

In sum, paid parking is less of an issue with more unusual destinations. A survey of most of the strong retail districts with paid parking in the United States, such as North Michigan Avenue in Chicago and Georgetown in Washington, D.C., indicates that they are supported by upscale urban residents and tourists willing to pay for relatively expensive parking. In other cases, such as Downtown Silver Spring and Circle Center in Indianapolis (discussed in more detail later in this chapter), parking fees are kept quite low for shorter stays so that the cost of parking will not be a significant deterrent to shoppers. Moreover, many other factors, such as downtown entertainment venues and the concentration and breadth of activities available, make these projects attractive to patrons.

Customers will tolerate parking at high prices to purchase goods or services they want or need and cannot get anywhere else. Hence the relatively high cost of parking for special events and at airports. Multiple parking options are often available for both those uses, differentiating price according to convenience.

As big-box discount operations begin to move into more densely developed urban areas with paid parking on neighboring parcels, even their customers now may pay for parking. In such locations, these discount retailers are serving an urban population that would have to drive a considerably longer distance to one of that company's stores in a suburban location to obtain free parking.

In sum, a reasonable charge for customer parking will not hurt an otherwise desirable destination. It is important both to create a special place and to carefully set the price of parking so that it will not detract from a project's appeal.

Employee Parking Charges: Pros and Cons

Businesses in downtowns and other established areas where paid parking is the norm may expect most employees to pay for parking or to take transit. Businesses have many different reasons for their location/relocation decisions. Some need to be convenient to customers or other destinations; for example, law firms oriented to litigation are more likely to choose to be near courthouses; specialty doctors who spend a lot of time at hospitals are more likely to choose a hospital-based medical office building than general practitioners. Other businesses may seek proximity to a particular residential area or labor pool.

It is relatively rare that parking costs are the primary factor in a decision to locate in an urban or suburban area, as indicated by the current attractiveness of several major city downtowns. Manhattan, Boston, San Francisco, and Washington, D.C., all have among the highest downtown parking charges, but all enjoyed substantially lower office vacancy rates in 2003 than their suburbs. The challenge is to assure potential tenants that the locations will be attractive to workers, regardless of parking charges.

When employees' parking costs as well as the availability and cost of transit do become key considerations, the real driver of the concern may be the employer's desire to recruit and retain employees. For example, hospitals considering development of structured parking in their current location often struggle with how much to charge employees due to the competition for nurses and other skilled staff members. They compete with all hospitals in the metropolitan area for employees. Few hospitals charge employees the full cost of providing parking, and even in urban areas where there are high parking fees, hospital employee parking is often subsidized to some extent.

Contrary to the hopes of many urban planners, pressure may increase for employers to include subsidized parking in their benefits packages. The predicted labor shortage as baby boomers retire may drive employers to move closer to where employees want to live, and recruitment and retention costs could also motivate employers to consider lower-cost options in suburban locations. These possible trends, combined with telecommuting and home-based companies, theoretically could starve downtowns and mixed-use developments of their daytime captive patrons. That would reverse the situation from that of the 1970s and 1980s, when most downtowns had ample daytime activity but had to work hard to attract uses that generated nighttime and weekend activity.

In sum, the cost of parking is just one of many competitive issues in a marketplace, and some differences in parking costs will usually not make or break a mixed-use area or site. If developers can absorb the costs of parking, whether surface or structured, they are likely to build it and provide it for free or at low cost to users. A certain amount must be charged before it makes sense to even use paid parking as a management strategy, due to the expense involved in collecting parking revenues. On the other hand, charging for parking where the market will bear it makes economic sense in many cases.

Parking Management Options: Controlling Who Parks Where

While the issues of paid parking and other parking management tactics are not unique to shared parking projects, the problems are significantly larger in many shared parking projects. Therefore parking management is often a key component of shared parking analysis. There are four primary options for parking management: maintaining free, uncontrolled parking; charging fees based on length of stay; charging market-rate fees but validating customers' tickets for reduced fees or free parking; and collecting flat fees from all users at all entries.

Free, Uncontrolled Parking

When parking is free and completely unrestricted, anyone can park anywhere. This approach generally works only where an adequate parking supply lies within a reasonable walking distance of all locations. For a shared parking plan, the site plan shown in Figure 6-1 would be inverted, with one large parking structure substituted for the ponds so that all parking spaces would be equally convenient to all destinations. However, the pedestrian linkages between uses would become significantly less desirable. Parking needs, quite justifiably, won't often win the argument in such cases.

When it is necessary to try manage who parks where at different times of the day or days of the week, the most common approach is to designate employee parking areas. Many shopping centers today paint a colored stripe a certain distance from the building and require employees to park beyond this stripe. This concept can also be used at other land uses.

At the first level of control, a designated employee parking area is usually operated on an honor system, which means it can be regularly violated. This approach relies on the cooperation of tenant managers to discipline violators among their employees; invariably, a few of the managers will be violators of the rules themselves. Security personnel may patrol the lots occasionally and stop obvious violators (such as those wearing tenant uniforms) to counsel them to follow the rules. When the problem is severe, particularly if parking is generated by adjacent properties, management may post a time limit for two- or three-hour parking in customer areas and issue violation tickets to those parking longer than this period. The ticket is designed to be a friendly notice that the time limitation has been violated. However, the license plates of violators are tracked, and repeat violators are identified and warned that their vehicles will be towed if they are parked in the time-limited area again. Private entities often have no legal means of forcing compliance except by towing the vehicles of repeat violators. Similarly, where there is spillover parking from adjacent land uses, it may be necessary to issue employees a sticker allowing them to use the designated locations for free employee parking.

Length-of-Stay Fees

When the problem is primarily keeping employees (either of the project/district or of adjacent properties) out of parking designated for customers, a common solution is to charge a fee based on length of stay. The charge for the first two or three hours is nominal, if not free, but it might be designed to recover the cost of fee collection. Relatively high fees are charged for longer stays; the employee must pay significantly more to park in the customer parking than in designated employee parking for this approach to be reasonably effective. For example, the fee could be $2 for the first three hours and $2 per hour thereafter. Employees working five eight-hour shifts a week would be paying $12 a day, or $240 a month for parking. If they can park elsewhere for free, or even for $100/month, the system is likely to be reasonably effective.

This strategy is generally not perfect, however, because of an employee's ability to leave work and move the vehicle. In one situation where a regional shopping center was located next to a high-rise office complex where parking cost several hundred dollars a month, an "entrepreneur" advertised a service to park office employees' cars at the shopping center and then move them every three hours for less than half the monthly parking fee at the office buildings. This forced the shopping center to institute parking fees for parking from the first hour, with a validation program to rebate fees for their customers, as discussed in the next section.

Generally speaking, holding the low-fee period to two hours is better than three or four hours, but today's retail/dining/entertainment venues tend to attract longer stays than a purely shopping-oriented center. Tenants such as cineplexes and anchor department stores will often try to get three or four hours of free parking for their customers included in the lease. Leasing personnel accustomed to suburban projects should be better educated about the ramifications of free parking on an overall shared parking system.

Validation Strategies

In the most urban situations, it is common for the first hour of parking to be relatively expensive. In Manhattan, the parking fee for the first 30 minutes may exceed $10, and overnight parking fees will often exceed $45. Charging a significantly lower fee results in a flood of parkers from fairly distant parking generators.

Another situation that sometimes calls for high fees is when event parkers are frequently present. It is becoming common to develop retail/dining/entertainment venues at or near event facilities. Mixed-use projects including such retail, dining, and entertainment uses are directly associated with new stadiums or arenas in Brooklyn, Cincinnati, Dallas, Los Angeles, Newark, Pittsburgh, and the Meadowlands in New Jersey. In many cities, stadiums, convention centers, and arenas are located in downtowns where independent development of properties is an ongoing process, and thus shared parking and parking management are challenges. See the further discussion of parking issues in downtown Indianapolis later in this chapter.

There are numerous ways to validate customers' tickets for reduced or free parking, and these have been significantly enhanced through the technology of machine-readable parking tickets. One of the problems with this approach occurs when employees can validate not only their own parking tickets but also those of acquaintances who work for other tenants that more closely monitor and control validations. The validation device used for each ticket can be electronically determined, tabulated, and tracked. Ideally, the entity validating the parking ticket will pay for at least part of the value of the parking validations, resulting in a natural incentive for the entity to use the validation device judiciously. Ultimately, validation programs require significant management time and investment and thus are often a less desirable option.

Flat Fees for All Users

Collecting parking fees on entry is the generally preferred method for event parking, and it may make sense to collect fees on this basis on evenings and weekends for all users when there is an arena nearby that generates 200 or more events per year. The processing rate is significantly faster than collecting fees based on length of stay at exit; in turn, fewer lanes and less staffing are required to collect fees. In addition, the exits would be controlled only to prevent people from entering there to avoid parking fees, so there is considerably less capital expense and space required for access controls. Options to be considered with this alternative include collecting fees only during appropriate time windows on event days or collecting lower fees on nonevent days and simply raising them during events. Another option is to collect fees at exit based on length of stay during daytime hours, converting to a flat fee on entry on evenings and weekends.

Options for reducing fees for retail/dining/entertainment (RDE) customers are as follows:

■ A coupon for free goods or services can be given to each arriving parker. The management could reimburse the tenant for each coupon when it is turned in; funds for the refunds would come from the parking fees collected on entry. Some parkers will not use the coupons. If the coupons are also issued to event parkers, it has the further benefit of encouraging event parkers to patronize the RDE uses before or after the event. However, employees choosing RDE parking would receive the coupons as well.

■ The parking fee or a portion thereof can be refunded at kiosks operated by facility management upon display of receipts. The amount refunded can be set on a sliding scale based on total value of the receipts, which can be a little more discouraging to employees. This system would be subsidized by the parking fees. The coupon approach is more customer-friendly but is more likely to be abused.

■ The parking fee or a portion thereof can be refunded at the time of purchase by the tenants. They can stamp a parking ticket so that other tenants will know whether the patron has already recovered most or all of the cost of the parking fee. With this scenario, the tenants essentially pay directly for the parking validation, and the parking operation keeps the fees collected.

In any of these discount/refund scenarios, employees can receive the benefits as well, but if the refunded amount is equal to the full parking fee, they would therefore not be discouraged from parking in the customer parking. Obviously, how discounts, refunds, and validations are accommodated can become a major factor in leasing negotiations.

Reserved versus Unreserved Spaces

A common problem with leasing is that tenants may request if not demand guaranteed or reserved parking. "Reserved" and "guaranteed" are not synonymous. To provide an adequate number of spaces to meet the peak demands of a shared parking facility, some land uses may require that a guaranteed number of spaces be provided to serve their customers or events within a specified distance of the entries to their space, or that a certain overall parking ratio be maintained through the life of the lease. Guaranteed spaces are thus part of the total number of parking spaces that have been determined to be necessary to serve the land uses within a multiuse project. They are not set aside and held exclusively for any one use or uses. The total number of spaces would still meet the requirements determined by shared parking methodology.

Reserved spaces are designated for exclusive use by either individuals or a group of users during a particular period. For example, convenience- and service-oriented businesses such as banks will often request convenient reserved parking for their customers, so that those users do not have to search all the spaces in the facility for a spot. Other convenience-oriented tenants may request that the spaces immediately in front of their stores be signed with time limits to assure convenient parking for their customers. A few reserved spaces will not damage the success of a shared parking plan, but those not having reserved parking who pass space after vacant space posted as reserved 24/7 for designated users may form a negative impression of the project as a whole.

Designating an area for employee parking may not necessarily result in reserved parking. Employees may be directed to park in a particular area, but customers may use it, too. In its least restrictive sense, "employee parking" simply means that employees are not allowed to park in any location.

As previously discussed, a space reserved for an individual user is one that cannot be shared, at least for the period it is reserved. Leasing representatives may feel intense pressure to negotiate deals, and they often lack a full understanding of the consequences reserved spaces may have for the overall parking plan. Some types of reserved spaces are more of a problem than others. To assist in communications with leasing personnel, the following discussion of reserved parking options is presented in a progression from least problematic to most difficult (from a shared parking/demand management perspective).

■ Reserved parking area for permit holders. The spaces are usually in less desirable locations such as the roof level of a parking structure and are priced accordingly. "Nested" parking controls may be employed to assure that the user parks in the less desirable area. Nested controls require the individual to use an access ID at the main entry/exit and again at the entry/exit to the reserved area; thus, the system can flag users who do not park in the designated area. The gates to the reserved area can be raised on evenings and weekends if appropriate to the shared parking plan. Generally, the area can be oversold, with 10 to 15 percent more permits sold than the capacity of the area.

■ Reserved spaces for permit holders in the general area, with time limitations. For example, the spaces may be reserved until 5 p.m. Any permit holder can park in any reserved space.

■ Reserved area with separate entry and controls. When it is clearly necessary to reserve parking for residential parking on a round-the-clock basis, the reserved parking should be separated if possible. The ideal location is one that is convenient but isolated, so that it cannot be searched easily by customers unfamiliar with the facility. The permit to park in the reserved area in this case becomes a "hunting license" for the first available space, rather than a ticket for an individually reserved space; the spaces thus can be more efficiently used.

■ Individually reserved spaces in a separate area. This strategy is similar to the reserved area approach, except that the spaces are individually reserved. Because the spaces cannot be oversold and may sit vacant when not occupied, the fee for this type of space should be significantly higher than for "hunting-license" permits.

■ Individually reserved spaces in a prime area.

At a minimum, leasing representatives should always negotiate the least restrictive type of reserved stalls possible. Most important, if more than about 5 percent of the total spaces are reserved, the time-of-day factors in a shared parking analysis must be adjusted to show demand for the spaces even if they are not likely to be occupied.

Off-Site Parking

A variety of circumstances may limit the number of spaces that can be provided on a project site or otherwise make off-site parking a reasonable component of a shared parking plan. In particular, when parking resources within a reasonable walking distance are underused during a project's peak hours, sharing that parking is in the best interests of all parties, including the local community.

Generally, more natural means of encouraging use of off-site parking are preferred to forced means. For example, on-site parking may be reserved for customers, with a paid parking plan that discourages use of the spaces by employees. Employees then may be offered low-cost parking in another location prearranged by the on-site management or be expected to choose from other market-priced public parking options. The latter option is more common and in fact more appropriate in downtowns and other activity centers, which offer public parking provided either by local government or by commercial parking operators. Overflow of customer parking to off-site facilities on evenings and weekends may also be desirable, as discussed in the case study of shared parking in downtown Indianapolis later in this chapter.

In other cases, off-site parking may require incentives for use, particularly if it is distant enough to require a shuttle service. An urban hospital in a relatively undesirable neighborhood, for example, was chronically short of parking for employees and staff. It ran a shuttle program from parking several miles away, leased from a shopping center. New employees were required to park at this location until a permit became available for on-campus parking. Far more permits at $10 per month were sold for the shuttle lot than occupancy of the lot indicated were being used. Apparently, employees were paying $10 per month to stay on the waiting list for on-campus spaces but were parking elsewhere in the neighborhood, despite a history of violent crimes (including at least one murder) against employees parking in the area. Employees and students clearly preferred to take that risk rather than ride a safe, convenient shuttle for a couple of miles.

The level-of-service criteria for walking distances shown in Table 6-1 suggest appropriate distances for walkable off-site parking. No one distance is appropriate for any and all circumstances, however.

When a shuttle is provided to maintain a higher level of service, such as a maximum 900-foot walking distance, some employees are still likely to walk significantly longer distances (as much as half a mile) during nice weather, using the shuttle only during poor weather. The availability of the shuttle is necessary to get them to use the distant parking regularly, but the shuttle service may be underused much of the time. Management can take advantage of this tendency by scheduling more shuttles with a decreased waiting time in the winter months and putting an extra shuttle into service during rainstorms, heat waves, and so on. When employees using the shuttle are predominantly working regular business hours, the shuttle service may only need to be run with frequent headways during peak arrivals (such as 7 to 9 a.m.) and departures (4 to 6 p.m.), with less frequent service in other hours. However, maintaining a shuttle service also incurs an obligation to get employees back to their cars at any time of the day or evening, including for extended overtime; such needs are usually best met by having a van or security vehicle perform on-demand runs to the shuttle lot rather than running the service for extended hours.

In situations where a lack of on-site parking may result in spillover parking into a neighborhood, the community may request commitments to maintain appropriate off-site parking that become part of the zoning approval by covenant or other legal document. This possibility is discussed in this chapter's section on recommended zoning requirements.

Entrance/Exit Capacity and Control

Adequate access capacity for paid parking depends on the type of controls, the volume of vehicles moving in and out of the facility, street capacities, and the effect of conflicts with pedestrians. In turn, the effectiveness of a parking facility's design and operation depends on the provision of adequate entrance/exit capacity and whether the facility is intended for mixed-use development (shared parking) or for a single land use. A methodology for properly sizing and laying out entries and exits for parking facilities is provided in chapter 4 of *Parking Structures*.[6]

A special consideration for facilities meant to house shared parking is the possible need to provide a separate access system for a particular land use within the project. For example, a reserved parking area may be necessary for residential uses, or valet parking may be required for a hotel.

Internal Circulation System and Parking Design

Typically, no special circulation considerations are involved in the design of a shared parking facility that would differ from those for a facility involving a single land use. A number of excellent references in parking facility design are available.[7]

Directional Signing

Signing is important in all parking facilities. The more complex the facility, the more critical the signing becomes, especially in a multiuse development with shared parking.

Effective signage includes:

■ Directional signs at the entrances to the development from all public streets and highways.

■ Signs at the development exits giving directions to the various streets surrounding the site.

■ Internal signs that direct parkers to various parking areas serving particular land uses.

■ Internal signs that direct drivers to available parking spaces. In larger, more complex facilities, areas with vacant spaces can be identified by electronic signs.

■ Information that directs parkers to and from their destinations. Memorable graphics and themed wayfinding systems are effective in assisting pedestrians to find their vehicles upon returning to the facility.

Two different approaches may be taken in aiding unfamiliar users arriving at a project. Encouraging patrons to park in the facility closest to a particular destination is often used when there is a well-developed ring road. Arriving patrons may thus circulate the site and select the parking facility

Photo 6-1. Changeable message signs switch among a few preset messages.
Photo Courtesy Daktronics

closest to their preferred mall entry or anchor tenant. A more urban solution is to encourage people to park in the first parking facility encountered, rather than to circle a project on public streets searching for the closest available space for a particular destination. In shared parking situations, changeable and variable message signs are critical to diverting parking to other facilities when the most desirable facility is full (see photos 6-1 and 6-2).

A number of cities in Europe and a few in the United States have developed an automated parking guidance system (APGS), in which the number of available spaces at nearby facilities is displayed at key points along the path of travel to the city center (see Photo 6-3). Variable message signs are also being used to direct parkers to particular locations in more campuslike settings. A related product, the automated parking availability display (APAD), is increasingly used inside parking facilities, particularly those with express ramps connecting flat parking floors, to reduce the number of spaces that must be searched to find an available space (see Photo 6-4).

Design of the Pedestrian System

Pedestrian links to destinations should be carefully planned for shared parking facilities, particularly in structures where users need to reach different destinations within a multiuse complex. Pedestrian paths can be of various designs. In downtown Minneapolis, for instance, an extensive second-level skywalk system links various buildings, land uses, and parking facilities. Other communities have used both upper-level and lower-level pedestrian systems. The Houston Galleria, Crown Center in Kansas City, and Crystal City in Arlington, Virginia, offer examples of large multiuse complexes with supporting shared parking facilities that have been effectively linked by signing and pedestrian paths.

Design considerations for pedestrian links include signing, safety and security, an attractive environment, lighting, and short, direct walkways. Locating parking spaces close to the building and stairwell-elevator cores will help orient visitors.

Photo 6-3. Signs using an automated parking guidance system (APGS) show drivers how many spaces are available near particular destinations.
Photo Courtesy Dambach

Photo 6-4. Automated parking availability displays (APADs) help drivers locate spaces within multilevel facilities.
Photo Courtesy Daktronics

Flexibility and Safety

The design and operation of a shared parking facility should be flexible to accommodate possible changes in rate structure, dimensions of parking spaces, addition or deletion of valet parking, and so on. The internal design should recognize the need for easy maintenance and cleaning, snow removal, and pavement markings.

Security and safety are, of course, critical. See *Dimensions of Parking* or one of the other texts previously listed for a complete discussion of security and safety concerns in parking.[8]

Shared Parking in a Downtown Environment: Indianapolis's Circle Centre

The renaissance of Indianapolis's downtown over the last 30 years offers a useful illustration of the benefits and challenges of shared parking in a downtown environment. The city long ago adopted a laissez-faire parking strategy that served its growth and development well. This strategy was

simply to let the market determine how much parking was required; therefore, parking has not been required by zoning for new developments in the downtown area. Even though tempted at times, the city did not intervene in the marketplace (by building municipal parking facilities, for example), except to provide parking for its own developments. As a result, when parking shortages developed, the private market met them.

The city has long had a thriving commercial parking sector with market pricing that encouraged private parking operators and developers to build parking to meet demand. Options for various price points have naturally developed; employees pay a higher price to park in the core area than they do if they are willing to walk a few blocks. At various times when shortages existed, private operators filled the gap with remote parking served by shuttle buses. If a recession affected occupancy of leasable space, and in turn the occupancy of core area parking, the commercial parking market nimbly adjusted rates and reduced shuttle services to maximize net revenue. In turn, the city has charged market rates for the customer parking it has developed to support its own projects.

Indianapolis was not immune to competition from the suburbs, and from the late 1960s onward its retail base was steadily eroded by the development of suburban shopping centers. Due to the presence of the state capitol and city and county government buildings (including the associated courts), as well as financial and corporate headquarters, office employment and development remained strong. But the city slowly slid toward ghost-town conditions in the evenings and on weekends. Many of the former retail store-fronts were occupied by service businesses oriented only to daytime customers and employees. Both of the locally owned department stores held on to market share by opening branches in the suburban shopping centers, but they still struggled, were sold to out-of-town interests, and ultimately their downtown flagship stores were closed.

Like many cities, Indianapolis took a number of actions to try to stem the tide. One of its first and ultimately most important actions was to merge the county and city governments, which gave a lot more people a stake in the success of the downtown. Economic development planners developed an imaginative marketing plan to position Indianapolis as a sports capital. The city built an arena for pro basketball and a minor-league hockey team and a domed stadium that today houses a pro football team. A convention center was built to support hotels and restaurants downtown, particularly on weekday evenings, so that they could attract residents and tourists alike on the weekends. The city lured amateur sports organizations, including the National Collegiate Athletic Association (NCAA), to relocate to downtown, and it built the facilities required to hold the Pan American Games in 1987.

What really turned the tide regarding nightlife, however, was Circle Centre. First proposed in 1979 as a $100 million enclosed shopping center, Circle Centre finally opened in 1995 as an urban retail/dining/entertainment project, at a cost of just over $300 million. The development required the resolution of numerous issues, not the least of which was parking. The fact that the city had a strong commercial parking sector with market-rate fees forced the question: would shoppers pay to park at Circle Centre? Parking could not be free as it is at suburban centers, because the more than 100,000 downtown employees would quickly gobble it up. Several newspaper articles questioned the viability of paid parking, with Richard Feinberg, director of Purdue University's Retail Institute, quoted as asking, on the eve of the center's opening, "Where else in Indianapolis do you have to pay to shop?"

The bigger problem was financing. The concept of downtown retail was a tough sell to both investors and tenants in the 1980s. The dining/entertainment focus added in the final push to get the project done was unusual at the time and considered equally if not more risky. As financing wavered, so did early commitments from anchors. The first of the old downtown buildings were torn down at a hopeful point in 1989, but financing again was lost, leaving gaping holes in the city streetscape. In the end, the city had to step forward and become essentially the majority investor in the project. Under the final financing arrangement, the city owns the project (land and buildings), and it provided $187 million, or more than 60 percent of the development cost. A consortium of 19 local companies invested $75 million, and the remainder came from two international banks.

One of the factors that made the project financially feasible was shared parking. At its opening, Circle Centre included roughly 630,000 square feet of retail and 78,000 square feet of restaurants. The entire fourth floor was devoted to entertainment uses, including restaurants, nightclubs, and a 2,700-seat cinema. If these components had been separately built in a suburban location without any consideration of shared parking, it would have required nearly 6,000 parking spaces.[9] However, Circle Centre was built with only 2,815 spaces, less than half that number. First, the application of time-of-day, day-of-week, and seasonal and captive-market adjustments for the combination of retail, dining, and entertainment reduced the peak parking need (as estimated in a shared parking analysis) by more than one-third. More important, no employee parking was provided, and the "new" parking was designed only to meet the incremental customer demand of the project on weekday afternoons when adjacent parking resources are occupied by area employees and visitors. A parking study found that the majority of the more than 12,000 parking spaces then existing within one block would be available to serve Circle Centre customers on evenings and weekends.

The sharing of parking proved extremely beneficial, both in terms of capital and operating costs. As previously noted, over half the parking spaces at a typical shopping center sit vacant for 40 percent of the operating hours. Circle Centre was not forced to build and carry spaces that are only used at peak times. The mix of dining and entertainment uses with retail keeps parking spaces well used in the evenings and on weekends, not only in December but year-round. A strong captive market exists for all the uses, not only by more than 100,000 downtown employees but also by visitors to the convention center, sports venues, and hotels.

Two other parking elements have been critical to the success of Circle Centre. One is the design of the parking. According to Tamara Zahn, president of Indianapolis Downtown, Inc., "Key elements that make Circle Centre parking successful are very affordable short-term rates, convenience, and a safe and comfortable environment." The parking facilities consist of two underground garages underneath the mall and one above-grade open structure across the street. The facilities are not interconnected; they are designed to get vehicles off the street and efficiently directed to an available parking space. They are not named or signed for a particular mall entry or destination. Parking is provided entirely on flat floors, giving users an ability to see pedestrian cores from anywhere on the floor. High lighting levels are provided, and the columns, walls, and ceilings in the underground facility are painted white. The underground facilities have proven particularly popular; users value the ability to leave heavy coats in their cars and return frequently to drop off packages.

The second key to Circle Centre's successful parking is sound management. The center does have to compete with suburban malls, restaurants, and cinemas that offer free parking, and it also needs to keep downtown employees from using its parking areas. Circle Centre's parking is relatively inexpensive at $1.50 for the first three hours, with a $3 maximum on evenings and weekends. However, all-day parkers are hit with $2-per-hour rates after the first three hours, resulting in a total parking expense for office employees that exceeds the cost of daily parking in nearby facilities. A few mall tenants validate parking, as does the cinema; most users consider the rates so reasonable that the hassle and expense of a high volume of validations were avoided. Another interesting fact for transportation planners is that Circle Centre is one of the few new regional malls ever constructed that did not require the construction of a single lane of road.[10]

Success has bred additional growth. Within one year of Circle Centre's opening, another $100 million in development came to fruition with three new hotels and seven more restaurants. The city has since constructed a new minor-league baseball park that shares parking with the state government buildings, replaced Market Square Arena with Conseco Fieldhouse, and worked with the state to develop White River State Park at the downtown's western edge, where aging industrial plants once stood. While the zoo moved there in the late 1980s, it remained disconnected from the rejuvenation of the downtown. The park now hosts the state historical museum, a renowned museum of western art, an IMAX theater, botanical gardens, event facilities, and the NCAA's headquarters and museum. An old industrial canal system was revived and transformed into Canal Walk, where people can stroll, bike, and rent paddle boats, and the pedestrian/canal system has been extended to and through the state park. Ultimately, Canal Walk has become the anchor of an entirely new, primarily residential district.

Because of the combination of world-class sporting venues and downtown activities that can be enjoyed by teams and their fans, the NCAA regularly rotates many of its national championships through Indianapolis, from rowing to swimming to gymnastics. In 2004, it committed itself to bringing the men's and women's basketball Final Four games to Indianapolis every fifth year and also to bringing either the men's or women's regionals to Indianapolis in the intervening years, for at least 20 years.

Public and private development in Indianapolis during the 1990s totaled more than $3 billion. Even more exciting, the small cadre of urban pioneers who first renovated historic housing on the edges of downtown has grown into a wave of new residential development of all types. Empty nesters and young singles alike are moving to downtown and its environs to be near not only to work but also to the vibrant cultural and entertainment activities, as well as to restaurants and shopping. More than 1,300 new housing units are in the pipeline as of this writing, which is significant considering there were 8,000 units downtown at the time of the 2000 census. The city's long-term goal is to double the 2000 census's 20,000 downtown residents to 40,000 by 2020. The influx of new residents has spurred the renaissance of a number of small neighborhood commercial areas, which now house art galleries, restaurants, and specialty shops.

Among the recent challenges has been the increasing number of evenings and weekends when event parking rates are charged for downtown parking. Market Square Arena was located far enough east that it did not generate much event parking in the core areas, nor did it conflict with retail and dining activities. However, Circle Centre is now bracketed by the football stadium and convention center one block to the west and the new Conseco Fieldhouse one block to the east. Between Circle Centre and the fieldhouse and stretching south is a restaurant and entertainment area known as the Wholesale District. The fieldhouse, which seats 19,200, was built with only 1,800 new parking spaces. Those spaces are used in the daytime by a nearby Fortune 500 corporation's employees and during events by arena suite holders, season-ticket holders for Pacers basketball, and public parkers as space is available. The remaining event parkers use public parking throughout the area. Shared parking has thus made the fieldhouse project more feasible as well.

Although the needed spaces are there, parking management is again a concern to the downtown community. Compared with the 20 or so significant event days a year at the football stadium, the Conseco Fieldhouse is scheduling at least 200 event days annually. The convention center has also been expanded, and the amenities of downtown Indianapolis have significantly increased the city's ability to draw national conventions and trade shows.

Thus, evening and Saturday parking needs are of growing concern as event parking rates have become the norm rather than the exception. While the restaurants and nightclubs downtown benefit from increased patronage before and after arena events, patrons arriving during events find parking to be more expensive than it used to be. Circle Centre charges market rates during events, but with a minimum purchase a validation is issued that reduces parking fees to nonevent rates. To assist smaller developments, Indianapolis Downtown, Inc., has developed a Best Bargains parking program, identifying more than 18 facilities in the core area that charge $5 or less for parking during events.

Zoning Ordinances

Most communities' zoning ordinance requirements for parking evolved from the exponential growth in private car ownership after World War II and were often designed to manage growth in outlying and suburban areas. Most ordinances are thus typically oriented to surface parking solutions. This perspective in turn reflects the lower cost of surface parking and the "more parking is better" philosophy. Moreover, seemingly minor revisions to what once might have been state-of-the-art model zoning ordinances have occurred so regularly that many ordinances have been altered beyond all recognition.

Parking provisions vary widely. The following list summarizes the primary variations in local requirements that can be found across the country.

■ Some ordinances have a single ratio for all commercial uses, ranging from two to five spaces per thousand square feet; others have 20 or more individual categories for commercial uses.

■ Some ordinances specify minimum parking ratios, some have maximum parking limitations, and others have no requirements for parking in certain districts.

■ Some allow on-street parking to be considered in supply; others do not.

■ Some allow a reduction in spaces due to proximity to public transit, others prescribe set reductions, and some do not allow any adjustment.

■ Some require that off-site parking be identified and "bound" to the project by easements or other legal measures; some allow any parking within a reasonable walking distance to be counted.

■ Some create boundaries to limit the use of shared parking, presumably based upon some walking-distance criteria.

■ Some localities specify that any deviation from the required ratios requires a variance that ultimately must be approved by the elected county or city council; others allow for administrative approval of adjustments within prescribed limits.

■ Some ordinances specify that shared parking be analyzed in accordance with the ULI methodology, perhaps requiring that it be done by a qualified traffic or parking consultant. Others provide for flat reductions in parking demand in certain areas or districts to allow for captive adjustments or within a certain distance of public parking.

When prescribed adjustments for proximity to transit or captive-market effects are overlaid on a single commercial ratio, it may be seen as "elegantly simple,"[11] but it can in fact be highly inaccurate. A project with a large amount of office space and a small amount of retail or restaurant uses might be permitted thereby to significantly undersupply parking, while one that has a complex mix of uses may be required to provide an excessive number. Clearly, ULI, the International Council of Shopping Centers, and the *Shared Parking* study team, as well as the Institute of Transportation Engineers' Technical Council Committee 6F-52, believe that careful, refined analysis of shared parking using the methodology described in this book offers the most reliable means of determining the appropriate parking supply for a particular mixed-use project or activity center.

Guidelines for acceptable transit use reductions, particularly for employees working in the daytime on weekdays, can be incorporated into an ordinance if local officials desire. It is not recommended that noncaptive ratios be specified in an ordinance, simply because they vary so significantly according to the specific types, quantities, and combination of land uses in the project.

A local entity can take the following steps to review and update its ordinances, incorporating significant changes in the understanding of parking requirements as well as flexibility into zoning practices. This process is paraphrased from *Flexible Parking Requirements.*[12]

1. Determine generic development characteristics (land uses present, employment densities, modes of travel, costs of parking, etc.).

2. Review parking experience elsewhere (read and assess relevant studies, literature, and other communities' zoning ordinances).

3. Survey existing uses' parking generation rates and problems (and submit them to ITE's *Parking Generation* database if possible).

4. Establish parking policy regarding the level of service to be provided.

5. Develop zoning requirements.

6. Monitor parking standards.

This book provides significant analysis of the design-day parking needs of 30 of the most common land uses, which certainly is a good place to start step 5.

Summary

The fundamental characteristic of shared parking facilities is that they are more efficient. Each space can be used more hours during the day, week, or month. This higher level of use is achieved through the combination of increased turnover and use of the space during more hours of the day. Increased turnover results from the rotation of different types of parkers using the facility during the day (for example, office parkers, then hotel guests), while the extended hours of use often result from the effects of the captive market.

Shared parking is practical and will work. In many places it currently is working extremely well and has contributed to vibrant central cities without sprawl. There are no significant operating and management constraints to preclude the development of a shared parking facility. A number of factors must be considered, however, to ensure the efficient design, operation, and management of shared parking facilities. These considerations must be addressed early in the project, when the shared parking analysis is being performed, to most accurately determine the appropriate number of spaces. Design, management, and operational decisions need to be made at the outset and subsequently adhered to in order for a shared parking plan to be successfully implemented. Developers, parking consultants, architects, and parking operators may need to confer to design and implement features necessary to meet the identified demands for shared parking. Following a project's completion, monitoring is often required to ensure that a facility is functioning efficiently or to make modifications where necessary.

Notes

1. John J. Fruin, *Pedestrian Planning and Design*, rev. ed. (Mobile, Ala.: Elevator World, 1987).

2. Anthony P. Chrest et al., *Parking Structures: Planning, Design, Construction, Maintenance, and Repair*, 3rd ed. (Norwell, Mass.: Kluwer Academic Publishers, 2001).

3. Mary S. Smith, "Parking," in *Transportation Planning Handbook*, 2nd ed., ed. John D. Edwards, Jr. (Washington D.C.: Institute of Transportation Engineers, 1999).

4. Jon Martens, "The Art of Maximizing Your Profits," *The Parking Professional*, September 2004, pp. 22–25.

5. International Council of Shopping Centers, *Shopping Center Executive Survey* (January 2005).

6. Chrest et al., *Parking Structures*, pp. 103–52.

7. See Chrest et al., *Parking Structures;* Ronald W. Stehman, ed., *Parking 101: A Parking Primer* (Fredericksburg, Va.: International Parking Institute, 2001); ULI–the Urban Land Institute and NPA–the National Parking Association, *The Dimensions of Parking*, 4th ed. (Washington, D.C.: ULI–the Urban Land Institute, 2000); and Robert Weant and Herbert S. Levinson, *Parking* (Westport, Conn.: Eno Foundation for Transportation, 1990).

8. ULI–the Urban Land Institute and NPA–the National Parking Association, *The Dimensions of Parking*, 4th ed. (Washington, D.C.: ULI–the Urban Land Institute, 2000).

9. Mary S. Smith, "Circle Centre: How Parking Helped Make Urban Retail/ Entertainment Development Work," *Parking*, September 1996, p. 25.

10. "Building a World-Class Downtown," Indianapolis Regional Center Plan 2020, www.indyrc2020.org (Summer 2004).

11. Steve Tracy, *Smart Growth Zoning Codes: A Resource Guide* (Sacramento, Calif.: Local Government Commission, 2003).

12. Thomas P. Smith, *Flexible Parking Requirements*, Planning Advisory Service report no. 377 (Chicago: American Planning Association, 1983).